The Rape Of The American Constitution

by
Chuck Shiver

Loompanics Unlimited
Port Townsend, Washington

This book is sold for information purposes only. Neither the author nor the publisher will be held accountable for the use or misuse of the information contained in this book.

The Rape Of The American Constitution
© 1995 by Chuck Shiver

Published by:
Loompanics Unlimited
PO Box 1197
Port Townsend, WA 98368

Loompanics Unlimited is a division of Loompanics Enterprises, Inc.

Cover design by Gene Fama

ISBN 1-55950-127-8
Library of Congress Card Catalog 95-76192

CONTENTS

Part I
The Background Of The Constitution

Part II
The Rape Of The Constitution

Dedication

This book is dedicated to my parents whose support and assistance has allowed me to follow my whims from rock star, to teacher, to lawyer, and finally to author, everything I have accomplished is due to them; to my grandmother Lillian whose financial support enabled me to continue in law school, without starving, while pursuing my dream to write; to Ken Matus for a decade of patient teaching of computer skills and for the creation of the impressive final copy of this manuscript; and to my 8th and 11th grade American history teachers, Fran Barger and Jon Ulbright, who gave me a love for history and respect for the Constitution.

AUTHOR'S NOTE

The Rape of the American Constitution analyzes the true history of the United States as it relates to constitutional law, examines examples of the abuse the Constitution has sustained, and answers the question: Is the Constitution just a worthless piece of paper as a result of being raped by those forces seeking tyranny? Part I describes the conditions that led to the crafting of that most amazing document, the United States Constitution, the sole reason for the maintenance of our liberties for more than 200 years. Part II describes the rape of our Constitution by examining examples of its abuse. Some may object to the use of the word "rape" in this context, but there is no more apropos description of what has been done to our Constitution. There are so many examples to choose from in our history that the most difficult task is to limit the selections to fit into a book of reasonable length. It also explores the implications for the future and a plan of action for avoiding totalitarianism.

This book is intended as a political manifesto. It is not a textbook, and not a dry technical recitation of history. It is intended for the common man, not professional historians. Therefore, it tells the story of American history in general terms without footnotes and the extreme detail which academia insists upon, but which so often makes history utterly boring to the masses. It also strives to avoid complex legal case analysis except in some areas where it is necessary to understand how the United States of America has become a "nation of the whims of judges, not laws."

This book makes no attempt to be politically correct. Those who value their liberty must refuse to adhere to the absurdities of this fad. Free speech and thought is all about protecting offensive speech, the response to which should be more speech, not less. The obscenity of PC, in an attempt to make everyone culturally sensitive, trashes the concept of free speech, but insofar as it is promoted by private parties, and not the government, the First Amendment does not apply. Like sheep to the slaughter. Don't people understand? The ignorant, liberal, alleged "intellectuals" who espouse this PC nonsense are just another group in a long list of groups who have historically attempted to tell us all how to live, act, think and speak. The result is less speech, less freedom, and division brought about by resistance to this brotherhood at the point of a bayonet. I hope this book is the epitome of what is politically incorrect.

INTRODUCTION

In January, 1776, Thomas Paine (1737-1809) published his pamphlet *Common Sense*. In it Paine openly criticized King George III for his tyrannical behavior towards the 13 American Colonies. Full of fiery rhetoric against tyranny and for the rights of man, the pamphlet is credited with converting thousands of Americans to the cause of freedom. This call to arms is widely acknowledged as an instrumental chapter in the fight for independence and liberty. Even with the ground swell of support caused by *Common Sense,* some historians believe that only one-third of the colonists supported the break with England. Without Paine's pamphlet it is unlikely that the war could have been carried out successfully. As Paine explained in another pamphlet, *Crisis* (1776-1783), those were the times that tried men's souls.

Another classic political literary work came in the late 1830s from Alexis de Tocqueville (1805-1859). The famous French historian traveled throughout America and wrote *Democracy in America*, an in-depth political analysis of this nation. In it he was very critical of the potential tyranny of the majority inherent in a democratic system. It is still the political scientists' handbook for the study of government.

The Rape of the American Constitution represents a modern-day cross between *Democracy in America* and *Common Sense*, a serious analysis of the nation and a call to arms. Today, the nation faces an even graver danger than that of 1776, from the growing tyranny of the United States government.

Tocqueville and the English-born Paine were, as outsiders, more able to take an objective view of matters. Like these famous authors, my perspective on American history has been shaped by external influences. It is a revisionist philosophy, a product of a foreign education. It is extremely critical of the United States and is based upon exposing the truth of this nation's rather inglorious past, rather than whitewashing its sins.

Many modern historians are extremely critical of a "revisionist" view of history. Even the term is disparaging in tone, as if there is something illegitimate about revising our interpretation of history. These learned men prefer to stick unquestioningly to the traditional understanding of events. Academia, though, misses several important points in their attacks on revisionism. First, historians writing at the time, or soon thereafter, are closer to the events as they actually occurred, however, they are also swayed by the emotion of the moment. Second, it is true, and has always been, that the victors write the history. These two facts guarantee that the history written by contemporary historians may not be accurate. Reflecting upon this, Napoleon Bonaparte once asked rhetorically, "What is history but a fable agreed upon?" The responsible historian, then, must strive to revise later when a clearer, more objective view can be seen.

Washington Crosses the Delaware: A complete lie

I was fortunate to spend my early school years outside the United States, in Canada and Australia. As a result I missed the propaganda lessons that constitute the American public schools' teaching of U.S. history, and I believe received a more realistic view of the country's past. In 1974 my family moved back to the United States. I developed an intense interest in American history, but immediately noticed the differences between the truth and the propaganda served up by the public schools. A classic example is the famous painting of George Washington crossing the Delaware River on his way to attack Britain's Hessian mercenaries at Trenton, New Jersey, in December, 1776. Every visual depiction in the picture is false; from the ice floes, to Washington's heroic stance, to the flag, and the boats. Clearing through these myths and legends became my goal. I specialized in history and government during high school and then completed a pre-law political science degree in college. Later work in secondary education and a Composite Certification to teach social studies led me back to the public school system, where I taught American History and Government.

During those years I took what some would call a controversial position on American history, exposing my students to the facts minus the propaganda. American schools, while failing on almost every count, have succeeded in one area: the subjugation of the minds of our children with lies and half-truths about America that would impress even the likes of Joseph Goebbels, the Minister of Propaganda in Nazi Germany. The myth that America is always just, fair, right, and good is hypocrisy unparalleled in the annals of man. Finally, after years of dealing with the stupidity and incompetence of public education, I decided I no longer wished to be a part of that failure, so I left and went to law school. A law degree, however, only taught me the extent of the abusive nature of the present government of the United States, for law has become the tool of totalitarianism.

As I look back on our nation's past and witness its modern decline, I share a sense of outrage. I am inclined, as in the movie *Network*, to go to the window and shout, "I'm as mad as hell, and I'm not going to take it anymore!" From our inglorious past, to the IRS, congressional malpractice, federal judges with no understanding of the Constitution, drug tests, affirmative action, gun control, idiot presidents, and censorship, some perspective needs to be applied.

The Founders of the Constitution, American heroes such as James Madison, a brilliant student of law and history, were determined to prevent the encroachment of government on the rights of the people. The great experiment in democracy, as the Constitution is often referred to, was really an experiment to see if government could be controlled. That experiment has increasingly been proven to be a resounding failure. Our government, indeed our nation, has trampled on the principles and the spirit of the Constitution with such abandon that it almost defies comprehension. The judicial branch, originally intended as the weakest in the federal triumvirate, has perverted the Constitution with the misguided and subversive doctrines of "substantive due process" and "necessary public policy" — theories that have absolutely no basis in law nor reality except in the senility-ridden minds of the life-tenured federal overlords. The judiciary has not been the only offender though, for the legislative and executive branches have played their parts, as have the American people, who in their uneducated, semi-literate state have allowed this process to take place and have at times led in the reduction of our liberties. For a classic example, one only need review the controversy over flag burning. The American people in their alacrity to rid the world of this evil violation of our national symbol, led the government in an attempt to amend the Bill of Rights for the first time in our history. I guess if our future depends on the wisdom of the American people, we are in dire straits.

As I watched the 1990 congressional debate on House Joint Resolution 350, the Anti-Flag-Burning Amendment, I was dismayed by the lack of historical knowledge displayed by our legislators. In one example, a black member of the House of Representatives, in a patriotic diatribe, pointed out that Crispus Attucks, also a black, was the first American to die in the American Revolution. Attucks died in the Boston Massacre on March 5, 1770, but, as every elementary student knows, the American Revolution did not begin until the battles at Lexington and Concord on April 19, 1775.

In another matter of mistaken history former Supreme Court Chief Justice Warren Burger, in a December, 1991, CNN interview, claimed that the Alien and Sedition Acts of 1798 had been repealed. His statement made it appear that the government had seen the error of its ways regarding these unconstitutional laws and acted to repeal them. Not only were these laws never repealed nor declared unconstitutional by the courts, they were used as a basis for later, similar laws. The point is that if such misstatements can be made by members of Congress and the Supreme Court, then expecting the American people to understand complex constitutional issues may be beyond possibility. This mistaken recall of history is a frightening and common occurrence. It may seem a trivial point, but to paraphrase the words of the Spanish-born American philosopher and poet Santayana (1863-1952), "those who forget their history are doomed to repeat the mistakes of the past." Forgetting the past begins with the details, and that is the danger we now face.

As I told my students, the Constitution is a worthless piece of paper if those in power do not follow it as it was intended. The original intent of each provision was based on a clear understanding of the abusive nature of power. Each provision then was to be a limit on the power of the government, to prevent abuse. However, understanding the intentions of the authors requires significant knowledge of these historical subjects, and that simply does not exist at any level in this country. Without it, combined with government leaders who wish to destroy the Constitution and consolidate their power, we may be on the road to a complete erosion of our rights and, eventually, totalitarianism. It is ironic that as the Eastern Bloc moves toward democracy, we are moving inevitably in the other direction.

The nation is indeed in serious trouble. Several amendments in the Bill of Rights are now dead. Parties on the right work feverishly, only to enslave the people with their pathetic and irrational religious dogma. Those parties on the left work feverishly, only to enslave the people with their perverted and socialistic views of morality. Adrift, without leadership, the nation declines; of that there can be no denial. In two hundred years, when the historians debate the reasons for the fall of the empire of the United States, they will pinpoint this period as the "critical time," and they will note the loss of our constitutional rights as a primary cause. Of course, this is supposing that there will be any freedom to think, speak, or write in the future. On the current course, that is highly unlikely. They will see in this critical period political parties concerned only about maintaining power so as to further their corruption, a people apathetic and functionally illiterate by government design, a system of democratic government that does not and cannot work, and a Constitution that should have acted as a wall to rising government tyranny, but did not, and the realization that the great experiment was a failure. Is this the future?

Our Constitution, the result of so many hard lessons in tyranny learned by Founders such as Madison, Hamilton, and Washington, has been weakened to a point where our liberties are more threatened now than they were in 1775 when the American Revolution broke out. In the 220 years since independence, our liberty has been almost completely stolen from us by our own government. It may already be too late to avert an Orwellian nightmare. This is the story of the rape of the Constitution.

PART I
THE BACKGROUND OF
THE CONSTITUTION

CHAPTER 1
THE NATURE OF POWER

Any study of the development of the United States Constitution must begin with an examination of the nature of power and the abuse of it by Britain during the colonial period. The colonists learned much about the abuse of power from Britain, and these lessons led them to craft the Constitution as they did.

Power seems to hold man in a trance-like grip, intoxicating him with its allure. British philosopher Lord Acton (1834-1902) expressed the very core and problem of power when he stated, "Power tends to corrupt and absolute power corrupts absolutely." This familiar aphorism has been repeatedly proven true throughout human history.

Ancient Rome, while making great strides in music, architecture, philosophy, and government, had a barbaric darkside. Roman emperors imbued with unlimited power achieved new lows in degradation, decadence, and abuses of mankind. Ranging far and wide across most of the known world, Roman legions savagely subjugated millions of people. At home, examples of government abuses were regularly found in the Roman Coliseum. The games which entertained emperors and the people forced criminals, opponents, and conquered leaders to fight to the death against each other and an assortment of odd devices and animals. Cries for blood emanated from the stands as emperors ordered Christians thrown to the lions. The true extent of the barbarity can only be understood by studying the lives of emperors such as Gaius Caligula who ruled from 37-41 A.D. They paint a picture of unbelievable atrocity on a grand scale.

Perhaps the most illustrative example of the abuse of power can be found in the history of the Roman Catholic Church and its popes, who have exercised tremendous power and done so in some of the most violent and abusive ways that the world has ever witnessed.

The abusive behavior of the Roman Catholic Church can clearly be seen in the infamous use of the Inquisition — an ecclesiastical institution organized to detect and punish heretics and others guilty of offenses against Roman Catholic orthodoxy. This practice began in northern Italy around 1224. In 1231, Pope Gregory IX adopted legislation requiring the penalty of death for the impenitent (unrepentant heretics). Beginning in France, but later spreading to almost all of Europe, the Pope divided nations into jurisdictions to be supervised by an Inquisitor whose role was to stamp out heresy. The Inquisitors were accountable only to the Pope, but in reality they answered to no one.

Inquisitors traveled throughout their jurisdictions and held tribunals. The procedure began with a sermon and a request that all those guilty of any of a long list of crimes against the Church come forward, confess, and repent. Those who did were usually let off lightly. Then a grace period of 15-30 days set in. After this period, the people were ordered to turn in known wrongdoers. This led to an intense search for suspects. Testimony from two witnesses was sufficient to commit an accused person to prison where hunger, lack of sleep, and physical abuses reduced their will to resist. They were then taken before the tribunal and told of the allegations, but never confronted by their accusers. No legal defense was allowed, on the grounds that an innocent person had nothing to fear and therefore did not need a defender. Defenseless, then, the accused was interrogated by the tribunal. By 1252 this subtle interrogation was not yielding satisfactory results, so Pope Innocent IV authorized the use of torture during the interrogation phase. Following the tribunal, the Inquisitor made a decision which, ironically, was always rendered on a Sunday. If convicted and still impenitent, the person was burned to death. All of their goods and property were confiscated so as to leave their descendants destitute. This is quite an interesting rite considering the

Bible includes a commandment that "thou shalt not kill." But then, religion has never had a particular problem with hypocrisy.

Inquisitions spread and increased in intensity over the next five centuries. During the infamous Spanish Inquisition (1480-1834), approximately 100,000 trials were conducted and 2,000 people were burned to death by the Church. This set off another inquisition in 1542, when Pope Paul III began the Roman Inquisition in an attempt to wipe out Protestantism. In order to carry this out, the Pope created the Holy Office, which existed until 1965.

Religion clearly has not been free from the negative influence of power. Torture, fear, mass murder, depravity of the grossest kinds, and heinous violations of the natural law are the reality of the Roman Catholic Church. The Inquisitions of the Middle Ages are but a few chapters in its infamous history. The Roman Catholics have murdered vast multitudes in the name of their god, yet they pretend to preach morality to the masses. That is, unfortunately, representative of several other world religions as well. Leaders and followers of these religions have been absolutely corrupted by power. If even the Church can be so corrupted, then power is a dangerous thing indeed. It follows from this that power is unquestionably an evil influence which must be carefully regulated.

In the late 17th century, America experienced the quintessential example of the results of power. The ordeal known as the Salem Witch trials began in March, 1692. At the beginning of that year, the church in Salem, Massachusetts, was without a minister. The town was locked in a struggle over the acceptance of the Reverend Samuel Parris as a replacement. The debate over his acceptance created animosity in the town due to his exorbitant salary demands. This conflict between families reflected a deeper division: a decades-old dispute over land. Inheritances were slowly changing the balance of power in the town by moving control of the land, and hence the power, from the families who owned the land (they were also the families who supported Reverend Parris), to those who did not (the families who opposed Parris). The majority won out and Parris was accepted. He, his family, and his West Indian slave, Tituba, moved to Salem and took up residence.

4

Soon after Parris began his term, his children and others became involved in games with the slave Tituba. These games involved incantations and fortune telling. The girls were caught in the midst of one of these blasphemous sessions and faced severe consequences. At that time, involvement in this type of activity was an offense of major proportions, a sign of witchcraft and satanism. The adults, who immediately panicked, demanded to know who had put the girls up to this evil business. The girls realized very quickly that they could escape the consequences of their acts by blaming others, which is exactly what they did. They began by accusing an old woman who lived in the town. She was a ripe target for paranoia, a strange old recluse. The girls claimed she was a witch who had cast spells on them making them participate in the evil games. The woman was arrested on charges of witchcraft and thrown in jail. The girls, feeling their power, began to accuse others, all of whom were arrested.

The trials of these suspected witches began and were run by the church, which completely rejected English judicial rules. The chained defendants were not even allowed defense counsel. The court accepted spectral evidence — testimony given by witnesses, the girls, about voices or apparitions perceived only by them. If a girl testified that the spirit of an accused person had attacked her, this was convincing evidence. Of course, there was no way to defend against such a thing.

On the basis of spectral evidence the hangings began. The terror spread, directed by Reverend Parris and the girls' parents (the landowning families who had supported Parris). The girls went after the other town families (the non-landowning opponents of Parris). Then, even the church and the girls' families lost control of the situation. Eventually, the girls rode from town to town in a wagon, across Massachusetts. In each community religious leaders dropped the names of suspects in the girls' ears. The girls would then go into their act of simulated fits and wild screaming, and accuse these people of witchcraft. They had, in effect, assumed control of the colony.

Finally, spectral evidence was rejected and the madness ended. By the time it was over, 19 innocent people had been hanged, and one crushed to death. Fifty had confessed (confession and repentance were the only way an accused witch could avoid the gallows), 100 were in jail awaiting trial, and another 200 stood accused. Years later, a few of those involved in this gigantic hoax admitted their crime and apologized.

The whole matter made people realize that the church should not control the government. Ignorant, paranoid intolerance cannot be the face of government. This feeling had much support from the Founders at the Constitutional Convention. This carried over into the passage of the Bill of Rights. The meaning of the religious freedom of the First Amendment has always been perceived as a protection for religion against government, and while that is partially true there was another goal as well. This other purpose was to protect the people and the nation from the abuses of religion. The Founders clearly understood that the mixing of church and state leads invariably to death and destruction.

The primary illustration of the abuses of power in Nazi Germany are found in the concentration camps. As the National Socialists rose to power under Adolf Hitler, they took barbaric revenge on all their opponents — Socialists, Communists, labor leaders, democrats, homosexuals, criminals, the Church, Free Masons, and Jews — only Germans at first, but later spreading to many nations. Eventually, the camp system comprised nearly 400 institutions. As German armies rampaged across continents conquering nations and subjugating the people, the mechanisms of internal security, chiefly under Reichsfuhrer-SS Heinrich Himmler, terrorized the people and raped their former countries of all value. Millions were sent to the camps.

Stalinist Russia, in the 1930s, murdered many people. Stalin, paranoid and psychotic, ordered the deaths of opponents in huge numbers. Those not killed outright were sent to the camps of Siberia.

These are not the only examples of abuses by government in world history. The list is endless. It reflects the corrupting nature of power which affects every person and government. In his 1994 book, *Death by Government*, University of Hawaii Professor R.J. Rummel compiled statistics on the number of people murdered by governments during the 20th Century.

6

Adolf Hitler and his paladins, 1935
(Reproduced from the Collections of the Library Of Congress.)

Name	Years	Murdered
Joseph Stalin (USSR)	1929-35	42,672,000
Mao Tse-tung (China)	1923-76	37,828,000
Adolf Hitler (Germany)	1933-45	20,946,000
Chiang Kai-shek (China)	1921-48	10,214,000
Vladimir Lenin (USSR)	1917-24	4,017,000
Hideki Tojo (Japan)	1937-45	3,990,000
Pol Pot (Cambodia)	1968-87	2,397,000
Yayha Khan (Pakistan)	1971	1,500,000
Josip Tito (Yugoslavia)	1941-87	1,172,000

This list, which includes only non-military civilian casualties, totals over 124 million people killed by government action in this century alone. Unfortunately, the list does not even include recent genocidal episodes in Bosnia, Somalia, Sudan, and Rwanda. In conclusion, Rummel sums up by saying, "Power kills. The more power a government has, the more it kills." A truer statement has never been uttered.

To govern means, by definition, "to control the actions or behaviors of; to guide; to direct; to make and administer public policy for a political unit." Government, in order to reach its objectives (public policy), must control the actions and behaviors of the people. To do so it must rely on the exercise of power. It does, however, display a disconcerting tendency to move toward maintaining, consolidating, and increasing its control. This is true of any government, be it Washington D.C., Moscow, Peking, or Baghdad. Government will use any means to achieve these ends. I wonder how many Americans, as they recoiled in horror at the massacre of protesting students in China during the summer of 1989, were aware that President Hoover used similar tactics when he sent tanks and troops against American World War I veterans as they peacefully protested in Washington D.C. in 1932.

A study of history forces us to accept two propositions: First, power is bad (Lord Acton); and Second, government relies on power to control. Logic then dictates that government must be inherently bad. The historical record shows this to be true!

8

A related proposition is that humanity, upon whom government rests, is by nature an evil entity disposed to do wrong. A treatise of infinite length would be required to fully develop this hypothesis. Let it suffice to say that if this were not true, then laws would not be needed to regulate human behavior. In addition, the history of mankind's acts prove this disposition. No amount of threats by the organized hypocrisy known as religion and its malevolent deities has ever, nor will ever, be able to change this fundamental point. With this behavior in mind, and because society needs control and organization, government becomes necessary.

The resulting paradox is that government will always be bad, but the human condition dictates that we must have it. The only other possibility would be to resort to a state of anarchy. This is not a real option, because mankind must have limits. Mankind's entire history is one chapter after another of serious abuses of other men. These abuses have occurred in societies under the control of government. The results can only be imagined if mankind were left to its own devices without any controls at all. Mankind simply cannot live in a totally unregulated state. Since anarchy is not an option, the only alternative is to have government that is understood by the people for its true character, and have clear written prohibitions against certain behaviors by that government.

The Founding Fathers had, through their experiences with Britain, gained a real understanding of this true nature of power and government. This explains why they built in many layers of constitutional protection to prevent our government from increasing and abusing its power. The Bill of Rights is the clearest example of this. The phrase, "Congress shall make no law," from the First Amendment, points to certain areas that our government may never enter. The Founders knew that this was the only way to stop a government from abusing its power, even a government that feigns worship of democratic ideals.

CHAPTER 2
THE COLONIAL CRISIS
WITH BRITAIN

To understand the development of the Constitution, one must trace the events that led to the Philadelphia Convention of 1787. That history begins with the colonial relationship between Britain and the 13 Colonies, and continues through the American Revolution, the Articles of Confederation, and the convention itself. It was the combination of these experiences that led the Founders to draft the Constitution, with each tenet based on some lesson learned from their past.

Trouble between Britain and the colonies took about 124 years to come to a head. The first step in that direction was the passage of the laws of trade and navigation (known as the Navigation Acts) by Parliament between 1651 and 1663. These laws, a four-point trade policy for controlling colonial trade, were the result of a new economic system known as mercantilism. This system, developed in 16th-Century Europe, required a nation, like a business, to maintain a favorable balance of trade — that is, to sell more than it bought. The goal was to create a self-sustaining empire that was totally independent of other nations. With many European countries pursuing this economic philosophy, it became difficult to find customers. Countries with colonies quickly realized that they could use them as purchasers for the mother country's goods. England, as a developing industrial nation, pursued this thinking. Its American colonies were forced to buy large amounts of goods from England in order to ensure a favorable balance of trade. To England the colonies existed solely to make the mother country rich. This put the colonies in a position inferior to England, a position that would not sit well with the developing spirit of colonial independence. The obvious drawback for a colony under mercantilism is that its wealth is bled off to the mother country.

The Navigation Acts represented classic mercantilism. These four laws required that in any trade involving the colonies:

1. The ship and a majority of its crew be English.
2. All manufactured goods would be purchased only from England. If England did not produce a particular good then it could be purchased from another location as long as it was shipped through England first with the additional expense (tax and shipping) added.
3. Certain colonial raw materials would be sold only to England.
4. The colonies were forbidden to make manufactured goods from their own raw materials.

The impact of these laws was widespread. Iron, for example, was mined in the Middle Colonies, but the colonists were forbidden to use it to make the tools they needed (4th law). They were then forced to ship the iron to England, even though other countries were willing to pay higher prices (3rd law). The ship that carried the iron and most its crew had to be English (1st law). Finally, the colonies were forced to buy the manufactured iron tools back from England even though other countries offered lower prices (2nd law).

The benefits to England were clear, as was the burden on the developing American economy. This upset some colonists, but as time passed both sides prospered from the extensive colonial resources. This did, however, set a precedent for English economic domination. The fact that there was no real resistance in the colonies suggested to England that the colonies were willing to be used by their mother country, an idea that would lead to more burdensome and offensive laws in the 1760s and 1770s. During this period of roughly 100 years, England grew, and in 1707, along with Scotland, became the United Kingdom of Great Britain.

By 1754, Britain and France were claiming the same land in North America. This land between the Great Lakes and the Mississippi River was known as the Ohio Valley. As Virginia planters moved into the area, settled, and began to sell the land, France responded by building a series of forts to keep the colonists east of the

Appalachian Mountains. It was then only a matter of time before war broke out.

The French and Indian War, as it became known, was started by a young Virginia militia officer. Colonel George Washington, disobeying orders, attacked French Fort Duquesne, the site of modern Pittsburgh, on July 4, 1754. His forces were soundly defeated by a combined force of French troops and Indians, and a world war was set off. In North America the French, the Indians, and later the Spanish engaged Britain and her colonies. The war went badly for the British in the beginning, but they made a comeback in 1758 by capturing Fort Duquesne and the French stronghold of Louisbourg. A British invasion of French Canada captured Quebec in 1759 and Montreal in 1760.

The war dragged on until it was settled by the Treaty of Paris in 1763. The treaty signified a great victory for Britain. In its most important provision, all French land in America, east of the Mississippi River, was ceded to Britain. This doubled British colonial holdings in that region.

As is often the case in the cause-and-effect relationship of history, this great victory for Britain turned out to be a disaster. After nine years of war Britain was broke, and its people — on the verge of revolt due to high taxes — were demanding relief. To add to this, Britain now had huge new territories to defend, conquered land containing former enemies that needed to be controlled, and the still-strong French threat that required continued military preparation. These things required huge new expenditures from a country that could not afford them. In January, 1763, the British debt stood at £122,603,000.

To solve the economic crisis the British government then made some tragic policy decisions. They felt that the war had been fought to protect the colonies; therefore, the Americans should share in its costs. Acts to raise taxes against the colonies were the next step. This was reasonable thinking, for the colonies had provoked the situation in the Ohio Valley and actually started the fighting, but raising taxes was not practical at that time.

12

The British government completely misunderstood the colonies for a number of reasons. First, members of Parliament were more concerned with battling each other over power and prestige than they were in developing coherent legislation. Second, they felt that the colonists were "country bumpkins" — convicts, religious dissenters, refugees, and foreigners. They remained unaware of the development of an educated elite and well-informed population in the colonies. Third, King George III suffered from mental illness. Fourth, the British government was badly divided among various political factions. Together, these problems caused the British government to embark on a course of action that would stir the independent Americans to revolt in only 12 years.

Shortly after the treaty that ended the war, a new threat arose in the area of the Great Lakes. In the spring of 1763, Indian Chief Pontiac led a major uprising that destroyed eight British forts. This revolt was caused by colonial incursions onto Indian land. The British government, in no position to finance another war, responded with legislation to avoid further Indian trouble. The Proclamation of 1763 created a buffer zone between the Indians and the colonists. It drew a line at the Appalachian Mountains and ordered the colonists to remain east of the line. All British land to the west was reserved for the Indians. The colonists were outraged. They claimed that they had fought for this land and now they were prohibited from moving onto it. Of course, this was a loose excuse at best, as the American desire for this land was motivated by greed. Some defiant Americans disobeyed the law. This defiance was interpreted by the British as lawlessness by the ungrateful colonists. The misunderstanding that would lead to another war had begun.

In 1764, Parliament passed the Sugar Act, making good on their intention to raise money for debts by taxing the colonies. While both Britain and the colonies prospered, Britain had been lax in enforcing its trade laws against the colonies. As a result, the existing tax on sugar and molasses was not being enforced. This new Sugar Act cut the old tax in half, but it was now to be collected. Opposition in America was generally confined to the business class involved in this trade. The tax, however, was not the greatest burden. The real problem came from the customs inspectors armed with Writs of Assistance. These were essentially blank search warrants that gave agents of the Crown *carte blanche* to enter and search anywhere without limitation. The abuse of this power created much colonial discontent.

In 1765 the Quartering Act was passed. This law required the colonists to provide shelter and food for British troops in America. The act was intended to reduce Britain's American defense costs, estimated at £350,000 per year at the conclusion of the French and Indian War in 1763. This was clearly a logical and reasonable step for the British to take; however, it was not practical at this time to tell the Americans that they had to take British troops into their homes and support them. The American position can be compared to that of a spoiled brat who expects everything to be done for him without fulfilling any responsibilities in return. It can be argued, however, that the inferior position of the colonies to the mother country in the context of more than 100 years of economic control and protection had created this attitude. Predictably, the Americans viewed the forced quartering of troops as the prelude to military occupation, and complained bitterly. The British continued to misunderstand the situation, and saw this as escalating disloyalty among the ungrateful colonists.

Also, in 1765, Parliament passed the Stamp Act, which placed a direct tax on legal documents, newspapers, dice, playing cards, and marriage licenses. A direct tax is by definition one that is placed directly upon the people. At the time of purchase, a stamp was bought to show that the tax had been paid. This tax was very obvious to all colonists and it immediately set off intense protests throughout the colonies. Petitions flooded Parliament demanding repeal of the law. Newspapers and political leaders urged the people to resist the act, and street demonstrations and riots broke out. Government property was destroyed, and British Prime Minister George Grenville was stoned and burned in effigy. The protests were most severe in Massachusetts, where the homes of a stamp-tax collector and the Lieutenant Governor were ransacked, and in Virginia, where Patrick Henry, speaking before the House of Burgesses, reminded King George III of the fates of earlier tyrants like Caesar and Charles I. The most important result of these protests was that they were held throughout the colonies, and helped develop a sense of cooperation and unity.

By the summer of 1765, the colonists began to boycott British goods and pledged not to use the stamps. Then, in October, came the Stamp Act Congress. Nine colonies sent representatives to New York City to organize protests against the Stamp Act. The result was the "Declaration of Rights and Grievances" which expressed loyalty to Britain, but demanded an end to taxation. The colonies had by this time developed rather republican forms of government and democratic ideals were inbred to the American spirit. The rallying cry of the time became "no taxation without representation." This alluded to the argument that there were no Americans in Parliament and thus Britain lacked the legal right to tax the colonies. It is interesting to speculate that had the British simply allowed some representatives from the colonies to sit in Parliament, the entire problem might well have been alleviated. Unfortunately, they did not, so colonial opposition began to spread from a few rabble-rousers to the general population. The British misunderstood the whole sequence of events and wrote it off as ungrateful disloyalty from a vocal minority.

Finally, the colonial boycotts had an economic impact on British merchants, who demanded that the Stamp Act be repealed. Under this pressure the act was repealed in March 1766. Simultaneously, embarrassed by this political defeat, Parliament passed the Declaratory Act to state that even though the Stamp Act was gone, "Parliament had the absolute right to make laws for British citizens everywhere in all cases whatsoever." It was, of course, a face-saving gesture. From this victory the Americans learned three lessons: the power of cooperation between the colonies; that Britain needed them as much as they needed Britain; and to distrust the mother country.

Following the embarrassing repeal of the Stamp Act, George Grenville was replaced as Prime Minister by Charles Townshend, nicknamed "Champagne Charlie" for his love of drinking. Considering the rising problems between the colonies and Britain, placing a drunk in charge of colonial policy was bound to worsen the situation. Nonetheless, Townshend went to work on the problem of raising money for British debts. He had no doubt that the money must come from the colonies. His plan was different in that he would try to get away with it by hiding the taxes. The Townshend Act of 1767 placed an indirect tax (one already included in the price of the product) on tea, paint, lead, and many other everyday items needed by the colonists. Import duties were established on these items so that the tax was paid by the merchants when the goods arrived in America. This meant that the colonists would not pay an additional fee at purchase, yet they were paying the tax. Champagne Charlie had found his method of taxing the colonists without their knowledge.

This was certainly a sensible approach, but in the climate of mistrust that existed it was also fraught with danger. Upon learning of these new laws, the colonists felt that Britain had resorted to trickery, and the protests started anew. It was a recurrence of the tactics of the Stamp Act protests, but this time they became violent. Boston was the hotbed of discontent and the center of the violence. As mob rule threatened law and order in Massachusetts during 1767 and 1768, Britain responded by sending troops to quell the disruption. This was another action based on Britain's misunderstanding of the situation, for troops could only aggravate the problem. With angry British troops in the same location as angry colonists who didn't want them there, trouble was bound to develop.

That trouble did indeed break out on March 5, 1770. An American mob, which in all fairness was totally responsible for provoking this trouble, had cornered a lone young British sentry. The growing crowd threw ice, sticks, and rocks and threatened to kill the man. British reinforcements were called up to escort the sentry from the hazardous affair. The crowd attacked the troops. What happened next has been much debated, but it seems that a rock hit a British soldier in the head knocking him to the ground. As he fell his musket went off. Some of the other troops, fearing that they had been fired upon, individually fired into the crowd in self-defense. Five colonists died in the confrontation.

This matter seriously raised tensions. Colonial newspapers now spread the story, along with an illustration of the event, throughout the colonies. The illustration, by Paul Revere, was an outrageous exaggeration, for it depicted an innocent, cowering and praying crowd of men, women, children and a puppy being ruthlessly and viciously attacked by an organized firing line of smiling British troops. The message that echoed across the colonies from Boston was that the British would mercilessly slaughter colonists to enforce their laws.

The Boston Massacre, March 1770: Totally False

Finally, Britain began to tire of colonial disloyalty. A climate of distrust and anger developed on the British side of the pond. The resulting "get tough" policy would not help matters.

Things simmered until 1773, when the Tea Act was passed. The Townshend Act boycotts on tea had seriously hurt British merchants, as valuable tea lay rotting in warehouses. Many members of Parliament owned stock in the East India Tea Company, one of the largest and most affected by the boycotts. They needed a way to move the tea, and they found it in the Tea Act.

Previously, the Navigation Acts required the colonists to buy all goods either directly from Britain, or if purchased elsewhere, shipped through Britain. This greatly increased the price of the goods. The Tea Act allowed the East India Tea Company to ship tea directly to America without going through Britain, which would significantly reduce the price of tea from this company. Parliament thought this act would be well-received by the Americans, who could then purchase cheaper tea, and it would also solve the crisis faced by the East India Tea Company, leading to increased profits for its stockholders.

The British were shocked by the unexpected and violent reaction from the Americans. But by this time, 1773, the colonists could best be described as paranoid. They were on the lookout for the next British attempt to subvert their liberties. The colonists claimed that Parliament's motive for this law was to create a monopoly. The Americans feared that this low-cost tea would bankrupt the competition, thus allowing the East India Tea Company to then raise prices to whatever level they chose. Whether the members of Parliament had such plans or not, and they probably did, this monopoly conspiracy never had a chance to develop, because the colonists in Boston held their famous tea party and things quickly became much worse.

The Boston Tea Party was the final straw for the British. They believed that they had protected and nurtured the colonies, and were being repaid with defiance and treason. It was time to punish the colonies.

Four punishment laws came in 1774 — the Coercive Acts, nicknamed the Intolerable Acts by the colonists. These laws closed Boston Harbor to all trade until the colonists paid for the destroyed tea, took tight control of the Massachusetts government, added a new tougher Quartering Act, and stated that British officials who committed crimes in America would have their trials in Britain. In the colonists' view, these laws starved Bostonians, deprived Americans of their rights of self-government and liberty, forced British troops into their homes, and gave license to British officials to get away with murder and then have their trials in Britain where they would not be convicted. American intransigence did not help matters. For example, a group of Boston merchants offered to pay for the destroyed tea, but the Sons of Liberty under Sam Adams and John Hancock forcefully prevented this from happening. They wanted confrontation. Soon they would have it.

Parliament also passed the Quebec Act in 1774, ostensibly to placate the French population in British Canada. This act made the Ohio Valley a part of Quebec, ending any possibility of colonial expansion into that area. This was widely viewed as another punishment law. Realistically, it could not have been anything else. As misguided as the British had been towards the colonies, there is no way that they could have failed to understand how the colonists would react to this. The very land that had started the French and Indian War and caused this entire series of events was now passed back to the French.

The Americans organized the First Continental Congress to meet in Philadelphia during September, 1774. The united representatives of 12 colonies appealed to Britain to repeal the Coercive Acts and restore peace, but that was not to be. King George III had decided that "blows must decide," and they soon would at the battles of Lexington and Concord in April, 1775. Following these battles, the Americans organized the Second Continental Congress representing all 13 colonies. This would act as the central government for the running of the war effort, and would last until the creation and acceptance of the Articles of Confederation.

The war itself is not relevant to the background development of the Constitution, except in that it helped create some problems between the colonies that made forming a postwar united government difficult. Suffice it to say that after eight years of hardship, trauma, amazing blunders on both sides, and French assistance for the Americans, the war ended with an American victory under the Treaty of Paris of 1783.

One event that cannot be so quickly passed over was the Declaration of Independence, which made a clear statement that due to Britain's obvious and severe abuses of power, it no longer had claim to the 13 colonies. The colonies declared themselves the independent United States of America. The Declaration of Independence also focused on an important concept of government that is the cornerstone of our country, that government is based on the consent of the governed, and when that support is lost the people have the right to dissolve that government and form a new one. This is one point that the current regime should remember.

CHAPTER 3
THE ARTICLES OF
CONFEDERATION

In May of 1776, the Second Continental Congress urged the 13 colonies to set up new state governments, a task that was completed by 1780. These new state governments reflected the colonists' fear of strong central power.

The states set up a variety of provisions to prevent strong government. To reflect their philosophy that a country should be ruled by laws and not by the whims of men, each state had a written constitution. All of the states gave the ultimate power to the people, saying that government existed solely to serve the governed, and that the people alone could establish or dissolve a government. Each state's constitution placed certain restrictions on the power of its government. These included bans on permanent armies and searches without warrants, and held that basic rights such as free speech and press, the right to petition the government for a redress of grievances, trial by jury, and due process of law could not be denied. In every state the power of the executive authority was reduced. Some states denied the governor a veto power; others limited the governor to a single term. Eight states placed the selection of the governor in the hands of the legislature, and Pennsylvania abolished the office altogether.

The thinking of the colonists followed a certain logic. They understood that Britain had been a strong government and that it had abused its power. From this the Americans inferred that strong government was bad. It then followed that weak government must be good. From this premise the Americans went about setting up weak governments in each state and on the national level.

20

The demands for cooperation and organization created by the war against Britain made a national government essential. In June, 1776, the Second Continental Congress began work on a constitution for the national government. The final product, drawn up by John Dickinson of Pennsylvania, was the first American Constitution. Known as the Articles of Confederation, it proposed a weak alliance among the states, which left the states with almost total sovereignty, and provided very limited power at the national level.

An omen of problems to come developed immediately, as the 13 states, which tended to act more like separate countries, became embroiled in a conflict over western land claims. Various states had their eyes on the British land between the Appalachian Mountains and the Mississippi River. Even at the very beginning of the war the colonists had plans to carve up this land, regardless of the fact that the colonies appeared to be losing. Nonetheless, several states extended their boundaries to the west, intending to add this valuable land to their territory. Virginia, though, based on her original land grant, extended her southern border to the west and her northern border to the northwest. This caused conflicting claims with Massachusetts, Connecticut, New York, Maryland, and Pennsylvania. The smaller states with no land claims also got involved by arguing that they would be forever dominated by the larger states if those states gained access to the new lands and resources. At a time when they most needed cooperation, the states spent four years fighting about land, as the war raged around them. This, of course, delayed any progress toward achieving a national government.

In 1779, Maryland suggested that all states give up their land claims and turn the land over to the national government when it was created. The following year Virginia finally gave in and rescinded her land claims. All other states did the same. With this settled, the Articles of Confederation were adopted in March, 1781. This squabbling over land claims was an unfortunate omen of things to come. It foreshadowed a struggle between small and large states that would force Constitution-shaping compromises at the Philadelphia Convention in 1787.

The league of friendship created by the Articles was intentionally weak. It gave the government a few specific powers, but denied five basic powers. First, the government could not tax. The still-fresh fear of British taxing abuses rippled through the American psyche. They reasoned that our government could not repeat those abuses if it could not tax.

Second, the government could not regulate trade. Britain had passed the Navigation Acts and others during more than 100 years of controlling colonial trade. The colonists had taken great offense at these laws and were very resistant to the idea of allowing the new national government to have this formidable power.

Third, the government could not prevent a state from issuing its own money. British monetary policy had crippled colonial economies, and once again no state was willing to relinquish this power to the national government.

Fourth, the government was not to have a separate executive. The great hatred felt for Britain at the time was centered on King George III and the various prime ministers he had used to carry out his colonial policies. Americans saw the executive authority as being responsible for the tyranny that affected America, and they therefore would allow no executive.

Finally, the government was allowed no national court system. Decisions made by courts were to be controlled locally. The states were surely afraid that national courts would have the power to settle disputes between the states and with the national government, reducing the sovereignty of the states. The states feared that in any conflict with the national government, asking a national court system to decide would be analogous to asking a referee to make a call in a game while he plays on one of the teams.

The Articles' government was to consist of a legislature only. This Confederation Congress was made up of two to seven representatives from each state. In the Congress, each state had only one vote, making all the states equal regardless of population. Congress could only be called into session when a quorum of nine states were present. The same number was required in order to pass any legislation. Finally, any changes in the Articles needed the approval of all thirteen states.

The intention of the designers of the Articles was to create a weak government, and in that they were highly successful. There were, however, unforeseen repercussions. For each of the five powers denied the national government, a new problem was also created.

The lack of a taxing power meant that the new government would be broke from the beginning. A government without money obviously cannot provide any of the services that define the institution itself. The most pressing concern was defense, as European nations hovered like vultures, ready to pick at the remains once the United States collapsed.

The inability to control trade also created numerous problems. Left to their own devices, the states passed laws to support their economies and trade, often at the expense of other states. Many states levied taxes on goods from other states. Virginia, for example, placed a tax on Pennsylvania farmers who crossed its roads on the way to the Carolinas. The resulting increase in prices pushed the Pennsylvanians out of the market in the Carolinas. Pennsylvania retaliated, as did the Carolinas. These approaches greatly hurt trade between the states and caused conflict. The economy of the country as a whole suffered immeasurably. On the international scene, other trade problems developed. It became extremely difficult for countries to negotiate trade agreements, as there was no one American voice with which to negotiate. Any time a foreign nation would propose trade with the United States, its envoys would be met by representatives of all 13 states and the national government, who would proceed to use every nefarious scheme available to gain the advantages of this trade for the entity they represented. The United States became a laughingstock to European nations with their obsession for diplomatic formalities.

The lack of control over money meant the states were free to issue any currency they wanted. Many states printed paper money without any responsible monetary policy. Basic economics dictates that money printed in large quantities, without backing such as gold, will lose value and eventually be worthless. This quickly became the case in the 1780s. Rhode Island put out so much worthless money that it was nicknamed "Rogue's Island" currency. Rampant inflation was not the only side effect. The lack of exchange rates resulted in confusion, and people refused to accept any money except that printed in their state. This further damaged trade between the states, and made international trade nearly impossible.

The lack of an executive brought about a lack of leadership and direction. Decision by committee is often slow and generally ineffective, and this held true in the 1780s. As the country faced mounting problems, the Confederation Congress moved in circles, going nowhere fast.

The lack of a national judiciary meant that national laws could not be enforced. Technically, the states were responsible for enforcing the laws of the Confederation, but this allowed the states to nullify any national laws they didn't like, which is exactly what they did.

Finally, the procedural organization of the Confederation Congress caused problems. If the Congress managed to achieve a quorum (a minimum number of representatives required to be on hand to carry out binding business), which was always a problem, it had difficulty gaining approval of the nine states required to pass legislation. The states, simply pursuing their own selfish goals, rarely cooperated. The most damaging factor was the requirement that all 13 states approve any changes to the Articles. The bottom line was that the Americans had created a system that brought chaos and then, because of its rigidity, they were locked into it.

By 1786, America was in serious trouble. Severe economic problems, rivalries between the states, low prestige at home and in Europe, and rising social unrest threatened independence. These conditions were perfect for breeding rebellion, and it wasn't long in coming.

By the summer of 1786, unrest was stirring again in Massachusetts. The farmers, many of whom were Revolutionary War veterans, were losing their ability to make their land mortgage payments. Just at this time the state legislature, controlled by the rich businessmen of Boston, shifted the tax burden from themselves to the farmers. Many farmers lost their farms and their livelihoods. A revolt erupted and turned into a mini-civil war. Revolutionary War hero Captain Daniel Shays led an armed band against courthouses in two counties. The attacks were designed to put an end to court actions against the farmers for debts. Next they moved against the arsenal in Springfield to seize ammunition. The governor organized a militia force to stop the revolt. The farmers were defeated, but the event had national implications. Across the land, fear spread with the news of Shays' Rebellion. It seemed that law and order were giving way to mob rule, and the national government was powerless to do anything about it. It became clear to most people that unless a stronger union was formed, there would soon be no union at all.

The Americans learned that a government that is either too strong or too weak is bad. Some realized a new plan was needed, one that would be strong enough to govern the nation but possessing built-in safeguards to prevent abuses. This thinking would lead to the Constitutional Convention in Philadelphia during the summer of 1787.

CHAPTER 4
THE CONSTITUTIONAL
CONVENTION

In 1787, the Philadelphia Convention was called by the Confederation Congress to recommend changes in the Articles of Confederation. Twelve of the states, Rhode Island being the only exception, sent delegates to the convention. These delegates began to drift into Philadelphia in May, and on the 25th they began their deliberations. Many of the most famous American leaders attended. George Washington was quickly elected president of the convention. Of the fifty-five delegates who attended, the average daily attendance was thirty-one. The convention ran immediately into disagreement as certain delegates had come ready to do more than just revise the Articles; they had come to throw them out completely and create a new form of government altogether. One of the first decisions was to keep the proceedings secret so that their debates would not be fought out in the public glare, and so that men could argue honestly without fear of reprisal. In a technical sense, the decisions of these delegates to exceed their authority and create a new government instead of revising the old one amounted to a secret plot to overthrow the existing government of the United States.

Two sides developed over the issue of creating a new form of government. The Nationalists wanted a strong national government. These men were very aware of the failures of the Articles which resulted from its weaknesses. However, those who opposed this idea clearly remembered the abuses of Britain's strong government. The Nationalists argued that if the union were not strengthened, all liberties would be lost in anarchy. Their view, persuasively argued, along with the great chaos in the country at that time, carried the day, and the convention decided to write a new Constitution.

Over the next four months the convention hammered out what has been called a "bundle of compromises." Several of the arguments almost ended the convention, and several delegates left Philadelphia during the proceedings with the declaration that they would do their best to defeat the plan. In the course of the heated debates, Ben Franklin was a consistent voice of compromise. Just as things would seem on the verge of disaster he would rise with a humorous tale, calm the situation, and present the need to reach an accommodation for the good of the country. The convention was able to compromise on issues that separated the large and small states, north and south, slave and free, and industrial and agricultural. The body of the document is found in Articles I, II, and III, and we owe most of the plan to James Madison, a delegate from Virginia. He would become known as the "Father of the Constitution and Bill of Rights."

On the third day of the convention, Governor Edmund Randolph rose to present the Virginia Plan as drafted by Madison. It proposed a government divided into three branches — the executive, legislative, and judicial. It would have strong new powers including the powers to tax, control trade, and control the printing of money. This proposal would address all of the major problems of the Articles of Confederation and create a strong nation under the control of a central government.

The delegates did not really have trouble with this plan until Randolph presented the make-up of the legislative branch. It would be comprised of a bicameral legislature (a body divided into two parts) called the Congress. Its two houses, the Assembly and the Senate, would have representation based on a state's population. Supporters of this plan pointed out that Virginia, with a population in excess of 800,000, had the same vote in the Confederation Congress as Delaware, with less than 100,000 inhabitants; that certainly was not democratic. But the small states were bitterly opposed to the Virginia Plan as it would put them under the domination of the large states in the new Congress.

James Madison: The Father of the Constitution
(Reproduced from the Collections of the Library Of Congress.)

In response, the small states developed the New Jersey Plan. William Paterson presented this plan, with a unicameral legislature where all the states had one vote. Many delegates pointed out, correctly, that this was nothing more than a return to the failures of the Articles of Confederation. The small states, however, clung to the position that given the nature of power, if the large states were in a position to dominate the small states, they would do so. The old issue of western land claims resurfaced and everyone was reminded of the actions of certain large states, like Virginia, which had attempted to monopolize the new lands. The small states feared that if the large states controlled Congress they could divide new land among themselves, thereby creating new resources and wealth. As these translated into new opportunities, population would grow rapidly in the large states, and this would increase their control in Congress. This was seen as the beginning of a vicious circle that was plainly bad for the small states. Delaware threatened to withdraw from the convention if the Virginia Plan was passed.

Roger Sherman of Connecticut presented the only logical compromise, considering that neither side was willing to accept the other's position. Sherman called for the Congress to be a bicameral legislature. One chamber, the House of Representatives, would be based on the population of a state, and the Senate would have an equal number of votes for each state. The passage of legislation would require the approval of both houses. This plan preserved the ideals of both sides.

It would seem that the small states had a legitimate complaint against any plan to base representation on population, as it would have doomed them to permanent subservience to the larger states. On the other hand, the small states attempted to maintain the undemocratic idea of equality between the states regardless of population. Both plans, then, were flawed. Logically, of course, this meant that the compromise, which used elements from both plans, was flawed as well. The small states got the better of the deal, as they could defeat any legislation in the Senate and ignore the more democratic House of Representatives. This problem became evident from 1819-1850, as the north/south conflict came down to the southern states, with significantly smaller populations, being able to block any legislation in the Senate.

If both of these plans were flawed, then what would have been an alternative? Considering the differences between the states and a general paranoia towards strong government, there may not have been a solution that was democratic, fair, and practical that could have been approved at the convention. The Connecticut Compromise was probably the best that could have been achieved under the circumstances.

On a more fundamental level, the question must be asked: Is republican (representative) government a workable form of government? Its underlying premise is that representatives are elected to run the government on behalf of the people. These representatives then make laws, generally by majority vote. This is supposed to represent the wishes of the majority of the people. The main problem is an internal and inherent paradox. If a member of Congress makes promises to his constituents, is elected, and is faced with legislation that is bad for the nation, but his constituents demand he vote for it as promised, what does he do? If he votes against it he protects the nation, but violates the very essence of representative government. If he votes for it he fulfills republicanism, but harms the nation.

Some argue that a member of Congress should represent the people by doing what he thinks best, but in the context of modern democratic thinking, that is an elitist attitude. Surprisingly, this line of thinking is close to that shared by most of the Founders at the Constitutional Convention. They felt the American people were incapable of dealing with the complexities of running a nation, so the people should elect representatives to run it for them. The representatives would be those with experience, competence, and knowledge of politics who could make the proper decisions. The use of the Electoral College in presidential elections is a perfect illustration. The Founders also believed, somewhat naively, that leaders would do what was right for the majority. Inevitably, though, this arrangement must fail. The political leaders, affected by the nature of power, will develop their own agendas, lead the nation in ways that benefit themselves and their supporting power structures, lose contact with the people, and move towards legislative dictatorship. This certainly has a familiar ring in the 1990s.

Philosophy aside, though, the body of the Constitution set up the structure of the new national government, but two important doctrines entered into the plan. First, the doctrine of separation of powers, the main idea behind Madison's Virginia Plan, divided the necessary powers of government into three separate branches. This meant that no one person or group could gain total control and abuse their power, because the powers of creating laws, carrying them out, and interpreting them each fell into different hands.

Second, the doctrine of checks and balances supplemented the separation of powers by setting up a series of controls that each branch has over the other two. Congress may pass bills into law, but the President may veto them. Congress may override a presidential veto if two-thirds of its members vote to do so. The Supreme Court may declare acts of Congress and the President to be unconstitutional and therefore void. Congress may, with the aid of the states, pass constitutional amendments to overturn decisions of the Supreme Court. The President may affect the makeup of the federal courts, including the Supreme Court, by making appointments to them, but the Senate must approve his choices.

After months of arguing, the final version was printed and approved on September 16, 1787. The delegates signed the document, and the next day George Washington adjourned the convention. The hard part — the ratification struggle — still lay ahead.

Madison's plan really was brilliant. Not only did it split up the power, but it also created a situation where the three branches would continually confront each other. Under such a system it seemed impossible for the government to consolidate, increase, and abuse its power. The modern dilemma is that this confrontational system does not promote swift, effective governing. In addition, the three branches now have more power individually than even the most extreme nationalist at the convention could have imagined for the entire government. Unfortunately, the result has become three tyrannical branches, each abusing the rights of the people in their separate ways.

Even with these faults, however, the Constitution has, for the most part, provided protection for the people against some severe abuses by the government. Together with a list of rights held by the people, the Constitution has allowed our nation to maintain political stability and liberty never before witnessed in the history of the world. It has not been a perfect system; indeed it has been far from that. The Founders only failing was that they created a piece of paper that required those in power to follow it as it was intended. The number of abuses at the hands of men has been disgraceful, though this does not take away from the document itself. As trampling reaches epidemic proportions in the 1990s it is not too late to return to the Constitution and its original intent. If we do not, we have only our liberty to lose.

CHAPTER 5
THE BILL OF RIGHTS

The Bill of Rights was not a part of the original Constitution. As the country struggled through the fight to ratify the Constitution, several states demanded the addition of a list of rights, to be held by the people, which the government could not violate. Some states conditioned their ratification upon this. The pro-ratification Federalists promised to propose such a list in the First Congress, and this helped swing many voices in favor of the Constitution. The Constitution required nine states to ratify it before it went into effect. New Hampshire was the ninth to do so on June 21, 1788.

Following ratification, elections were held, and the First Congress then took up the issue of a Bill of Rights. Numerous amendments were proposed by the states, and finally twelve were presented by Congressman James Madison. Of the original twelve, ten amendments were ratified by the states by December 15, 1791.

The demand for a list of rights had come from the more radical states, the ones which had suffered the most under British rule. The Bill of Rights uses two major approaches. First, it lists specific actions that the government may not ever take. These are clearly spelled out in the words, "Congress shall make no law..." in the First Amendment. Second, it lists a series of rights that the people possess which cannot ever be taken away, such as gun ownership and the right to have the assistance of counsel when accused of a crime. With rare exceptions these rights are absolute and not open to interpretation, though this has not prevented the courts from doing so.

The amendments in the Bill of Rights fall into several categories. The First Amendment lists general religious and political rights which

34

all Americans enjoy. Amendments 2-4 include basic protections for all Americans. Amendments 5-8 protect Americans involved in the judicial system. Amendments 9-10 reserve all other powers of government to the American people and the states on an equal footing with those granted to the federal government. These amendments are listed in order of importance. This is a concept known as "preferred position," which reflects the concerns of the Founders. These rights were intended to be absolute. Unfortunately, that has not been the case.

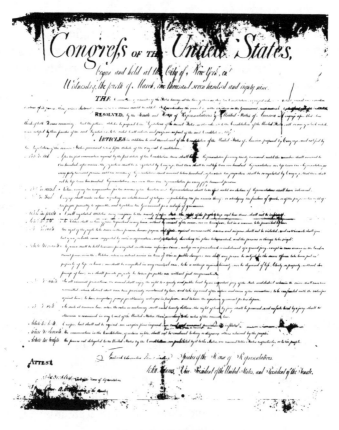

The Bill of Rights
(Reproduced from the Collections of the Library Of Congress.)

In order to understand each of the amendments, it is necessary to examine the text, a list of the rights, and their general historical development. Many of these issues are examined closely in Part II.

Amendment 1 — Religious And Political Rights
Congress shall make no law respecting an establishment of religion, or prohibiting the free exercise thereof; or abridging the freedom of speech, or of the press; or the right of the people peaceably to assemble, and to petition the Government for a redress of grievances.
1. Congress may not pass laws to establish, benefit, or limit religion, nor any law that interferes with the people's right to worship as they wish.
2. Congress may not pass laws to limit free speech and press, the people's right to gather and protest, or the people's right to demand that the government correct a wrong.

Amendment 2 — The Right To Bear Arms
A well regulated Militia, being necessary to the security of a free State, the right of the people to keep and bear Arms, shall not be infringed.
1. The government shall not interfere in the people's right to own guns.

Amendment 3 — Quartering Of Soldiers
No Soldier shall, in time of peace be quartered in any house, without the consent of the Owner, nor in time of war, but in a manner to be prescribed by law.
1. During peacetime the government may not place troops in the homes of the people without their permission.
2. During wartime troops may only be placed in the people's homes according to the law as established by the Congress.

Amendment 4 — Search And Seizure
The right of the people to be secure in their persons, houses, papers, and effects, against unreasonable searches and seizures, shall not be violated, and no Warrants shall issue, but upon probable

cause, supported by Oath or affirmation, and particularly describing the place to be searched, and the persons or things to be seized.

1. There shall be no searches or seizures of persons, houses, papers, or effects without a warrant.
2. A warrant must be obtained from a court under the following conditions:

   Probable cause to believe a law has been broken or that evidence exists.

   Must be supported by testimony.

   Must describe the exact location to be searched and the persons or things to be seized.

Amendment 5 — Life, Liberty, And Property

No person shall be held to answer for a capital, or otherwise infamous crime, unless on a presentment or indictment of a Grand Jury, except in cases arising in the land or naval forces, or in the Militia, when in actual service in time of War or public danger; nor shall any person be subject for the same offence to be twice put in jeopardy of life or limb; nor shall be compelled in any criminal case to be a witness against himself, nor be deprived of life, liberty, or property, without due process of law; nor shall private property be taken for public use without just compensation.

1. Before any federal trial there must be a grand jury indictment (this does not apply to the military during wartime).
2. Once found not guilty, a person may not be tried a second time for that crime at the federal level.
3. A person cannot be made to testify against himself.
4. A person cannot be deprived of life, liberty, or property without following the due course of law.
5. The government cannot take private property without paying a fair price for it.

Amendment 6 — Rights Of The Accused

In all criminal prosecutions, the accused shall enjoy the right to a speedy and public trial, by an impartial jury of the State and district wherein the crime shall have been committed, which district shall have been previously ascertained by law, and to be informed of the nature and cause of the accusation; to be confronted with the witnesses against him; to have compulsory process for obtaining Witnesses in his favor, and to have the assistance of counsel for his defence.

1. The accused has the right to a prompt and public trial by jury.
2. The jury must be chosen from the state or district where the crime occurred.
3. The accused must be told what the charges are.
4. The accused must be faced by all witnesses against him in court.
5. The accused must be allowed to call witnesses for his defense.
6. The accused has the right to a lawyer.

Amendment 7 — Right To Jury Trial

In Suits at common law, where the value in controversy shall exceed twenty dollars, the right of trial by jury shall be preserved, and no fact tried by a jury, shall be otherwise reexamined in any Court of the United States, than according to the rules of the common law.

1. In a suit, at common law, of more than $20, a trial by jury is guaranteed.
2. A decision of a jury may only be reexamined according to the rules of common law.

Amendment 8 — Bail And Punishment

Excessive bail shall not be required, nor excessive fines imposed, nor cruel and unusual punishments inflicted.

1. No excessive bail.
2. No excessive fines.
3. No cruel and unusual punishment

Amendment 9 — All Other Rights

The enumeration in the Constitution, of certain rights, shall not be construed to deny or disparage others retained by the people.

1. This amendment is a catch-all to cover other rights possessed by the people that were not expressly written in the document. The

rights listed are not the only rights that exist, and other rights are not made less important by not being listed.

Amendment 10 — Rights Of States And The People

The powers not delegated to the United States by the Constitution, nor prohibited by it to the States, are reserved to the States respectively, or to the people.

1. The people and the states have all the power that is not given to the federal government.

For many Americans, the colonial period (1651-1775) was a time of increasingly intrusive British abuses. Almost all the rights included in the Bill of Rights stem from these acts. The religious rights, however, are rooted in an earlier period. Most of the 13 American colonies were established by groups searching for their version of religious freedom. There were the Anglicans at Jamestown, the Pilgrims at Plymouth, the Puritans at Massachusetts Bay, the Catholics in Maryland, the Quakers in Pennsylvania, and so on. Each of these groups left persecution in Europe and came to America for religious freedom. Many then went about setting new standards for religious intolerance. Some of these groups persecuted their members so intensely that it became desirable to escape to other colonies or back to Europe. The colonies of Connecticut and Rhode Island were established by those fleeing the authoritarianism, despotism, and tyranny that were the norm in the Puritan colony of Massachusetts Bay.

The early American colonies were religious dictatorships controlled by the church. This mixing of church and state sank into depravity in all instances and was made worse by the hypocrisy of the preachings about supposedly-just gods. Religious rights, then, were seen as necessary not only to avoid abuses of religion by the government, but also abuses of the people and the government by religion.

In 1763, following the French and Indian War, the British initiated a taxing and regulation policy which generated significant opposition. As Britain began to abuse her power, people in America, such as Samuel Adams, complained. This opposition took the form of town meetings, soapbox speeches, newspaper articles, protest marches, and petitions. Britain responded with harassment, persecution, and prosecution. These lessons provided the basis for the political rights, freedom of speech and freedom of the press (or rather freedom of expression) listed in the First Amendment.

As opposition to British abuses mounted, and violence spread, the British responded by trying to disarm the Americans. The battles at Lexington and Concord, the first shots in the American Revolution, occurred as British troops marched to capture an American arsenal at Concord. This resulted in the Second Amendment.

The Quartering Acts of 1765 and 1774 required the colonists to provide housing and food for British troops in America. The American complaint was that this amounted to occupation by a foreign army. These troops were later placed in the homes of suspected patriots to harass and spy on them. This violated the privacy of people's homes and became one of the most offensive acts carried out by the British, and the most hated by the Americans. This was the basis for the Third Amendment.

Unreasonable searches and seizures by the British began with the Sugar Act in 1764. British authorities used customs agents and inspectors to enforce collection of the taxes on sugar and molasses. These inspectors had the power to search ships, warehouses, houses and anyplace else that could possibly hide untaxed cargoes. The British Navy was widely used to intercept and search American shipping. In the years following the Sugar Act, this power was seriously abused; as American protests increased, it became a way to harass rebel leaders. Following the Townshend Acts in 1767, marauding tax collectors were aided by Writs of Assistance, essentially blank search warrants, which authorized searches of anyplace at anytime. The people were not safe, even in their own homes, from the invasion of these inspectors. As this power was misused to intimidate and harass for political reasons, the people grew to hate it. The result was the Fourth Amendment.

As British tyranny increased, it became a common practice to hold a trial when no evidence existed, as this tied up a person's time and resources. Persons were tried over and over, and forced to testify against themselves. Very often, penalties were carried out with total disregard for the law. Authorities seized property at will and generally manipulated the legal system to harass opponents of British policy. These practices led to the Fifth Amendment.

British authorities held people in jail for extended periods of time without charges and without trials; they allowed convictions based on written testimony from people who never appeared in court; they did not allow the accused to cross-examine a witness; they did not allow the accused to call witnesses in his defense; and they denied the right to a lawyer. Judges, appointed by the Crown, ruled without juries. These were certainly signs of tyranny and power gone astray. They led to the Sixth Amendment.

The British used their royal legal appointees to judge civil cases involving colonial protesters, and to deprive these protesters of considerable resources, as harassment. Protection in the form of a right to a trial by jury in civil cases was added with the Seventh Amendment.

Excessive bail was used to keep people in jail for long periods. Besides causing hardship, this stopped the defendant from developing his defense. Excessive fines were used to harass and break a person financially. Torture was common. An example of colonial-era punishment was to hang a person, cut him down while still alive, disembowel him, and cut him into quarters. This kind of punishment is beyond the laws of nature, and so the prohibition of cruel and unusual punishment was written into the Eighth Amendment.

Following years of these abuses the Americans came to understand the inherently bad nature of government and power. Their solution was a central government of limited power wherein the people and states retained all powers not explicitly granted. This principle was established in the Ninth and Tenth Amendments.

One may analyze this Bill of Rights and come to the conclusion that the British were an evil people, but their abuses were limited to them and at a different time, so there is no real need to enforce these rights at the present time. Frankly, anyone who reaches this verdict should prepare to live in a totalitarian system, because that is what we will have if we abandon these rights. Make no mistake: Given the kind of power that was held by the British, our government would react in exactly the same ways. Or is it already? Nicknamed the American Gestapo, the IRS, which is well-known for its tactics of humiliation and intimidation, functions in the same manner as abusive British authorities. The IRS is a classic example of abuse of power in our system. Anyone who doesn't think it can happen here is living in a dream world. Such a person simply does not understand the very nature of power! An examination of history shows that every government that has ever existed has abused its power. It is also true that all those governments came to an end because of their abuse of power, as will ours!

The Bill of Rights originally applied only to the federal government. In recent years the courts have applied some of the amendments to the states. This judicial process is known as "incorporation." It is thoroughly illegitimate, as is the 14th Amendment upon which it is based. Nonetheless, at this time most of the protections in the Bill of Rights also apply to the state governments.

Words are imprecise. And of course laws are based upon words. There is, then, an inherent imprecision in all laws. This creates a need to interpret the meaning of laws so that they can be applied, and that is the basic role of judges.

The Constitution is written in broad language. This has led to many legal questions requiring interpretation of the meaning of constitutional wording. For example, what is cruel and unusual punishment, and what is a speedy trial? A major question comes out of the necessity to interpret the Constitution: how does one determine the meaning of the words used? Two views have developed. First, the doctrine of Original Intent, and second, the dogma of modern judicial activism. Original Intent requires the judge to follow the Constitution as it was intended by the Founders. Judicial activism allows the judge to hold the law is whatever he wants it to be. These two views have clashed and created intense controversy.

What is Original Intent? Former Supreme Court Justice Brennan has been one of the most severe critics of this doctrine. In 1985, in a speech at Georgetown University, Brennan said:

"In its most doctrinaire incarnation, Original Intent demands that Justices discern exactly what the Framers thought about the question under consideration and simply follow that intention in resolving the case before them. It is a view that feigns self-effacing deference to the specific judgments of those who forged our original social compact. But in truth it is little more than arrogance cloaked as humility. It is arrogant to pretend that from our vantage we can gauge accurately the intent of the Framers on application of principle to specific, contemporary questions."

This is a great mischaracterization. No proponent of Original Intent has ever suggested this view. A requirement that the judge know the specific intentions of the Founders regarding the case at hand is simply, utterly, unobtainable. If they had to have such knowledge they could never make a decision. If such specific knowledge were available, judges would never disagree with one another and we would have no need for appeals. As Judge Bork has noted, "Justice Brennan demolished a position no one holds, one that is indefensible, but undefended."

In *Democracy and Distrust: A Theory of Judicial Review*, John Hart Ely, former professor of constitutional law at Yale and dean at Stanford, well described the meaning of Original Intent.

"What distinguishes interpretivism [Original Intent] from its opposite is its insistence that the work of the political branches is to be invalidated only in accord with an inference whose starting point, whose underlying premise, is fairly discoverable in the Constitution. That the complete inference will not be found there - because the situation is not likely to have been foreseen - is generally common ground."

In short, all that a judge committed to Original Intent requires is that the text, structure, and history of the Constitution provide him not with a conclusion, but with a major premise. That major premise is a principle or stated value that the Founders wanted to protect against hostile legislation or executive action. The result of following Original Intent is that a judge should look to the language and meaning of the Constitution, and, if the cause before him is not resolved by that language and meaning, then he must abstain from the decision, because the matter does not offend the Constitution. If the result is harsh, then the solution to the matter is for the people, through the democratic process, to amend the Constitution.

The Bill of Rights represents a limit on government power and also on the power of the majority to rule. Anything not specifically listed is open to control by the majority through the democratic process. In a sense, the Bill of Rights preserves democracy in those areas of life that the Founders intended to leave to the people's self-government. Anytime a court expands upon the Bill of Rights, it removes such an area from the control of the people.

Legal theorists of recent years have declared Original Intent, which used to be the dominant theory of constitutional law, to be outside the mainstream. They do so because it does not allow judicial activism, which is the purported road to salvation as far as Ivy-League law faculties are concerned. Their criticisms are that Original Intent is unknowable; the Constitution must change with the times; there is no reason the living should be governed by the dead; the Constitution is not law; and the Constitution is what the judges say it is.

Most of these "theories" are not worth the time to consider. Analysis of two will make this point. First, the Constitution is not law. This is a position proposed by some, including a former Dean of Stanford Law School. However, Article VI of the Constitution clearly states:

> "This Constitution, and the Laws of the United States which shall be made in Pursuance thereof; and all Treaties made, or which shall be made, under the Authority of the United States, shall be the supreme **Law** of the Land." (emphasis added)

Second, Original Intent is unknowable. This would be true except for the following: James Madison, the force behind the Virginia Plan, which became the body of the Constitution and the primary drafter of the Bill of Rights, took copious daily notes at the Philadelphia

Convention in 1787. They include the details of the debates which took place; *The Federalist Papers* written by John Jay, Alexander Hamilton, and James Madison to explain the meaning of the provisions of the Constitution to the people during the ratification struggle; the legislative history of the First Congress as it debated the twelve amendments Congressman Madison introduced which became the Bill of Rights; and the extensive writings of the other Founders.

Analysis of the legislative history of laws today is a primary instrument in legal interpretation. It is accepted by all as a useful tool. Why is it that some of these same people reject what amounts to the use of legislative history for the Federal Constitution?

This question is readily answered by modern judicial activists. Following the Original Intent of the Founders limits a judge to the law, but the modern dogma of judicial activism, which completely ignores the intent of the Founders, allows a judge to dictate the law as he sees fit. Judicial activism is pursued by liberals who want government without limits and morality without restraint, and by conservatives who want government with too many limits and morality with total restraint. This is not limited to Democrats on the left, but also to Republicans on the right. And they have both done great damage to the Constitution and the liberties it protects.

The modern results of judicial activism are depressingly infamous: the legalization of abortion; prohibitions on religious ceremonies; the coddling of criminals; whole areas of speech not entitled to free speech protection; the power of police to search private homes without warrants; and defendants who do not have the right to be faced by their accusers in court. And on and on *ad infinitum*!

Alexander Hamilton, member of the Constitutional Convention and co-author of *The Federalist Papers*, was opposed to the addition of a bill of rights to the Constitution on the ground that it was unnecessary. He stated that the federal government was a government of delegated powers, and it was not granted the power to intrude upon fundamental personal rights. His opinion relates the potential danger of misguided judicial interpretation. He argued, "I go further, and affirm that bills of rights are not only unnecessary in the proposed Constitution, but would even be dangerous. They would contain exceptions to powers which are not granted; and on this very account, would afford a colourable pretext to claim more than were granted. For why declare that things shall not be done which there is no power to do? Why for instance, should it be said, that the liberty of the press shall not be restrained, when no power is given by which restrictions may be imposed? I will not contend that such a provision would confer a regulating power; but it is evident that it would furnish, to men disposed to usurp, a plausible pretense for claiming that power."

Hamilton was prophetic indeed on the subject of usurpation. Instead of a government with powers limited to those enumerated in the Constitution, the Bill of Rights, in the hands of modern day usurpers, has been used to assume such a regulating power through interpretation of the amendments themselves. In Part II, this historical rape of the Constitution is explored. Its modern effects are listed below.

Current Status Of The Bill Of Rights

Amend.	Right	Condition	Current Status
1	no establishment of religion	20% dead	Lemon v. Kurtzman Test is appropriate though religious fanatics on local level increasingly ignore the law
1	free exercise of religion	80% dead	Employment Division v. Smith allows government to regulate religion to enforce a compelling state interest
1	free speech	70% dead	5 major areas of exceptions now exist; as well as time, place and manner rules; and special context rules
1	free press	10% dead	Courts often use gag orders to prevent news coverage of trials
1	right to assemble/petition	70% dead	HUD Housing efforts

46

2	right to bear arms	90% dead	Crime Bill of 1994 banned 19 types of semi-automatic rifles
3	no quartering of soldiers	0% dead	
4	no searches without warrants	100% dead	Limited by definition of reasonable expectation of privacy; 11 exceptions to warrant requirement; and United States v. Leon good faith rule
5	Grand jury indictment required	0% dead	
5	no double jeopardy	80% dead	The Wheeler and Heath cases allow prosecution by the Feds and multiple states while the Blockburger line of cases allows multiple prosecutions resulting from the same conduct
5	privilege against self-incrimination	40% dead	The Schmerber and Muniz cases have reduced this protection to only the extremely limited category of testimonial evidence.
5	due process	100% dead	Expanded way beyond original intent to create bureaucratic nightmare
6	speedy trial	90% dead	Under Barker v. Wingo Test defendants have been made to wait as long as seven years before trial takes place
6	right to jury (criminal case)	30% dead	Batson line of cases places rights of jurors over the fair trial rights of defendants
6	confrontation by witnesses	100% dead	Maryland v. Craig allows witnesses to testify from other rooms or even on videotape without any chance to cross examine

6	right to counsel	10% dead	Applies only in cases where actual incarceration is imposed
7	right to jury (civil case)	0% dead	
8	no excessive bail or fines	100% dead	Both excessive fines and bail are regularly used now
8	no cruel or unusual punishment	100% dead	Expanded by liberals well beyond its intended meaning, which has resulted in coddling criminals
9	nondisparagement clause	100% dead	Expanded by liberals well beyond its intended meaning. Used to support Roe v. Wade which legalized abortion
10	reserved powers clause	100% dead	Garcia v. San Antonio Metro Transit Authority killed the 10th Amendment, Federalism, and all hopes for control over congressional power

PART II
THE RAPE OF
THE CONSTITUTION

CHAPTER 6
THE ALIEN
AND SEDITION ACTS 1798

In 1797, following the election of John Adams as President, the fledgling United States government was dominated by the Federalist Party. A new crisis developed immediately. The new French government ordered the seizure of American ships carrying goods to Britain. This course of action threatened America's delicate attempts at neutrality and caused great concern, because the United States was hardly in a position to contest France or anyone else. It would lead to anti-French sentiment and help inflame the rivalry between Federalists and Democratic-Republicans in America. This inter-party squabbling would then take a new and serious turn with laws passed by the Federalists that were a slap in the face to the new Constitution.

This French interference in American sovereignty prompted Adams to send a three-man commission to Paris. These diplomats were refused an audience with Minister of Foreign Affairs Talleyrand until certain conditions were met. Talleyrand then sent three commissioners, later known as X, Y, and Z, to insist that the United States apologize for certain anti-French statements made by the President, approve a loan to France, and pay a $250,000 bribe directly to Talleyrand. The incident became known as the XYZ Affair, and when Adams allowed a report on the matter to become public the American people were outraged. A clamor for war with France arose and Adams took steps to increase the American military. Although war was not formally declared, a quasi-war broke out. The American Navy responded, capturing 80 French vessels by the end of 1798. By 1799, France had a new government, and Adams realized a real war would greatly harm the young nation. He initiated a second American peace overture which was accepted by the French. Popular resentment against France remained strong, however.

The anti-French position taken by the Federalists was opposed by the Democratic-Republican Party, generally known as the Republicans, under the leadership of Thomas Jefferson. Relations between the parties were bitter, each willing to do whatever was necessary to protect the country from the policies of the other. In that spirit, the Federalist-dominated Congress passed four laws, known as the Alien and Sedition Acts, in 1798. Presented as national security measures, their real target was the Republican Party.

The party of Jefferson, with its roots in the Antifederalist sentiment of the ratification fight, feared strong government. The Republicans represented the common man — small farmers and the poor — and spoke for a small, non-meddling national government. To the large numbers of European immigrants arriving at that time, many of whom were escaping governmental oppression in their homelands, these views had great appeal. They joined the party in droves. It became inevitable that this groundswell of support would eventually lead to Republican control of the government. Jefferson organized a grass-roots campaign for a run at the presidency in 1800. His method was based on harsh criticism of the ruling Federalists to stir up opposition.

The four Alien and Sedition Acts were designed to solve these problems for the Federalists. The first was the Naturalization Act. It extended the residency requirement for citizenship from five to fourteen years. This law was intended to choke off the growing Republican support from immigrants, who would have to wait an additional nine years before gaining citizenship and therefore the right to vote. Second, the Alien Act allowed the President to expel foreigners if he thought their presence dangerous to the peace and safety of the United States. Third, the Alien Enemies Act gave the President the power to imprison or expel foreigners considered dangerous in time of war. This and the Alien Act allowed the President to silence criticism by foreigners in the United States, during peace or war, by expelling or imprisoning them. This was also a subtle attempt to discourage foreigners from joining the

Republicans. Many people fled the United States, fearing persecution by the Federalists. Finally, and most offensive, was the Sedition Act. It "barred American citizens and others from saying, writing, or publishing any false, scandalous, or malicious statements against the U.S. government, congress, or the president." Persons doing so faced a $2,000 fine and two years in jail.

Thomas Jefferson
(Reproduced from the Collections of the Library Of Congress.)

Under vigorous enforcement of the Sedition Act, twenty-four Republican newspaper editors were arrested soon after the law's enactment. In this list were some of America's most able journalists, including Benjamin Bache, the grandson of Benjamin Franklin. Franklin, who in his role as peacemaker at the Constitutional Convention had helped make the Constitution possible, and had died in 1790. That was probably a good thing, for this insult to the plan he helped create surely would have killed him.

The most prominent victim of this law was Vermont Congressman Matthew Lyons. He was sentenced to four months in jail and fined one thousand dollars for asserting that "President Adams had turned men out of office for party reasons," and for referring to the President's "continual grasp for power" and his "unbounded thirst for ridiculous pomp, foolish adulation, and selfish avarice."

After circulating a powerful petition calling for the repeal of the Sedition Act, Jedidiah Peck was dragged from his bed in Oswego, New York, placed in manacles and marched 200 miles to New York City, where he was tried for sedition. In a similar case David Brown, an illiterate Revolutionary War veteran from Massachusetts, was sentenced to eighteen months in prison and fined $400 for assisting in the erection of a liberty pole bearing the inscription: "No Stamp Act, no Sedition, no Alien Bills, no Land Tax; downfall to the tyrants of America, peace and retirement to the president, long live the Vice President, and the minority; may moral virtue be the basis of civil government."

These four laws were clearly moral violations of the spirit of a democracy, but the Sedition Act was also a blatant violation of the First Amendment, which provides, in part, that "Congress shall make no law abridging the freedom of speech or of the press." Yet this act created criminal penalties for political speech against the government.

Many of the Founders objected to these laws. Alexander Hamilton, a leading Federalist and Cabinet minister in Washington's administrations, declared them foolish and provocative and warned that they "carried a threat of civil war." Republicans, including James Madison and Thomas Jefferson, were outraged. In response to the laws, Jefferson drafted the Kentucky Resolutions and Madison drafted the Virginia Resolutions. These works proposed for the first time a doctrine known as the "states rights" or "compact theory" of the Constitution which asserted the right of a state to nullify any federal law which was harmful.

The amendments in the Bill of Rights are a direct result of experiences with abusive governmental authority. Political and religious rights having been the most seriously violated, and of the greatest concern in the future government, were to be protected by the First Amendment, a position whose importance is self-evident. Regardless, in 1798, only seven years after the passage of the Bill of Rights, our government was already trampling on the Constitution with a desperate attempt to protect its power by unconstitutionally limiting free speech. This law was never ruled unconstitutional by the courts, and never repealed.

It might seem that this law was an anomaly, a one-time thing, and that the nation learned its lesson. Unfortunately there have been several more laws like this in our glorious history. The Sedition Act of 1918 made it a crime to "say or do anything which could obstruct the sale of government bonds, or to utter or publish words intended to bring into contempt or disrepute the form of government of the United States, the Constitution, flag, uniform; or to incite resistance to the government or promote the cause of its enemies." The Smith Act of 1940 again directed an attack against subversion, and among its provisions were ones calling for punishment of anyone who:

1. knowingly or willingly advocates or teaches the duty or propriety of overthrowing the government of the United States by force or violence;
2. disseminates literature advocating such overthrow with the intent to cause such overthrow;
3. organizes any society, group, or assembly of persons to teach, advocate, or encourage such overthrow;
4. becomes or is a member of any such society, group, or assembly knowing the purposes thereof.

If Thomas Jefferson had witnessed this abuse of power by the American government and had written the Declaration of

Independence while the Smith Act was in effect, he would have been arrested, found guilty, and sentenced to jail for subversion.

These laws represent three clear examples on the long list of sedition legislation passed throughout our history and it all has stemmed from the Alien and Sedition Acts. This is exactly the kind of governmental abuse that the Founders experienced and tried to prevent with the First Amendment, but, after all, the Constitution is just a piece of paper.

CHAPTER 7
THE REMOVAL OF
THE CHEROKEE INDIAN NATION
1828-1838

With the election of Andrew Jackson to the presidency in 1828, the United States seemed to be entering a new, more democratic era. Jackson was devoted to ending the influence of the rich and the elite and turning power over to the common man. Jackson's reign, which is an appropriate term to describe his "royal rule of the poor," was marked by two major issues. First was the "slaying of the monster," and second was Indian removal. Jackson's handling of the Indian problem was one of the most disturbing episodes in the nation's history; a story of horrible abuses and constitutional trampling by Jackson, the government of the State of Georgia, and its good citizens.

Jackson's dealings with the Second Bank of the United States were an indicator of the way in which he would deal with the Indians. Together, these two events certainly break the myth surrounding Jacksonian Democracy. In running for president, Jackson had campaigned against the bank, nicknamed the "monster" by opponents. With his backwoods mentality, Jackson feared that the bank stood for privilege and special treatment — odd thoughts from a man who would give new meaning to "political patronage" during his reign. This national bank had been chartered in 1816 for a 20-year period. Jackson arranged a subterfuge that forced Congress to recharter the bank in 1832, four years earlier than required. He then vetoed the recharter bill, which put the bank out of business. With the death of the national bank came financial calamity. The loss of the bank made national regulation of money impossible; paper money with little or no value quickly flooded the market. The Panic of 1837 followed: state banks collapsed, inflation ran rampant, small business owners and

58

farmers were ruined. The nation suffered greatly from Jackson's lack of vision and failure to anticipate the results of his actions. These shortcomings would not bode well for the Indians.

Andrew Jackson
(Reproduced from the Collections of the Library Of Congress.)

For all of Jackson's rhetoric about standing up for the common man against the powerful, he did not apply this philosophy to the American Indians. He had risen to national prominence during the War of 1812 by defeating the British in the Battle of New Orleans, a battle that was fought more than two weeks after the signing of the Treaty of Ghent, which officially ended the war. He had also earned a reputation for slaughtering Indians. He would continue with his animosity against the Indians and reach new depths with his actions towards them. A particular target was the Cherokee Nation in Georgia.

During Jackson's administration, almost all the Indians east of the Mississippi River were dispossessed — driven out of their homes and off their lands so that whites could have access to those valuable resources. They were forced to move west, beyond the Mississippi, to "Indian Country." This area on the Great Plains was thought to be a desert, and therefore useless for white settlement. Twelve major Indian nations were forcefully moved west. Countless numbers were murdered. The Cherokee Nation did not go without a fight. It was not the vicious head-scalping, savage massacre that the American media has always portrayed; it was a legal battle.

During the American Revolution the Cherokees had fought with Britain against the colonies. After the British sued for peace in 1783, the Cherokees fought on until 1785 when the Treaty of Hopewell ended hostilities. This treaty placed the Cherokee Nation under the protection of the United States; however, their rights to self-government and inviolate territory were not at all affected. Citizens of the United States were not even allowed a right of passage through the Cherokee country. When the new constitution of the United States was adopted, the Treaty of Hopewell was confirmed. In 1791 the Treaty of Holston was made, acknowledging that the Cherokees were under the protection of the United States, and of no other sovereign. The Cherokees agreed to allow the United States to regulate their trade; to deliver Cherokees who caused injury to Americans for trial and punishment; and to allow a right of way in one direction through the Cherokee country. In exchange, the United States agreed to protect the Indians; to punish American citizens who caused injury to the

Cherokees; to prohibit whites from hunting on Cherokee lands, or even entering the country without a passport; and to a solemn guaranty of all Cherokee land. Over the next 36 years the Cherokees faithfully executed their responsibilities under these treaties.

During the early 1820s Georgia became insistent on taking control of the millions of acres of Cherokee land which could be opened up to white settlement. Georgia asked President James Monroe to remove the Indians by force, but he refused to do so. Monroe did, however, request congressional appropriations to extinguish by treaty the Indian title to all lands in Georgia. When the Cherokees were approached about this in 1823 they flatly refused to give up one more foot of their land.

Voluntary emigration of Cherokees to the Louisiana Territory had begun in 1817, and by 1823 approximately one-third of the Indians had moved west. The remainder refused to go, as stories filtered back from the west indicating that the emigrants had suffered terribly from sickness, wars, and other disasters. In order to reinforce their determination to stay, the Cherokees sent a delegation to Washington in 1824 which was received with full diplomatic courtesy, and its representatives attended to as those of a foreign power. The Indians, relying on clauses in the Declaration of Independence, dulled efforts to drive them west, temporarily. This was also assisted by the passive support of John Quincy Adams, newly-elected President in 1824.

Over the next few years the Cherokees progressed rapidly. They continued to develop as a civilized people with a wonderful culture, a written language of their own, a weekly newspaper, and a settled way of life as farmers. In 1827, a convention of Cherokee representatives adopted a national constitution establishing a republican form of government modeled upon that of the United States. It also asserted that the Cherokee Nation was sovereign and independent, having complete jurisdiction over its territory, to the exclusion of any other authority.

The cultural modernization and moves towards democracy were ignored in Georgia. The state's focus remained steadfast on taking the Cherokee land. In December, 1829, Georgia extended her laws over all whites and Indians in the Cherokee Nation, effective June 1, 1830.

It also declared that, after that date, all laws made by the Cherokee Nation were null and void. The law also began a process to survey the Indian lands and distribute them to Georgians through a lottery system. At the same time, Jackson's administration passed the Indian Removal Act, which authorized the federal government to seize most Indian land so long as some compensation was paid for the property.

In July, 1829, gold was discovered on Cherokee land, and within a year there were 3,000 whites intruding on Indian territory. This violated the laws of the United States, Georgia, and the Cherokee Nation. American troops were sent in to enforce the law and protect the Indians, but Georgia sent a request to Andrew Jackson, newly-elected President, to remove them so that Georgia could control the affair. Jackson immediately did so. In December, 1830, Georgia passed laws to prevent intrusion and disorder. By the same act the state made it unlawful for any Cherokee council or legislative body to meet (except for the purpose of ceding land), prohibited any Cherokee courts, and required all white residents in Cherokee territory to possess a license granted by the governor to those who took an oath to support and defend the constitution and laws of the state. Violations of these laws carried penalties of not less than four years confinement in the state penitentiary. The Georgia judge into whose jurisdiction fell the Cherokee Nation expressed his unequivocal support for Georgian policy when he exclaimed that he would disregard any interference by the United State Supreme Court in cases which might arise over the acts of Georgia.

The Cherokees appealed to the U.S. Supreme Court with a motion for an injunction against these Georgian laws, asserting that they violated numerous treaties with the United States. The Indians had every reason to be hopeful, as Chief Justice John Marshall was an opponent of Jackson and Indian removal. In the case of *Cherokee Nation v. Georgia* (1831), Chief Justice Marshall, writing for the majority, had stated sympathetically that, "the Cherokee Nation is a domestic dependent nation with an unquestionable right to the lands they occupy, until that right be extinguished by voluntary cession to our government." However, the Court decided that it lacked jurisdiction to hear the matter, and dismissed the motion for an injunction.

Article III of the Constitution lists several cases to which the judicial power of the federal courts extends, including "controversies between a state or the citizens thereof, and foreign states, citizens, or subjects." Supportive as the majority were, they did not consider the Cherokee Nation a foreign state. Rather, its relationship with the United States was described as that of a "ward to his guardian." Notably, it was a 3-2 decision with a dissent that shredded the majority argument and proved unquestionably that the Cherokees were a foreign state.

Georgia took steps to prevent any cases with proper jurisdiction from going up to the federal courts. Cases involving the Cherokees were allowed to drag in the Georgia courts so as to prevent any defendants from carrying their case to the United States Supreme Court. However, a Cherokee named Corntassel was sentenced to hang by a Georgia court. He sued out a writ of error which was issued by Chief Justice Marshall and sent to the Georgia authorities. The state legislature then declared that the United States Supreme Court had no jurisdiction over the subject, and in defiance of the court order had Corntassel immediately executed.

Finally, in July 1831, another case arose involving a number of white missionaries, arrested for being on Cherokee land without the required Georgia licenses. It was orchestrated intentionally to get the case before the United States Supreme Court. Two of the missionaries, Rev. Samuel Worcester and Rev. Elizur Butler, were convicted and sentenced to four years hard labor in the state penitentiary. As this was a final judgment, it was open to appellate review for violations of law, and since this involved a citizen of Vermont against a state, the case was properly placed before the United States Supreme Court. In *Worcester v. Georgia* (1832), Chief Justice Marshall, writing for the court, held that "the Cherokee Nation is a distinct community, occupying its own territory, in which the laws of Georgia can have no force, and which the citizens of Georgia have no right to enter, but with the assent of the Cherokees themselves. The act of Georgia under which this defendant was prosecuted, is consequently void, and the judgment a nullity." It was a tremendous victory for the Cherokees.

Unfortunately, Georgia ignored these rulings, as did President Jackson to whom is attributed the comment, "John Marshall has made his decision; now let him enforce it." The President of the United States then went about not only ignoring the decisions, but also leading in the Cherokee removal, thus violating the law of the land as decided by the Supreme Court. The Court frequently makes highly debatable rulings, but this was clearly a correct decision in favor of the Indians.

Article II of the Constitution contains two particularly relevant clauses that describe the function of the president. Section One states that, "the executive power shall be vested in a president of the United States of America." The commonly accepted meaning of executive power is the power to carry out the laws. Section Three states that, "he [the president] shall take care that the laws be faithfully executed." As President, Jackson was required to enforce Supreme Court decisions, the law of the land, and should have used all measures available to the federal government to prevent white encroachment onto Cherokee land. Instead, Jackson intentionally disobeyed a ruling of the Supreme Court, thus violating the law and his duty to uphold the Constitution. He had carried out offenses that should have resulted in his impeachment. He wasn't impeached, of course, and the Cherokee Nation was the big loser.

Over the next three years Georgia carried out a campaign designed to oppress the suffering Cherokees and to induce them to leave voluntarily. The great majority of the tribe stood firmly on their rights and resisted. Federal agents, appointed by Jackson to carry out the removal, and the state of Georgia resorted to all manner of intrigue to harass the Indians. Mixed-breed Indians were paid to circulate among the Cherokee and argue for removal; a Georgia law denying Indians the right to testify against a white in court was employed to rob Indians of their livestock and other property with impunity; and, plied with liquor, the Indians were charged for debts for which their property was taken without due process of law. Under these conditions the spirit of the Indians was broken, and thousands would

64

have emigrated except for the stern opposition of their leaders, even though some did move west during this time.

The Trail of Tears 1838
(The Philbrook Museum of Art, Tulsa, Oklahoma)

In 1835, two delegations of Cherokee arrived in Washington; one, the National Party, headed by Chief John Ross, came prepared to fight to the end for their homeland. The other, headed by John Ridge, a prominent subchief who recognized the battle was lost, came to negotiate for removal. A treaty was negotiated with the Ridge party providing that the tribe would give up all its territory and move west. The treaty was signed in March with the understanding that it be ratified by the tribe in full council. In October the tribe met to consider the treaty, which was overwhelmingly rejected. The government then demanded that the Cherokee meet in New Echota in December to negotiate another treaty. Included in these demands was the threat that those who failed to attend the meeting would be counted in favor of any treaty made. Over the next two months the Cherokee were bombarded with threats, bribes, and inducements to attend the meeting. Chief John Ross was arrested and held without charges, and the national paper, *The Cherokee Phoenix,* was closed. Even with these Draconian measures, only about 300 Indians out of a population of sixteen thousand Cherokees actually showed up. The American commissioners drew up the Schermerhorn Treaty with this tiny minority, and presented it to the U.S. Senate for ratification. Despite the fact that Cherokee national delegates protested in the Senate on behalf of nearly 16,000 Indians, the Schermerhorn Treaty was approved. President Jackson ordered that no Indian council would be allowed to meet to discuss the treaty, and that any efforts by the Cherokee leadership to prevent the carrying out of the treaty would be suppressed. He also sent in troops to disarm the Cherokee and prevent opposition. Nonetheless, the Indians stood resolute and declared they would die before they would leave their homes.

A deadline for the final removal of the Cherokee was set for May 23, 1838. Up until this time small bands continued to leave voluntarily, but when the date arrived 15,000 Indians remained. The President then sent 7,000 troops under General Winfield Scott to drive them westward at bayonet point. The first stage was to imprison the Cherokee in a series of forts. In his book *Indian Removal*, Grant Foreman describes several eyewitness accounts of this brutal disgrace:

*"Multitudes were allowed no time to take anything with
them, except the clothes they had on. Well-furnished houses
were left prey to plunderers, who, like hungry wolves, follow
in the train of the captors. These wretches rifle the houses,
and strip the helpless, unoffending owners of all they have on
earth. Females are driven on foot before the bayonets of
brutal soldiers. Their feelings are mortified by vulgar and
profane vociferations. It is a painful sight. The property of
many has been taken, and sold before their eyes for almost
nothing — the sellers and buyers, in many cases having
combined to cheat the poor Indians. The poor captive, in a
state of distressing agitation, his weeping wife almost frantic
with terror, surrounded by a group of crying, terrified
children, is in a poor condition, and in most cases is stripped
of the whole of his property in one blow. Many of the
Cherokees, who, a few days ago, were in comfortable
circumstances, are now victims of abject poverty."*

It was only to get worse. Beginning in June, 1838, the hottest part
of the summer, the Cherokee were forced westwards. The people of
Georgia celebrated their victory and the theft of over 800,000 acres of
Indian land. A great drought, along with numerous outbreaks of
disease, brought intense suffering to the Cherokee. Finally, General
Scott decided to suspend the removal until September when the
weather turned cooler. The death march resumed in October after the
drought ended. There were no more delays, and the Indians then faced
winter conditions on a four-month march of nearly 1,000 miles to
Oklahoma. Several thousand died on the way. The survivors called it,
"The Trail Where They Cried." This infamous defilement of every
principle upon which the United States was founded became better
known as "The Trail of Tears."

Along the way a Kentuckian who witnessed this forced march
observed:

*"The sick and feeble were carried in waggons (sic), a
great many ride on horseback, and multitudes go on foot —
even aged females, apparently nearly ready to drop in the
grave, were travelling with heavy burdens attached to their*

backs on the sometimes frozen ground and sometimes muddy streets, with no covering for their feet except what nature had given them. We learned from the inhabitants on the road where the Indians passed, they buried fourteen or fifteen at every stopping place."

Another observer noted:

"She could only carry her dying child in her arms a few miles farther, and then she must stop in a strange land and consign her much loved babe to the cold ground, and that too without pomp or ceremony, and pass on with the multitude. When I past (sic) the last detachment of those suffering exiles and thought that my native countrymen had thus expelled them from their native soil and much loved homes, and that too in this inclement season of the year, I turned from the sight with feelings which language cannot express and wept like childhood then."

Unfortunately, this wasn't the only such case of Indian abuse that can be attributed to Jackson. Prior to the Cherokee, the other Indians of the South and Northwest suffered similar fates. In Illinois, the Sauk and Fox nations were driven west, in 1831 after squatters took their land. When they encountered enemy Indian nations to the west some of them, led by Chief Black Hawk, returned to Illinois for protection, but they were not welcomed. In 1832, an Illinois militia unit attacked and massacred about 1,000 of these starving refugees. In 1835, the Seminoles of Florida resisted American efforts to deport them beyond the Mississippi River. Chief Osceola bravely led his people's fight until 1837, when he was treacherously captured by an American general who had invited him to talk peace under a flag of truce. Almost all of the Seminole Indians were killed. It really makes one proud to be an American.

This is the true history of this country. One cannot but be shocked and disgusted. The nation's excuse for genocide was that Manifest Destiny, a silly semi-religious idea that God had graced this nation and given it the right to spread from shore to shore, supposedly justified this nation in destroying entire cultures. The Constitution should have stopped the President and the states, and prevented these atrocities from happening, but after all, it is just a piece of paper.

CHAPTER 8
SECESSION 1860

In 1860, following the election of Abraham Lincoln, seven Southern states seceded from the Union of the United States. They had made quite clear their intention to do so if Lincoln, the candidate of the pro-abolition Republican Party, won the election. These states had been forced more and more into a corner by the North over four decades, and they had had enough. The only way out was to leave the Union. Lincoln, after taking office, pursued a course of action, namely the calling up of troops, that provoked the Southern states, like the 13 colonies before them, to fight for their independence from an oppressive government. At this point, four more Southern states left the Union, and soon a war erupted. The Civil War cost the lives of approximately 618,000 Americans. It should not have happened, as secession is and always has been a legal right of an American state. When John Wilkes Booth jumped to the stage after shooting Abraham Lincoln he yelled, "Sic Temper Tyrannis," — Thus Always to Tyrants. In this he was accurately describing Lincoln, for the prosecution of war against legitimately seceding states was indeed the act of a tyrant.

The question of secession that arose in 1860 was not a new one. There had been significant debate from the likes of Jefferson, Madison, and Jackson. The issue was first raised in a national sense at the time of the passage of the Alien and Sedition Acts in 1798. Upon witnessing these vile laws, many in the country were concerned that the states and the people were helpless when the federal government passed oppressive laws. The reaction was focused in the Kentucky

70

Resolutions by Thomas Jefferson and in the Virginia Resolutions by James Madison. These documents expressed the states' rights, or "compact theory" of the Constitution. This theory stated that the states had created the federal government to act as their agents in certain matters, and that a state had the right to criticize the federal government, and, if necessary, nullify its laws.

618,000 dead as tyranny triumphs
(Reproduced from the Collection of the Library Of Congress.)

Compact Theory must be explored as a legitimate constitutional doctrine for the very reason that James Madison supported it to the degree that he did. Madison, commonly known as the "Father of the Constitution," drafted the Virginia Plan, which became the body of the Constitution. He also proposed the amendments which became the Bill of Rights. In this sense he holds the position of ultimate arbitrator of constitutional questions. He clearly pointed out in the Virginia Resolutions that if a federal law violated the rights of a state without redress, then that state could nullify the law. If the federal government were to persist in its violating of that state's rights, then the logical continuation of the compact theory argument is that the state may eventually secede from (quit) the Union. It only makes sense that a governing entity such as a state may leave a larger governing body it has voluntarily joined to promote its own welfare, if that association is harmful to it.

The 10th Amendment guarantees certain powers to the states. This amendment recognized that a state did not give up its sovereignty entirely just by joining the Union. Only if a state had given up all rights to self-determination would it be logical to argue that they must continue in a Union where that continuance is harmful to the state.

In 1814, another region of the country stood up for Compact Theory at the Hartford Convention. In December of that year, a group of Federalists met secretly in Hartford, Connecticut, to organize a protest against the War of 1812, and to declare that the states had a right to reject those national policies and laws they found hateful. New England thus joined the clamor for this idea.

In 1828, a series of events would lead South Carolina to declare a federal law null and void. The Nullification Crisis, as it became known, almost led to a civil war in 1832. This crisis began in 1828 with congressional passage of a very high protective tariff, a tax on imports, that was designed to help the industrial mid-Atlantic states. The South rallied against these laws nicknaming them the "Tariff of Abomination," as they would greatly harm the consumer economies of that region. The South's position was spelled out by John C. Calhoun in the "South Carolina Exposition and Protest." His bottom line was that a state had the right to nullify any federal law that threatened its welfare.

The crisis quickly came to a head — and almost to blows — when South Carolina voted to nullify the Federal Tariff Act of 1828, as well as the compromise tariffs of 1832. Their next step was to declare that no federal customs would be collected in South Carolina. Finally, they voted funds for a military force. President Jackson vowed to send troops to force the state into compliance with federal law. This promise was backed by Congress with the Force Bill of 1833, which approved the use of federal troops to collect the duties in South Carolina. Realizing they stood alone, South Carolina retreated and accepted compromise. But the ground for a later crisis was laid, and it had little to do with slavery.

The best evidence of the legality of secession is that the states were asked to ratify the new Constitution in 1787 and the Bill of Rights in 1791. Ratification, defined as "to approve," allows the option of not approving. North Carolina and Rhode Island stayed out of the Union for several years after its creation. These two states felt that participation would be detrimental to their welfare. Since a state had the option of declining participation in the Union based on its fear of harm from such participation, it follows logically that if a state joined the Union and conditions later became harmful, then a state must retain the right to end that participation and leave the Union. Arguments to the contrary put one in the seemingly untenable position of supporting the idea that "an organization voluntarily joined cannot be voluntarily departed." Now, this may be the way things are done in the Mafia, but it should not be the rule in a democracy.

While secession was a valid legal exercise of a state based upon Compact Theory, it is also a constitutional doctrine that can stand entirely on its own; one cannot, however, fully support the right of a state to nullify federal laws. The states had agreed to join this Union, and that includes all of its provisions. The power to determine the constitutionality of a law was granted to the Supreme Court and, if disagreement arose, the amending process could be used. One of the core problems of the Articles of Confederation was the ability of the states to nullify acts of the Confederation Congress, and this caused great hardship. After contracting with the Union, a state did not and does not have a right to violate the terms of that contract; that would amount to a breach of contract. However, continuing the contract law analogy, secession is not a breach. It is a basic principle that a contract may be excused if it is unconscionable or if performance becomes impracticable. This can easily be analogized to secession of a state whose performance in a contractual Union becomes a severe and unreasonable burden. Based on Compact Theory, a state does have a voluntary right to leave a Union that it voluntarily joined. This is especially true when the perpetuation of those ties threatens the welfare of the state.

Those opposed to secession offer one principle argument in opposition: that the nation could not survive this voluntary right to leave. But is this necessarily true? It should not be assumed that allowing states to exercise the right of secession would continually threaten the Union, as one after another aggrieved state would attempt to secede over every minor conflict. In reality, a state would only consider secession as a last recourse following the most offensive, and unredressed, abuses by the federal government. The lesson of Rhode Island is a poignant example. This state refused to join the Union for almost two years after the Constitution was ratified. During that time they were subjected to intense pressure from the other states. Interference in trade and harassment took place which resulted in near-total isolation. The situation became intolerable, and they joined. Knowing that such difficulties await a seceding state, no state would leave on a whim. Fears of disunion were unfounded, as a state simply had more to lose by leaving the Union.

There is, in fact, constitutional doctrine to support secession. The Constitution does not discuss secession, so preventing it is not a delegated power of the federal government. Nor is secession prohibited, by the document, to the states. It is, then, a power reserved to the states or to the people. This reflects the wording of the "reserved powers clause" of the 10th Amendment in the Bill of Rights.

After the war, Radical Republicans in the North continued their claims that secession was illegal and that the Southern states had not actually left the Union. This claim gave justification for the war to many people, especially since most Northerners totally rejected the idea that they fought to free blacks. They argued that all the horror and carnage of this war were not in vain; that it was to preserve the Union from those in rebellion against the lawful government. However, numerous acts were committed by the Northern government during Reconstruction that proved the Southern states had left the Union.

In 1865, Radical Republicans in the Congress denied seats to the duly elected representatives from the Southern states reconstructed under Johnson's plan. Yet Article V of the Constitution declares that no state, without its consent, shall be deprived of its equal suffrage in the Senate. The North argued that the Southern states never left the Union because they couldn't legally do so, but then turned around and denied them equal suffrage in the Senate, which could only be done if the Southern states were not actually states; in other words, they had left the Union. In 1867, the radicals declared the legally elected Southern state governments illegal, returning them to the status of territories under military control exercised by Congress. This followed Southern refusal to ratify the 14th Amendment. There is no constitutional authority whatsoever for the federal government to do such a thing. There is a constitutional procedure for allowing new states in, but no language dealing with removing them. This presents a problem of logic for the Northern argument that states could not leave the Union. After all, didn't the North just fight a war to declare that states could not leave the Union, and now the North was removing states from the Union?

With the legality of secession established, was the Southern states' belief that their welfare was threatened valid? The answer must be a resounding "yes!" A starting point for regional conflict between North and South is hard to pin down, but in 1819 the national government openly dealt with slavery for the first time in a way that fostered inter-regional hostility. It must be understood, as it is by most modern historians, that slavery was not the pivotal cause of the Civil War. The role of slavery in the Civil War could be analogized to that of a football in a football game. The ball does not cause the game, but it does give the two battling sides something to throw around.

The single most relevant fact in support of this position is that five Southern slave states (Missouri, Kentucky, Maryland, Delaware and West Virginia) fought all or part of the war with the North against the South. Slavery fit into the larger context and the real cause of the war — a clash between the industrial manufacturing economy of the North and the agricultural consumer economy of the South. Both sides had greatly divergent needs from a government and views of where the power should be in that government. The tariff crisis of 1828-33 was one of many examples of this. The North supported these import taxes to protect its manufacturing from foreign competition and believed this was the role of the federal government. The South was opposed to the taxes since they caused price increases in a region that produced little and consumed much. They also felt that this power was not appropriate for the federal government. Into this economic/political clash stumbled the issue of slavery. To the South, whose economy rested on the "peculiar institution," these Northern attacks increasingly appeared to be another step taken to subjugate the South, and this had to be prevented. Slavery became the issue pragmatists on both sides saw as the final battle over where the powers of government belonged — in the federal government or the states. Protecting their particular view began to translate into maintaining or ending slavery.

The Tallmadge Amendment was proposed by Representative James Tallmadge of New York, in 1819. His plan was to ban further slavery in the Missouri territory and to free all children of slaves there when they reached the age of 25. The amendment was passed by the House, but defeated by the Senate. By this time, the larger Northern population had given that region control of the House, but the number of Northern and Southern states, known increasingly as the Free and Slave states, was equally divided at eleven each, leaving a tie in the Senate. Even though the amendment was defeated, it caused shock and anger in the South. It also set off a power struggle between the two regions for control of the Senate. Each side recognized that the South had, in effect, a veto over the North in that chamber. The North worked to end this balance, the South to preserve it. This awkward balance was maintained until 1850. Every time a new territory was ready for statehood, the necessity of the balance created a nasty battle between the two regions. This was a primary reason why Texas was kept out of the Union for nine years (1836-1845) by the North, so as to avoid a Southern advantage in the Senate.

In 1820, the Missouri Territory applied for admission to the Union as a state. The debate raged over whether it would be admitted as a free or slave state, with the obvious Senate ramifications. The Missouri Compromise of 1820 temporarily lessened the tensions. It allowed Missouri to join as a slave state and Maine to join as a free state. It also dictated that slavery would be banned north of 36° 30' N in the Louisiana Purchase, except for Missouri. This opened up approximately half the new territories to slavery. The Senate balance was maintained and calm returned. In a prophetic note shortly thereafter, Thomas Jefferson wrote that the Missouri dispute, "like a fire bell in the night, awakened and filled me with terror."

The 1830s saw the Nullification Crisis, and then the rise of the abolitionists who began to agitate for the end of slavery. They used newspapers, books, and other methods to stir up opposition to the South. Their attacks were virulent and barely true, but they began to have the desired effect in the North. They also created rage in the South. Attacks of a different kind occurred as well. In 1831, Nat Turner led a bloody slave uprising in Virginia; it was one of many. Frightened Southerners, afraid that the revolts could spread, appealed for strong new slave laws, which were soon passed. Fear and misunderstanding between the two regions increased.

The next major problem developed in 1846, when Pennsylvania Congressman David Wilmot proposed an amendment to ban slavery in any territory gained during the Mexican War. Like the Tallmadge Amendment, it passed the House, was defeated in the Senate, and created a tremendous uproar in the South. As the war ended, the issue arose again, and with the potential admission of California into the Union, in 1850, things became much worse. By that time the Free and Slave states were balanced at 15 each. A major compromise was worked out by Henry Clay and guided through the Congress by Stephen Douglas. It admitted California to the Union as a free state, divided the land won from Mexico into the territories of New Mexico and Utah with no restriction on slavery, paid Texas $10 million for land removed and given to New Mexico, abolished the slave trade in the District of Columbia, and established a new, strong Fugitive Slave Law. While the government was attempting to balance the needs of both sides, the Southern states got the worst of the deal, and it is hard to see why they agreed to this in the first place. The bottom line was that the North got California, which gave them an advantage in the Senate, and the South got a new Fugitive Slave Law.

The compromise may have suited the politicians, but it did not suit the people. By this time both sides had become a little paranoid, and harsh words were being exchanged. The North was accused of abusing the powers of the federal government to unconstitutionally limit the spread of slavery, powers which Southerners, following the States' Rights view, claimed the federal government did not have. Southerners widely believed the North's goal was to destroy the Southern economy and way of life. The South was accused of trying to spread slavery throughout the land, including the North. This was further exacerbated by the implementation of the new Fugitive Slave Law, which required Northern law enforcement personnel to actively assist in the hunting down of runaway Southern slaves in the North. Northerners were unwilling to do so and actively refused such assistance. The result was that the only concession to the South, from the Compromise of 1850, was not enforced. This was seen by Southerners as proof that Northerners would not live up to their agreements. Bitter feelings spread and intensified.

In 1852, Harriet Beecher Stowe wrote *Uncle Tom's Cabin*, a book that told the story of slavery and the whites that ran it. The book was generous in its portrayal of the South, but it pointed out that slavery hurt everyone who was involved in it, white and black. It became a best seller in the North, where it was hailed, and banned in the South. Southerners blasted it as a book of lies that defamed their society.

In 1854, Senator Stephen Douglas introduced and led in the passage of the Kansas-Nebraska Act to deal with the Nebraska territory. The land was to be divided into two territories, each of which would follow the principle of "popular sovereignty," which dictated that the people of a territory would vote on being free or slave. Much of this land was north of the old 36° 30' N line of the Missouri Compromise of 1820 which prohibited slavery in this area. For this reason, the act was viciously attacked in the North. It now appeared that the South could not be trusted to keep their word, as they tried to spread slavery into Northern territory. The debate over this law set off a violent struggle in Kansas as that territory prepared to enter the Union. From both sides came large numbers of people determined to sway the vote to their point of view. Over the next two years Kansas bled as the various forces vied for control. Massacres were commonplace. The violence even spread to the floor of the U.S. Senate when Representative Preston Brooks of South Carolina, in a near-fatal attack, used a cane to beat Massachusetts Senator Charles Sumner, who had made anti-Southern speeches. The Kansas-Nebraska Act also spawned the anti-slavery Republican Party.

In 1859, the South's greatest fear seemed about to come true. John Brown, a northern abolitionist fanatic, who had committed a well known massacre in Kansas, organized a group to attack the federal arsenal at Harper's Ferry, Virginia. His plan was to seize the weapons, free and arm the local slaves, spread a slave revolt throughout the South, and create a free black republic. After taking the arsenal, they were defeated and captured by U.S. Marines under the command of Colonel Robert E. Lee. Brown's hanging in Virginia made him a martyr in the North; he was even compared to Jesus. Southerners compared him to Satan and were outraged at the Northern reaction. This event greatly intensified the animosity between the two regions.

The election of 1860 provided the final step towards secession. Abraham Lincoln, the nominee of the Republican Party, was opposed to the spread of slavery. If elected he would be the first President to hold this view. He had, however, not always held this position, but took it on at that time because it was politically expedient. Lincoln shared the prejudices of all other whites and did not think the slaves should be freed and allowed to take up co-equal positions alongside whites. At one point in his career Lincoln had even supported the Back-to-Africa movement which proposed shipping all blacks back across the Atlantic. The African nation of Liberia was actually founded for such a purpose in 1847. Lincoln's position had not really changed by 1860. At the start of the war he was widely quoted as saying it was not a war to free the slaves, only a war to restore the Union.

Abe and his worthless proclamation.
(Reproduced from the Collections of the Library Of Congress.)

Lincoln is best known, mistakenly, for freeing the slaves through the wartime Emancipation Proclamation. This underhanded political trick did not free a single slave. It applied only to states and parts of states that were in rebellion against the United States. This meant the Confederate States, which Lincoln had no control over anyway. Southerners laughed at Lincoln and ignored the Proclamation. It did not, of course, apply to the five slave states that were fighting with the North. If the thing was worthless, why was it issued? The year of 1862 saw some major Confederate victories, and there was an international perception that the South would fight to a draw, if not an outright victory. France and Britain, both hurt by the Union blockade of Southern cotton, were sympathetic to the South. By late 1862 it looked as though one or both of these nations would diplomatically recognize the Confederacy. If this was done, these nations would re-establish trade with the South, which would break the Union blockade and greatly help them in the war against the North. If the Union blockade attempted to prevent British and French ships from trading with the South, it would be an act of war. It came very close to being France, Britain, and the Confederacy against the United States. With this as the backdrop, Lincoln needed to do something to prevent diplomatic recognition. When he issued the Emancipation Proclamation, effective January 1, 1863, it made the war appear to be a war over slavery. If France and Britain were to join with the South, it would mean they were fighting to uphold slavery, and this their people would not allow. The Proclamation, along with Southern defeats at Gettysburg and Vicksburg in July, 1863, ended any possibility of European intervention in the war. Even in the face of these clear historical facts, the myth surrounding Lincoln as the Great Emancipator hangs on. More than anything, it is an example of typical American history: pure garbage.

Nonetheless, in 1860, Southerners reasoned that they would no longer be able to defend their rights with Lincoln as President. They insisted they would secede if Lincoln won. In the election he was not even on the ballot in 10 Southern states and did not receive a single vote from them, but he won a majority of the electoral college due to the populous Northern states anyway. The election victory, though, cannot be used to show any widespread support for Lincoln or the policies of the Republican Party. By this election the Democratic Party, the only other major party, had disintegrated and split into feuding Northern and Southern factions, each of which ran a candidate. In addition, the border states supported the candidate of a fourth party — the Constitutional Union Party. With the opposition split among three parties and many Northerners totally opposed to supporting any of them, they turned their votes to the Republicans as the best of the worst, and Lincoln won.

After viewing the relationship between the regions it is clear that the Southern states did have a legitimate reason to secede from the Union following many years of unredressed abuse by the North. Even though slavery was the dominant topic of these many years, it must be remembered that it was not the major cause. When the war started, only 10% of Southerners owned any slaves at all. The South increasingly saw its agricultural aristocratic society as under attack by the North. Two sides with such different economies and societies and such differing needs from a government could not long stay under one government. A split was inevitable and legal.

In December, 1860, following Lincoln's election, South Carolina seceded as promised. She was followed by Mississippi, Florida, Alabama, Georgia, Louisiana, and Texas. Together they formed the Confederate States of America, with their capital in Montgomery, Alabama. After Lincoln's aggression at Fort Sumter, Virginia, Tennessee, Arkansas and North Carolina seceded and joined the Confederacy. A long period of Northern abuse was over, or so the South thought. But the greatest abuse was yet to come in an illegal and unwarranted war that would virtually destroy the South.

Lincoln's attempt to force the reunion of these eleven states was clearly illegal. His only basis for requiring continuation of the whole Union was a sort of silly, semi-religious misconception that this country must exist. For this, 618,000 Americans died, almost as many soldiers as have died in all of America's other wars combined. Lincoln had absolutely no constitutional grounds for launching this

82

immoral war, but that's nothing new in a country where the Constitution is, after all, just a piece of paper.

CHAPTER 9

JOHNSON'S IMPEACHMENT 1868

In 1868, Congress turned the impeachment process against President Andrew Johnson, and in so doing provided another example of constitutional trampling. This whole mess originated during the Civil War as President Lincoln developed a strategy to deal with the defeated Southern states once the hostilities were successfully concluded. Lincoln's plan for Reconstruction advocated forgiveness and leniency, perhaps believing that such a crushing defeat was punishment enough. This was totally unacceptable to the Radical Republicans who wanted harsh punitive measures taken against the South. This difference of opinion would develop into a bitter struggle between the Congress and the President that nearly toppled our system of government.

Towards the end of the Civil War, the Radical Republicans in Congress drafted their own reconstruction plan in the Wade-Davis Bill of 1864. Lincoln's pocket veto seriously inflamed the Radicals who were already greatly upset at Lincoln's mishandling of the war. Then on April 14, 1865, just days after the surrender of Confederate General Robert E. Lee at Appamattox effectively ended the war, Lincoln was assassinated by John Wilkes Booth, a disgruntled Southern actor.

The assassination of Lincoln has a darker side, that is, the conspiracy behind his death. Lincoln had many enemies: Southerners, the Radical Republicans, and his own military, including Secretary of War Stanton, who criticized his running of the war. The plot to kill Lincoln included other targets as well. On the night Lincoln went to Ford's Theater, Vice President Johnson and Secretary of State Seward were also to be killed. The attack on Seward left him critically wounded, while Johnson's assassin failed to carry out his mission. One conspiracy theory suggests that Northern forces, especially the military, were involved in a coup attempt. Evidence shows that Booth was able to escape from Washington without confrontation across an always heavily guarded bridge; the search for Booth was purposely held up until the following morning; and certain telegraph lines had been cut so that word of Booth's escape could not be sent. At that time there was no constitutional provision for a transfer of power if both the president and vice president were removed from office, though the secretary of state was commonly believed to be the next most powerful position. Successful attacks on all three would have created a vacuum. Power being what it is, the only result of this would have been a power struggle by various forces. Of course, only the military was in a position to take control and enforce it. As Secretary of War Stanton was implicated, along with the military, this only gives credence to the theory. Regardless of who was involved, the President was dead and the power of that office was transferred to Vice President Andrew Johnson. It would take three years for this crisis to create a much darker one.

Following the assassination, Andrew Johnson assumed the presidency and tried to continue Lincoln's lenient plan for reconstruction. Lincoln's popularity with the people probably would have allowed his plan to work, but Johnson lacked such popularity, as well as the ability to compromise. He attempted to force Lincoln's plan into effect, mostly while Congress was not in session from April through December, 1865. By December, 1865, Johnson had guided all the Southern states, except Texas, back into the Union, these states having followed all the requirements mandated by Lincoln's plan. This also meant that the Southern states sent their newly elected representatives to Congress. To the horror of the Radicals, these new representatives included former Southern officials such as Confederate Vice President Alexander Stephens.

On top of this, the Southern states had passed a series of laws to regulate the former slaves. These laws, known as Black Codes, restricted the activities of blacks. They segregated blacks socially, required them to work, and denied the rights of voting and serving on juries. Southerners argued that these codes were enacted to deal with the strains caused by of large numbers of freed blacks who had no role in Southern society. The Radical Republicans saw these laws as attempts to reinstate slavery by states that refused to accept defeat.

Totally dissatisfied with the course of presidential reconstruction and the apparent defiance of the Southern states, Congress began to pass measures designed to allow it, instead of the President, to control Reconstruction. Upon reconvening in December, 1865, Congress began to assert its will. Their first act was to refuse to seat the new Southern representatives. Next they formed the Joint Committee of 15. Composed of six senators and nine representatives, this committee was designed to control Reconstruction. Two measures from the committee immediately faced President Johnson: the Freedmen's Bureau Bill and the Civil Rights Act. The Freedmen's Bureau Bill was to allow the continuation of a wartime measure that gave assistance to ex-slaves and provided them with federal protection. The Civil Rights Act guaranteed citizenship to blacks and gave the federal government the power to intervene in the affairs of the states to protect the civil rights of blacks.

Johnson vetoed both bills, claiming that they unconstitutionally intruded upon the powers of the states and the President. Unfortunately, Johnson had been touring the country, launching vicious and undignified attacks on the Radical Republicans. His verbal abuse and intemperate language backfired, eventually costing him the support of moderate Republicans in Congress. Combined with the moderates, the Radicals were then able to consistently wield the two-thirds vote necessary to override a presidential veto, a power which they began to exercise with the Freedmen's Bureau and the Civil Rights Act.

Next came the 14th Amendment, which the Radicals proposed in 1866 in order to protect the Civil Rights Act. Knowing that the act violated the very spirit of federalism, as well as constitutional divisions of power between the states and the federal government, the Radicals were concerned that the Supreme Court would rule it unconstitutional. Their solution was to propose the 14th Amendment and legalize their unconstitutional intrusion into the power of the states. The most important features of the amendment granted citizenship to blacks and stated that, "no State shall make or enforce any law which shall abridge the privileges or immunities of citizens of the United States; nor shall any State deprive any person of life, liberty, or property, without due process of law; nor deny to any person within its jurisdiction the equal protection of the laws."

The amendment was then presented to the states for ratification. It is interesting to note that it was also presented to the Southern states. They had been denied their seats in Congress with the excuse that they were not legally back in the Union; but on the other hand, they were allowed to ratify the amendment.

Article V of the Constitution provides the process by which the Constitution may be amended. Such amendments may be proposed by either the Congress or by a convention called by an application of the states. These proposals must then be "ratified by the Legislatures of three fourths of the several States, or by Conventions in three fourths thereof." The use of the word "State" is clear. In order to ratify an amendment a political subdivision of the nation must be a "State." It would follow that a "territory" would not be allowed to ratify a constitutional amendment. At this point, in 1866, the Congress had refused the former Confederate states their seats in Congress. The question arises — can Congress deny seats in Congress to a state legitimately in the Union? The answer is an unequivocal no! Article V of the Constitution also provides, in the amending process, as a limitation on future amendments, that "no State, without its Consent, shall be deprived of its equal Suffrage in the Senate." Congress had, as we have seen, deprived all the Southern states of their representation in the Senate and the House. In effect, Congress had reduced their suffrage in the Congress to zero. This would be in violation of Article V, unless, that is, the Southern states had been somehow demoted from the status of "states" to some lower status such as "territories". This would mean that the Southern states had no right to be involved in the ratification process as only a legal "State" can do. But is that possible? Article IV gives Congress the authority to admit states to the Union, but does not include the power to remove them. Congress has no such enumerated power in the Constitution to demote a state.

President Johnson, who understood the congressional intent of the 14th Amendment, led the opposition to it in the South where 10 of the 11 former Confederate states voted against it, thus defeating the measure. If Johnson thought this would be the end of the matter, he was sadly mistaken. The Radicals were outraged at this defeat, and in March, 1867, over Johnson's veto, they began Radical Reconstruction run totally by Congress. They passed a series of measures that included:

1. The governments of the 10 states that refused to ratify the 14th Amendment were declared illegal. These states reverted to territories over which Congress had complete control.
2. The ten states were divided into 5 military districts. The military commanders of these districts had the power to institute special military tribunals instead of the civil courts.
3. A list of steps was established that the ten states must follow before being readmitted into the Union. These included a requirement to ratify the 14th Amendment.

When these conditions were met, a state would be readmitted to the Union and its representatives allowed to return to Congress. Until then, these states were under military rule without representation. The trampling of the Constitution in these events is simply astonishing. Two years after the war was over, Congress deprived 10 states of their legally chosen governments, placed them under military law during peacetime without any constitutional authority to do so, and blackmailed them into approving the 14th Amendment. Besides problems with Southern states, the Northern states of Ohio and New Jersey voted to withdraw their ratification of this amendment. Reconstruction was indeed reflecting the nature of abusive government the fear of which had forced secession in the first place.

The amending process as described in Article V of the Constitution states that an amendment must be ratified by three-fourths of the states before being added to the Constitution. Ratify means "to approve," and this logically implies a state has the option of not approving; however, in this case the Southern states were required to pass the 14th Amendment as a condition to removing Draconian measures taken against them. This surely qualifies as blackmail. The 14th Amendment, having been added in a devious and unconstitutional manner, is invalid, as are all subsequent legal decisions that have been based upon it.

After leading the opposition to the 14th Amendment, Johnson was in a desperate situation. A united, and highly offended, Congress began to pass measures to strip the President of his power. One such act was the Tenure of Office Act of 1867. It required the President to get consent from the Senate before removing any officeholder who required Senate consent to be appointed. Since this made an addition to Article I, Section 2, Clause 2 of the Constitution, it was clearly unconstitutional, but this made no difference to Congress as they prepared to trap Johnson. Congress knew that Johnson wanted to fire Edwin Stanton, the only Radical in the Cabinet, and this was their motivation for the new law. Congress also knew that Johnson would challenge the constitutionality of the act. But the Supreme Court does not give advisory opinions, so the law would have to be violated in order to reach the court. Johnson stepped right into this trap and fired Stanton without Senate approval. The Radicals in the House then led that body in drafting articles of impeachment. They alleged vague accusations that the President had defamed Congress (though surely criticism of Congress was protected by the First Amendment), and that he had, by firing Stanton, violated the Tenure of Office Act, a law which was clearly illegal. In February, 1868, when the House passed these articles, Andrew Johnson became the only President ever to be impeached. It was clear that he was impeached for his political stand against the Radicals in Congress, as it related to Reconstruction in the South.

Even with these trumped-up charges, Congress had no legal recourse to the impeachment process. Article II, Sec. 4 of the Constitution explains the necessary conditions for impeachment. That section provides that an official, "shall be removed from office only if found guilty of treason, bribery, or other high crimes and misdemeanors." Certainly, in this case, no treason nor bribery had been committed. That left only the clause of "high crimes and misdemeanors." In the context of 1787, the Founders intended this phrase to mean serious criminal abuses of power. Again, that had not taken place in this incident. Johnson's violation of the Tenure of Office Act, which was done in order to gain a judicial decision on its constitutionality, certainly does not fit into this category. So, in the final analysis, Johnson had not committed any act that could legally warrant his impeachment. He was impeached for his political disputes with Congress.

Ticket to Johnson's Impeachment Circus
(Reproduced from the Collections of the Library Of Congress.)

90

After his impeachment by the House, Johnson faced a removal trial in the Senate, where the Radicals had more than the two-thirds vote necessary to remove him. This trial dragged on for more than two months, and became a complete circus. It also consumed the time of the Congress. In the end, it seems that seven Republicans suddenly realized they were on the verge of destroying the executive branch and instituting a parliamentary system in the United States, and that their actions were an affront to the Constitution. As a result, the seven voted against removal. Johnson was saved by one vote. Even though he remained in office, his influence was gone; he was sent packing in the election of 1868. As for the seven Republicans who voted against removing the President, their careers and lives were destroyed by the furious Radicals.

This entire episode is more the rule than the exception in our long and colorful history. It was an almost unparalleled trampling which most certainly should have been prevented, but after all, the Constitution is just a piece of paper.

CHAPTER 10
THE BONUS MARCH 1932

In early May, 1932, as a result of hardships brought on by the Depression, a group of 250 ex-servicemen, veterans of World War I, began a march from Portland, Oregon, to Washington D.C., with the goal of pushing Congress into approving early payment of their Adjusted Service Certificates (war bonuses). During a serious confrontation with railroad officials in East St. Louis, they attracted nationwide attention and became a rallying point for people dissatisfied with economic conditions in America. By June, over 22,000 veterans had converged on Washington, much to the chagrin of the Hoover Administration and the government of the District of Columbia. The Bonus Expeditionary Force (B.E.F.), as they became known, set up camp and proceeded to exercise their First Amendment rights of peaceful assembly and petitioning the government for a redress of their grievances. President Hoover responded by sending in the Army with cavalry, tanks, bayonets, and tear gas to forcefully evict the men, women, and children of the B.E.F. from the nation's capital. The shameful result was described in December, 1932, by Congressman Loring Black (D-NY) as "the greatest crime in history." The whole affair brings to mind images of the 1989 massacre of protesting students by the Chinese Government, for on July 28, 1932, the United States was in the same league as the murderers at Beijing.

During the early 1930s, the world was suffering through a tremendous economic depression. The large corporations and banks had abused the system with their greed until the inevitable collapse resulted. In the United States, businesses went under, banks collapsed, and millions of people lost their life's savings. Unemployment, homelessness, and starvation ran rampant. Herbert Hoover was the Republican President whose policies and actions, controlled by industrialists like Andrew Mellon, had helped bring about the Depression. Republican concern for the human suffering was expressed in a 1932 administration statement that "there is no starvation in America." This was, of course, in the middle of the Depression.

But people were starving, and many of them were ex-servicemen. In Portland, Oregon, there were approximately 1,800 veterans with families, and many others, without dependents, living on the streets. They searched for jobs, begged for food and money, and engaged in all the other desperate measures that a man will take when he is starving. As they marched off to war in Europe in 1917, these veterans had been told that they were being sent to fight for their nation. It seemed by 1932 that all they had done was fight for a place in which to starve. Ex-sergeant W.W. Waters was one of these veterans in Portland, and his story was typical.

Waters was sent overseas in the winter of 1917, and served on the front lines in France from July through November, 1918. Following the armistice, his regiment was ordered into Germany as part of the forces of occupation. He returned to the United States in July, 1919, and was honorably discharged with the rank of sergeant. Through the 1920s, he worked in various enterprises, and had risen to assistant superintendent in a cannery before being laid off in December, 1930, as a result of the Depression. Over the next year, he could find no work either at home in Idaho or elsewhere in Oregon, so he and his wife settled in Portland, as the city seemed to offer more opportunities. Within that year their savings were used up and their belongings found their way, one by one, to the pawnshops. By March, 1932, they had nothing left except the clothes on their backs.

Waters joined many others beating about the city in the forlorn hope of finding work which would provide the bare necessities of life. The story was the same in every other American city. Families half-clad, in threadbare clothing, paced the streets in soleless shoes. The poverty seemed to destroy them not only physically but also emotionally. The receipt of charity from public and private services helped them survive, but also took away their self-respect. Desperately they searched for jobs that did not exist, their plight worsening daily. There was profound discontent with conditions and a desire for change. Their frustration was compounded by their total ignorance of how to bring it about, but more and more they looked to their Adjusted Service Certificates, more commonly known as the "Bonus," as a solution to their problems.

The Bonus was not a gift, but rather a payment of money to compensate those men who served in the military for the difference in pay between them and non-servicemen. Those who stayed home had not risked their lives nor endured the significantly lower pay of the military. This was a well-deserved compensation to the troops whose lives were disrupted by fighting for their country. Such compensation was not a new idea. Veterans of every American war had received significant government assistance. Traditionally, the reward consisted of a bonus of land or a pension plan for the veterans and their dependents. Over the years, 75 million acres had been taken out of the public domain for settlement by veterans. Pension payments, which had been a fairly small part of the national budget until the Civil War veterans were provided for, grew to consume 43% of all federal outlays by 1893. This was not controversial, as most people agreed with the medieval concept of rewarding soldiers for their service to the nation.

When World War I ended in 1918, Congress was already considering several proposals to assist the returning veterans. Again, most people agreed that the veterans should be compensated. The pro-Bonus position was offset, however, by a concern for economic conditions. A post-war nation inevitably suffers an economic slow-down from the full-scale production that is required to fuel a war effort. Productivity goes down and unemployment goes up. With this in mind, many industrialists and their Republican allies were unwilling to support a plan that would greatly increase government expenditures. Besides, these same people supported tax cuts to help their rich friends. Their propaganda line stated that they were very grateful for the sacrifice of the troops, but the government couldn't afford to compensate them at that time. Surprisingly, the struggling economy did not prevent Republicans from making multi-million-dollar government gifts and loans to banks, corporations, and other countries.

The struggle over compensation legislation lasted six years. It passed the House of Representatives early in the game, but was defeated by the more conservative Senate. Eventually, the Senate passed the bill. Subsequent versions were vetoed by Presidents Warren G. Harding and Calvin Coolidge. In a viciously stinging veto message, Coolidge questioned the patriotism of the Bonus supporters. Congressional reaction was sharp and immediate. Both houses voted to override the veto. By May, 1924, the Bonus was law.

Congress set the adjusted service pay rate at $1 a day for domestic service and $1.25 for overseas service, with maximums of $500 and $625. The Adjusted Service Certificates would equal the adjusted service pay plus 40%, plus 20 years compound interest to be paid when the certificates matured in 1945. A veteran with $625 coming in adjusted service pay was given a certificate with a maturity value of $1884.15. The law allowed veterans to borrow against the value of their certificates, at 7% interest, after two years from their issue, and included a provision for immediate payment of the total amount to the veterans' heirs in case of death. It amounted to a fair deal for the veterans that they could enjoy in their later years.

Just prior to the crash in 1929, several bills had been introduced into Congress to allow the full and immediate cash payment of the veterans' Bonus certificates. One of these was introduced by freshman Representative Wright Patman of Texas, who would become the outspoken and influential leader of the pro-Bonus forces. Following the crash, the world settled into depression. Many veterans joined the unemployment and food lines, and began to look at the certificates as a postdated check which they desperately needed to cash, but couldn't. As conditions worsened, a clamor arose from the veterans for early payment of the Bonus.

Administration opposition to immediate payment was strong and effective, but by February, 1931, Congress made some major changes to satisfy the veterans. A bill was passed and became law, over the

President's veto, increasing the allowable loan basis to 50% of face value, and reducing the interest rate on these loans to 4-1/2%. It was estimated that if all eligible veterans borrowed the maximum allowed, it would cost the government $1.6 billion. The administration had stopped immediate cash payment, but they were beginning to lose ground. Their best argument, the cost to the Treasury, began to assist the immediate cash payment forces whose counterargument, known as the "Theory of Stimulation," claimed that since this money would be immediately spent by the veterans, it would stimulate the economy with a sudden injection of several billion dollars of much-needed capital. The result would be good for the entire country. The Republicans did not see it this way, nor did northern liberal Democrats, conservatives, the Progressives, big business, or the media.

Meanwhile, Congressman Patman had been busy with a nation-wide effort to promote the legislation. Through the congressional recess of 1931, he toured and spoke across the country. He established groups to fight for the Bonus, and worked with organizations such as the American Legion and the Veterans of Foreign Wars. He raised funds, started petition drives, joined radio talk shows, built lobbying efforts, and wooed the media. In the winter of 1931, Patman introduced H.R. 1, one of several immediate-payment bills introduced in the 1931-32 session. He then launched a full-scale effort to impeach Andrew Mellon, the powerful anti-Bonus Secretary of the Treasury. All of Patman's maneuvers had little effect. The House Committee on Ways and Means did not even consider his immediate-payment bill until April, and the result was predictable. Conservative Democrats voted with the Republicans to shelve the plan. Next, Patman attempted a discharge petition to get the bill out of the committee for consideration by the House. Under newly relaxed rules he only needed 145 signatures, but he had barely 100 when Congress broke for the Memorial Day holiday. At this point, the 300 members of the Bonus Army left Portland on their march to Washington. When this group, led by W.W. Waters, descended upon the Capital, things changed dramatically.

For several months veterans in the Portland area had contemplated a march to Washington. It was done by other small groups, but to most it seemed like an unnecessary effort. The perception was that petitions and letters to Congress would do the trick. By March it became clear that Congress was playing games with the issue, and when Patman's bill was shelved by the House Ways and Means Committee in May, the Portland veterans were stirred into action. Eventually, about 250 men were loosely organized along military lines. A command structure was established with elaborate titles. The men were required to show evidence of military service and to swear allegiance to the Constitution and the flag. Their stated goal as they left Portland around May 11 was to travel to Washington and petition Congress to give them their Bonus.

Their march had an auspicious beginning. As they had no cars or trucks, the only possible means of transportation across the 3,000 miles to Washington was by train. With flags flying, the column of men marched to the freight yards of the Union Pacific Railroad and prepared to board the night train out. Union Pacific had other ideas. A company vice-president had found out about the plan, so as the veterans waited to board the train it raced through without stopping. This seemingly minor affair almost spelled the end of the Bonus Army. Chaos broke out as some men deserted, some searched for food, others argued over what course of action to take, and some went to sleep. By morning some minimal supplies were thrown together, and as the remaining men waited for the next train a curious comradeship developed. As they exchanged stories about their war experiences and about their struggles with poverty, a bond formed. The veterans finally threatened to stand on the tracks, so Union Pacific gave in and let the men ride to Pocatello, Idaho.

Important changes then took place. A new commander-in-chief was elected for advance organization. Walter W. Waters rose from a lower position to Regimental Commander and began to institute real organization and discipline. A transportation committee was established, a supply officer was selected, and a military police unit was created. The men complained that this wasn't the Army, but they followed the strict discipline nonetheless.

The march continued after this short organizational delay. Continuing to ride the freights, the men stopped in Cheyenne, Wyoming, where Regular Army kitchens provided a hot meal. After a week the Bonus Army arrived in Council Bluffs, Iowa, where city officials and the American Legion post worked tirelessly to provide supplies and assistance. The next stretch required the men to board a train in the Wabash freight yards, where they had another run-in with railroad officials. When they were refused passage, the men continued to uncouple the cars, preventing a loaded freight train from leaving. Finally, the railroad gave in.

The Wabash line delivered the veterans to St. Louis on May 22, 1932. The men were confronted by a major police presence upon disembarking the train. They immediately paraded to a nearby field, where the police chief complimented them on their discipline, made a donation to their cause, and sent his men home. That afternoon began a run-in with Baltimore and Ohio Railroad officials which would bring the march to the attention of the nation. The railroad made it clear they would not allow the veterans to ride on their line, and they had an injunction to prevent them. The next day the Bonus Army moved into the B&O yards in East St. Louis. For the next three days B&O tried to sneak trains out of the yard. Every time they did, the veterans ran forward and boarded them, at which time B&O would uncouple the engine and let the train sit. The affair escalated quickly. National headlines depicted the struggle of a peaceful band of ex-servicemen, trying to get to their nation's capital, against a major railroad company. The constant attention drew the focus of the nation. It angered other veterans who felt their buddies were being given a raw deal, and it angered the common folk who were already resentful against the powerful corporations, utilities, and railroads. By May 25, several thousand civilians had encircled the rail yards and were in a nasty mood. They were threatening trouble against the railroad. B&O requested National Guard troops from the Governor, and five companies arrived on the scene. As a clash seemed imminent, the national headlines continued to scream, the people grew angrier, and thousands more veterans left their homes for Washington.

During the day of the 25th, B&O continued to sneak freight cars out of the yard one at a time to be reassembled at Caseyville, seven miles away. As an engine and caboose left, the veterans figured out what was happening. A number of them jumped aboard while the rest chased after. Civilians with their cars carried many of the veterans. They came together again at Caseyville, where they took over the reunited freight train. Finally, the Illinois governor broke the impasse and ordered the National Guard units to transport the veterans by truck to the Indiana line. This was done on May 26, and from there it was an easy trip. National Guard and state police units transported the Bonus Army across Indiana, Ohio, Pennsylvania, and Maryland. It seems that no governor wanted this problem on his hands, nor the blame for holding up these national celebrities. On May 29, 1932, the Maryland National Guard delivered the veterans to the boundary of Washington D.C. The trip had taken eighteen days, started a national debate on the bonus issue, and set off a stampede that would lead to the arrival of over 22,000 veterans.

Washington had known about the marchers from the constant headlines for some time, but did almost nothing to prepare for them. The single exception was the newly hired police chief, former Brigadier General Pelham D. Glassford, who acted on his own. The District of Columbia is administered by the federal government. Congress provides the money, and the President appoints a board of three commissioners to run the city. At this time, President Hoover had appointed all three Commissioners and their actions, or rather lack thereof, would contribute to the trouble to come. The Commissioners had recently hired Glassford who, upon hearing of the approaching marchers, took immediate charge of the situation. Glassford, an ex-serviceman, played on both sides. He organized a program to discourage the veterans from coming to Washington, but also took numerous steps to provide assistance for them once they arrived. He felt that they were legitimately exercising their First Amendment rights to petition the government, and as long as they assembled peacefully there would be no problems. He did, however, make it clear that no disruptive behavior would be tolerated, and also that he would use force to control the veterans if necessary.

Glassford requested tents, cots, bedsacks, rolling kitchens, and other equipment from the numerous local military camps. Secretary of War Patrick J. Hurley flatly refused, saying that "the federal government could not recognize the invasion." Glassford also went to the Capitol to ask senior members of Congress to unbottle the Bonus Bill from the Ways and Means Committee and bring it to a vote. He correctly pointed out that as long as the bill was shelved it would act as a magnet to veterans thinking they could influence its passage. The congressmen refused. He also tried to meet with the President for the same purpose, but he was not allowed to see him and was told that the administration would do nothing to help. Glassford's efforts to assist the veterans were designed to prevent trouble; however, the administration and the D.C. Commissioners saw these acts as proof that Glassford was in with the veterans. This would earn him the personal wrath of Hoover and the Commissioners.

By May 26, while the Oregon Bonus Army was still in Indiana, 500 veterans had already arrived in Washington. On this date they held a meeting at which Glassford made speeches and took charge. He urged them to organize in order to provide discipline and control. They formed the Bonus Expeditionary Force and elected Glassford secretary-treasurer.

He then continued to make preparations for the influx to come. Over the next couple of days he established shelter for the veterans in a number of vacant and abandoned buildings around the city, and also arranged for the overflow to settle on federal land on the Anacostia Flats. This narrow strip of land was separated from the city by a creek. A drawbridge provided access. Two Washington, D.C. National Guard rolling kitchens were obtained from a personal army friend of Glassford's, money was raised to procure food from Ft. Myers, wholesalers contributed food, bakeries agreed to donate day-old bread, and medical facilities were set up. By the time the Oregon Bonus Army arrived on the 29th, the city was as prepared as Glassford could make it.

The rise and fall of the B.E.F. is outlined in the following numbers:

May 29 -	1,000
June 7 -	5,000
June 15 -	15,000
June 28 -	20,000
July 17 -	22,000
July 28 -	10,000

As their numbers increased, W.W. Waters became the Commander of the entire B.E.F. They set up shop in various abandoned buildings and on the Anacostia Flats. They soon began to march and protest at the Capitol. With the ominous presence of so many veterans, Congressman Patman's discharge petition suddenly gained new interest. It received the necessary signatures and was filed on June 4th. The bill was discharged from committee on June 13th and debate in the House started the next day. Veterans filled the visitors' galleries and surrounded the building to wait for the results. The debate continued on the 15th, and the House voted 232 - 197 to pass the Patman immediate-payment bill. It was a victory, but it was not enough votes to override the expected Presidential veto. The bill was then sent to the Senate, where it was brought to the floor for debate on the 17th. The rhetoric flowed until the evening, when the Senate voted 68 - 28 against the bill. As the Capitol was surrounded by veterans, everyone expected a riot to break out, but instead Commander Waters led the men in singing "America" before returning quietly to their camps. The government widely believed that the B.E.F. would then break up and go home, but they were wrong. The veterans claimed they would live up to their motto of staying until they got immediate payment of the Bonus, or until the certificates matured in 1945. Their army continued to grow as did the now clear no-win situation. Secretly, Waters and Glassford agreed that leaving would be the best course of action, but the men were determined to stay. At least there was hope for the Bonus while Congress was still in session. Their adjournment was not scheduled until July 16th, so the B.E.F. presence continued.

The B.E.F. exercising their constitutional rights on the steps of the Capitol.
(Reproduced from the Collection of the Library Of Congress.)

Over the next month, as the siege of Washington continued, the administration and District Commissioners were increasingly upset by the affair. The story remained on the front page across America and was a daily reminder to the nation of the government's failure to fix the economy. This was intolerable to Hoover, whose re-election campaign was getting under way, so a subterfuge was arranged. Stories began to leak that the B.E.F. was really made up of communists and criminals, so as to discredit them and reduce their popular support. There was a small communist presence, but the B.E.F. had nothing to do with them. In many cases the police had to protect communists from the veterans, who were staunchly anti-communist. The government propaganda began to have an impact. Increasingly, veterans were begging throughout the city and generally causing a nuisance which tarnished their reputation. The general population saw no reason for their continued presence and became angry. The city's social services, and thus its ability to take care of its own citizens, were steadily being drained as well. Congress passed a joint resolution providing transportation home to any veteran who wished to go. Few left at this point. Actually, the B.E.F. continued to grow.

The veterans, though, were getting tired of Commander Waters' passive policies, and a new activism was developing. It was really sparked by the July 9th arrival of 1,500 California veterans under the leadership of Royal Robertson. They refused to sit and wait. They began to picket the Capitol and sleep on the Capitol grounds, which created great concern. On July 13th the Vice President and the Speaker of the House ordered Glassford to enforce the regulations and prevent the veterans from sleeping on the grass around the Capitol. The regulations did not prevent walking, so Robertson's group took advantage of this loophole and began to walk all night on the sidewalks around the Capitol. The national press dubbed this the "Death March," due to the haggard appearance of the veterans. The Capitol Police now feared for the safety of the congressmen. On July 14th, Glassford was called to a meeting with Chief of Staff Douglas MacArthur, in which procedures were outlined for calling out federal troops.

On July 16, Congress adjourned. Waters and Glassford stepped up their program to get the veterans to leave. Many took advantage of the cheap transportation arranged by Congress and went home. From July 18th on, about 1,000 veterans left each day. The B.E.F., however, was not surrendering. They intended to maintain a semi-permanent colony on the outskirts of town with a force of several thousand hard-core members who would continue the pressure. So the slow fading process began. Unfortunately, President Hoover decided this evacuation was not quick enough. Seeing the potential for a campaign issue over his handling of radicalism in the country he staked out a law-and-order position. What he needed was an opportunity to show the country he could put down lawlessness. Since, as he claimed, the B.E.F. was not really a group of veterans, but communists and criminal agitators engaging in disruptive behavior, he could evict them from the city, reinstitute control, and use this to win in November.

The administration plan to provoke the remaining veterans into an uprising began on July 20. First, they revoked permission to use various abandoned and partially demolished buildings. The government insisted the buildings were to be evacuated by midnight July 24th. The next day, they pressured local groups and individuals who had allowed their property to be used as shelter to do the same. The District Commissioners ordered the return of all National Guard equipment by August 1, and the evacuation of Anacostia Flats by August 4th. Glassford tried in vain to warn the Commissioners of the danger in this course of action, but their minds had been made up from above. There was no turning back.

For the next several days a rather farcical series of events took place. The Treasury Department tried to carry out the eviction of the veterans from a series of buildings along lower Pennsylvania Avenue. Assorted legal maneuvers resulted from the government, the B.E.F., and from Glassford. By the 27th nothing had been accomplished. On that afternoon Waters was called to a meeting with the Commissioners. He was not allowed to see them personally, but forced to relay messages back and forth to them through Glassford. Waters negotiated a plan whereby the veterans would leave the disputed buildings by August 1, and to this the Commissioners agreed. What they didn't tell him was that they had already arranged the forced eviction of the veterans in these buildings for the following day, July 28th.

In a surprise attack early the next morning, Glassford, under orders from the Commissioners, peacefully evicted the squatters from one of the buildings. By noon, however, hundreds of veterans began to stream into the area around the disputed buildings. Finally, a confrontation, involving only about 50 persons, was started by a communist. It developed into a five-minute brick-throwing melee. Glassford then met with the commissioners who went to the trouble site, returned to their office, and called out federal troops at about 1:30 p.m. Shortly thereafter another fight erupted. Two veterans were shot dead and three policemen were injured. By this time the troops were on their way, and things rapidly got out of hand.

At 4:30 p.m. cavalry and infantry wearing gasmasks, with tanks supporting, moved in under the command of General Douglas MacArthur. The cavalry, making liberal use of their sabers, cleared the veterans away from the downtown area while the infantry routed veterans out of their shelters in the buildings at bayonet point. Teargas was used in abundance. By 7 p.m. the tattered, gasping mob of veterans had been cleared from Washington proper. Hastily and in a state of panic they fled into the country. As the evening wore on the troops attacked Anacostia Flats and burned the encampment. These veterans fled also. It was estimated that 1,500 teargas bombs had been used against the 10,000 members of the B.E.F., which included approximately 700 women and 400 children. One of the most distasteful incidents involved Joe Angelo. During World War I, Angelo passed through a heavy German bombardment in the Argonne to rescue a wounded American officer. He returned from the war, rewarded for this bravery with the Distinguished Service Cross. Unemployed for a long time, he came to Washington and camped with the B.E.F. at Anacostia Flats. During the eviction he was chased from the field at bayonet point by a group of soldiers commanded by the very officer he had rescued during the war. The eviction was over by 2 a.m.

Tanks are prepared to attack the Bonus Army
(Reproduced from the Collection of the Library Of Congress.)

The number of killed and wounded was low. The attack was so swift and powerful that the veterans had no real chance to fight back, so they ran. It was clearly an excessive use of force in the face of a basically peaceful law-abiding group of veterans. There is also much evidence that Hoover did not actually order the troops to be sent in, but rather the attack was orchestrated by MacArthur who later earned a very public reputation for doing his own thing. Nonetheless, the government had evicted the veterans and Hoover was in charge of the government, so rightly he got the blame. In the aftermath the country was outraged, and in the election of 1932 Hoover was soundly defeated. It is quite clear that sending the troops against the B.E.F. played a major role in that defeat. In 1936, the veterans received immediate payment of the bonus.

It must be made clear that the overwhelming majority of the veterans continued to be peaceful and law-abiding. Two minor incidents occurred, both as a result of police pushing the veterans as part of a wider plan to provoke them to riot. Much credit should be given to the veterans for remaining under control in the face of this provocation. The government's reaction was totally out of proportion to the events, but Hoover's government needed to prove it could handle radicalism in America.

It may have been, as Congressman Black described it, "the greatest crime in history." These veterans had fought for their country, but only 14 years later their government ignored them, refused to assist them, called them criminals and communists, humiliated them, teargassed them, and chased them from their capital city with bayonets, sabers, and tanks. What a disgusting episode. It certainly was one of the greatest examples of constitution-trampling in our history. One really must wonder how Hoover and his cronies could justify the eviction of peaceful protesters in the face of the First Amendment. The people have the rights to peacefully assemble and petition the government for a redress of their grievances. Our Constitution should have prevented this police state affair from taking place, but after all, it is just a piece of paper.

CHAPTER 11
JAPANESE-AMERICAN
INTERNMENT 1942

The most outrageous example of constitution-trampling in the nation's history occurred between 1942 and 1945. It was an episode that began shortly after the Japanese attack on the U.S. naval base at Pearl Harbor, Hawaii. In short, the United States government rounded up 110,000 people of Japanese ancestry who were living in this country, and imprisoned them in concentration camps. Of that number, approximately 70,000 were American-born citizens. It was supposedly done due to "military necessity," an excuse governments often fall back on when they need to deprive the people of their rights. In reality, typical American ethnic intolerance was the true cause, and it was, as later events proved, totally unnecessary. As if the internment wasn't bad enough, the Supreme Court actually upheld the constitutionality of this heinous act, though the internment clearly deprived American citizens of their 5th and 14th Amendment rights of life, liberty, property, and due process.

This story has its roots in early Chinese immigration to California in the mid-1800s, as a result of the discovery of gold. The Chinese soon came into competition with "Americans" in many industries. They were a cheap source of labor that was tapped by American business. This was perceived as a threat by many people on the West Coast, which led to discrimination and violence against the Chinese. By 1857, newspapers were reporting the slaughter of hundreds of Chinese during the preceding five years. At this time, California passed a law forbidding Chinese from testifying against whites in court. In Los Angeles, a white man was killed by a Chinese, and the ensuing mob stormed the Chinese section of town, hanging even women and children. An orgy of violence against the Chinese swept San Francisco, Tacoma's Chinese section was burned to the ground, and the Workingman's Party of California rose to power with its slogan, "The Chinese Must Go!" The West Coast, especially California, developed an intense hatred of the Chinese.

It was into this atmosphere that Japanese immigrants arrived on the West Coast in the latter half of the 19th Century. As they arrived they filled a void that was being created by the departure of many Chinese back to China, in the face of severe discrimination. The Japanese began to move into farming and railroading, which also caused competition with whites. This put the Japanese in the same position as the Chinese. From that point until 1942, Japanese-Americans faced increasing hostility not only from the locals, but from the local, state, and federal governments. They were attacked by American newspapers and literature as being a threat to the American way of life. The media even went as far as to report plots such as a purported Japanese/Mexican invasion plan against the United States. As had been the case so many times in our history, propaganda was effective in stirring up the masses. In 1913, California passed the Alien Land Law which prevented the Japanese from purchasing land. In a highly debatable 1923 decision, the U.S. Supreme Court ruled that since the Founding Fathers had not anticipated Japanese immigration, they were not eligible for naturalization, the process a foreign-born person follows to become a U.S. citizen. An assortment of anti-Japanese groups rose up on the West Coast to stop Japanese immigration, to remove the rights of the ones who were here, and, finally, to kick them out of the country. Paranoia reigned supreme on the West Coast.

With the benefits of competitive capitalism shining through the treatment of the Japanese, on the national level the United States had, by the use of economic blackmail, forced Japan into a corner by 1941. They were left with no choice but to attempt to cripple American military power in the Pacific, move against other nations in the region, and seize the raw materials they desperately needed in spite of the American embargo. The first step on this course took place at Pearl Harbor on December 7, 1941. The U.S. naval presence in the Pacific was, for a time, crushed. This also brought a terrible vengeance against those of Japanese ancestry on the West Coast.

Monday, December 8, opened with a federal order freezing the bank accounts of all persons of Japanese descent. People could not get their money for living expenses, employers could not pay their employees or their bills, businesses crumbled, lives were ruined. This was only the beginning. Next came thousands of arrests. The FBI, Naval Intelligence, and Army Intelligence made the arrests and, after countless investigations, they obtained a conviction against just one person of Japanese descent. Next came violence as seven Japanese-Americans were killed and many hurt in racial attacks in the weeks following Pearl Harbor. The military stoked the fires by claiming Japanese submarine attacks were occurring on shipping along the Pacific Coast, and radio communications were taking place between land-based spies and lurking submarines. Later investigation proved these claims to be false. The clamor to remove the Japanese from the West Coast grew, and had indeed become deafening by January, 1942. All the old hate groups were involved, along with the media and the military, in demanding relocation of all Japanese from the West Coast into the interior of the nation. Some interesting voices were heard, for example California Attorney General, later Supreme Court Chief Justice, Earl Warren, who insisted on relocation. Warren added that the political approach to relocation was too slow, but the Army could avoid the ills of democracy and move them out immediately.

Lieutenant General John L. DeWitt was in command of the military region that included the West Coast. He was also a leading proponent of relocation. Wheels started turning so that by the end of January the U.S. Attorney General issued a set of orders establishing strategic areas along the West Coast and ordering the removal of all persons of Japanese descent from those areas. The residents of these areas were given as little as twenty-four hours to uproot their homes, families, and lives and to move to designated Assembly Centers. On February 19, President Roosevelt issued Executive Order No. 9066, authorizing the removal of any or all persons from military areas. With this, he forever joined the ranks of the great rapers of the Constitution.

The planning for this assault on the liberties of the Japanese would take time, as bureaucracy needed to be set up. At first it was the Wartime Civil Control Administration, but after the Army stood aside it became the more permanent War Relocation Authority (WRA). On March 2, General DeWitt issued Public Proclamation Number One. It was the first of 108 Civilian Exclusion Orders. These orders removed 110,000 Japanese, of whom 70,000 were American-born citizens. They were taken out of their homes, schools, colleges, jobs, activities, relationships; in short they were taken out of their lives.

The first step was to remove them to sixteen temporary Assembly Centers while the tarpaper barracks could be built at the desert War Relocation Centers. The inmates (an appropriate word to describe these people) were allowed to leave their homes for the Assembly Centers with only the possessions they could carry. Meanwhile, their vacated property (homes, businesses, cars) became fair game for anyone who wanted to take it. The good "Americans" of the West Coast did indeed greedily help themselves to much of this property.

The Santa Anita Assembly Center was a typical example of the conditions the inmates faced. It was a racetrack that became home to approximately 18,000 people. The inmates were assigned a place to reside by stable and stall number. The accommodations often contained manure covered floors. In a procedure similar to that used in the Nazi concentration camps, the inmates were assigned numbers for identification. A typical meal consisted of boiled potatoes and bread. As most of the inmates were broke by this time, a pay scale was established to cover work that was needed in the camps. A doctor or other professional earned $16, skilled workers received $12, and unskilled workers got $8. This pay was for a month's work of 40-hour weeks and was substantially below normal wages in the private sector. It only barely avoided a problem with the 13th Amendment's prohibition against slavery.

The 40,000 Japanese in California made up only 2% of the state's population, while Hawaii had 137,000 Japanese, constituting 37% of its population. The military command in Hawaii did not relocate their Japanese. This is the greatest proof that the "military necessity" of West Coast relocation was a farce. Hawaii was even under martial law, which allowed the military total control. California was not, which reflects a lack of concern for the safety of that area. The California relocation marks the first time in our history that this type of authority was wielded by the military in a non-combat zone. In Hawaii, the Japanese worked with the military and civil authorities in labor corps, and in their traditional jobs. On the plantations they produced 90% of the food grown in the islands. In Hawaii, an active war zone, the Japanese were not relocated, but rather made a valuable contribution to the war effort. It is estimated that the West Coast relocation removed $70 million from the local economies, and the cost of maintaining the camps was another $70 million for the first year. All in all, it was an unconstitutional, racist, impractical, expensive and unnecessary plan. By June, 1942, the Japanese Fleet had been smashed in the Battle of Midway. With this defeat there was no longer any possible threat to Hawaii or the West Coast, but the relocation continued anyway.

Soon the ten War Relocation Centers were ready to be occupied. These concentration camps were mostly built in desert areas in California, Arizona, Idaho, Wyoming, Colorado, Utah and Arkansas. The most infamous were Manzanar and Tule Lake, California. As the inmates arrived at Manzanar they found fourteen barracks. Only two had showers and toilet facilities. The barracks were divided into apartments measuring 20'x 25' which were to be shared by two families of 8-10 people each. There was no furniture, but the Army supplied straw-filled mattresses. The inmates were put to work on various projects including the manufacture of camouflage netting, but this caused problems as it violated the Geneva Convention for the treatment of prisoners.

Through this misery, the response of most Japanese-Americans in the camps can only, and surprisingly, be termed as heroic and patriotic. They purchased war bonds, joined the Army, and displayed great affection for the United States. They embodied all that America was supposed to stand for, when it wasn't imprisoning its citizens in concentration camps.

Manzanar: An American Concentration Camp
(Reproduced from the Collection of the Library Of Congress.)

The right to join the military did not come easy, but it was finally won. Concerning military service by the Japanese-Americans, President Roosevelt stated, "No loyal citizen of the United States should be denied the democratic right to exercise the responsibilities of his citizenship, regardless of his ancestry." This was an interesting comment from the person who issued executive Order 9066 and denied the exercise of citizenship to 70,000 people. Nonetheless, Japanese-Americans joined the military *en masse* and attained an extremely distinguished war record, even while their parents were being held in American concentration camps. The most decorated military unit in American history was the famous 442nd Regimental Combat Team. This unit, made up entirely of Japanese-Americans, suffered 9,486 casualties and won 18,143 individual decorations during World War II. Their loyalty was, however, in question and they were only allowed to fight in the European theater. In another embarrassing twist, there were Japanese-American veterans from World War I who were interned in the camps. The ultimate stupidity was that even Japanese-Americans in our military were not allowed to enter the military zones on the West Coast.

As the war continued, a movement developed on the West Coast to prohibit the Japanese from returning after the war, or ever. At one point, a friend of three Japanese-Americans who died fighting with the 442nd in Italy sent a copy of the newspaper article reporting their deaths to California State Assemblyman Chester Gannon, who was chairman of an Assembly committee that was working to keep the Japanese from returning to California. Attached to the newspaper article was a note to Gannon saying, "Here are three Japanese who will not be returning to California." Assemblyman Gannon promptly returned the article to its sender with the comment, "Glory! Hallelujah! Hallelujah! Hallelujah!" In a another incident, Presbyterian minister Dr. John Carruthers, testifying before the California State Senate, stated, "It is our Christian duty to keep the Japanese out of this Western world of civilization. I would urge the deportation, by every means possible, of all the Japanese from the American continent." It seems that the Bible meant as much to Dr. Carruthers as the Constitution did to our government, though one could never claim that religion was anything but hypocritical and intolerant.

A great debacle developed in the camps as the WRA tried to register all adult inmates. The questionnaires included questions about swearing unqualified allegiance to the United States. The whole process was done in a haphazard sort of way that led to much confusion on the part of the Japanese. Serious misunderstandings developed over the ramifications of certain answers. Many inmates answered "no" to these questions in the mistaken belief that this answer would lead to being sent to Tule Lake Camp in California. This was widely seen as the first step to returning home. There were, of course, many who answered "no" as a protest against being interned in a concentration camp. This was certainly an under-standable reaction. These people would have been justified in joining spying and sabotage activities as a result of this disgusting atrocity that was carried out against them. Of the 75,000 who were to register approximately 10,000 answered "no." This was seen by Americans as a sign of disloyalty and as a justification of the relocation effort.

Meanwhile, conditions in the camps deteriorated to such a point that the Japanese government called for an investigation by a neutral country, Spain. The investigation found military guards, tanks, barbed wire, guard towers, dogs, a lack of food and milk for the children, ineffective heating, censorship, tension, inmates held in stockades without charges or trials, and inmate strikes. These were conditions much like what the Allies found in the Nazi concentration camps.

Finally, the legality of the military's actions were questioned, as two cases reached the Supreme Court. First came the ruling in *Hirabayashi v. United States* (1943). Gordon Hirabayashi, a California resident, was convicted for violating the Army curfew shortly after the Pearl Harbor attack. The Court found, unanimously, that the curfew of citizens, residing in areas not under martial law, was constitutional. In the second case, *Korematsu v. United States* (1944), Fred Korematsu had violated an exclusion order and remained in Oakland, California. He was arrested by the FBI, tried, and convicted. His case questioned the legality of the relocation to the camps. In a 6-3 decision the court held that since the military saw an urgency, which demanded removal of all Japanese from the West Coast, it was constitutional to remove them. Absolutely a wrong decision and one of the most offensive ever made! It is not constitutional to allow the military, in an area not under martial law, to put citizens in concentration camps, thus depriving them of their 5th and 14th Amendment rights to life, liberty, and property. It truly makes one ashamed to be an American.

The philosophy of military necessity really must be questioned. Throughout history that phony excuse has allowed governments to step on the rights of men. Yet another significant fact of history is that all governments end. Ancient Egypt, Greece, Rome, the Holy Roman Empire, the British Empire, the Soviet Empire, and many others have risen, dominated the world, and then come to an end. The decline of the United States, already well on its way, is indisputable as well. Knowing, then, that all governments end, how far should a nation go in allowing the government or military to infringe upon the rights of the people in order to preserve that government? A process that is doomed to inevitable failure, this relocation was surely an example of the military going too far.

Finally, as the war began to draw to an end, so did the need to keep the Japanese-Americans in the camps. On January 2, 1945, the exclusion orders were revoked and the inmates were allowed to leave. Of course, most had nowhere to go, their property and jobs were no more, and they faced harassment and discrimination in all quarters. By July, nearly 44,000 inmates remained in the camps. The affair was brought to an end on June 30, 1946, when the War Relocation Authority officially expired. The only matter that remained was the fight by the Japanese-American Citizens League to gain compensation for the losses faced by the inmates during four years of imprisonment. In July, 1948, President Truman signed a compensation bill into law. The law paid out $38 million to the former inmates. Their estimated losses ran to $400 million. The compensation law paid a pathetic ten cents on the dollar. By the summer of 1991, Congress finally got around to making restitution to the survivors of the camps. They were given an insulting payment of $20,000 each. The only reason it took so long to provide this paltry sum is the government wanted to pay as little as possible, and the longer they stalled, the lower the number of living survivors who would have to be paid.

Ironically, the Allied Powers — the United States, Great Britain, France, and the Soviet Union — moved swiftly in 1945 to punish the civilian and military leaders of Nazi Germany for war crimes and atrocities committed during the war. The same was done to the Japanese. In October, 1945, the Allies established the International Military Tribunal to conduct trials which took place in Nuremberg, Germany, beginning in November of 1945. The charter authorizing the trials defined the crimes for which war criminals were to be indicted, tried and punished. The listed crimes were: crimes against peace; war crimes; crimes against humanity; and, conspiracy. A crime against humanity was defined as: "murder, extermination, enslavement, *deportation*, and other inhuman acts committed against any civilian population, before or during the war; or persecutions on political, racial or religious grounds whether or not in violation of the domestic law of the country where perpetrated" (emphasis added). Through these ex post facto laws, the surviving major leaders of Nazi Germany went on trial. Some were executed and several were imprisoned. Acts of deportation of civilians on racial grounds were punished by execution or imprisonment in Germany, yet the same conduct in the United States against Japanese-Americans was sanctioned by the Supreme Court. Of course, to the victors go the spoils, and in this case the victors were more concerned with covering their various crimes than really seeking justice for acts committed by Nazis. The Americans had the crime of Japanese-American internment, the French had their total and cowardly collaboration with the Germans during the occupation, the British had ruthlessly firebombed German cities during the war (including Dresden where possibly more than 100,000 civilians were killed in totally unnecessary raids only eight weeks before the end of the war), and the Russians had committed political mass murder for decades. In addition, the United States, Great Britain, and France may themselves have been involved in mass murder. In his 1991 book — *Other Losses: The Shocking Truth Behind the Mass Death of Disarmed German Soldiers and Civilians Under General Eisenhower's Command*, Canadian author

James Bacque established the fact of the death of as many as a million surrendered Germans, who were held prisoner by the Western Allies after the war ended. So much for the might of right.

Today, nearly everyone agrees that the mass removal of Japanese-Americans was militarily unnecessary, that it accomplished little more than an all-around waste of manpower and gave the Axis powers excellent propaganda material that proved democracy did not always work. There are, however, future implications from the Korematsu decision, which still stands today. In Justice Jackson's dissent he stated, "a military order, however unconstitutional, is not apt to last longer than the military emergency, but once a judicial opinion rationalizes such an order to show that it conforms to the Constitution, the Court for all time has validated the principle of racial discrimination in criminal procedure and of transplanting American citizens. The principle then lies about like a loaded weapon ready for the hand of any authority that can bring forward a plausible claim of an urgent need." We now have only to wait for that hand to come forward, and it certainly will. The nature of power guarantees it.

We have a Constitution that is supposed to protect the people's rights to life, liberty, and property, but as the Japanese-Americans' relocation of 1942 proved, it is, after all, just a piece of paper.

CHAPTER 12
McCARTHYISM 1950-54

The 1950s were a time of national embarrassment characterized by a fear of communism that went well beyond paranoia. It also became a time of serious trampling of the Constitution. This period, which witnessed the beginning of the Cold War between the United States and the Soviet Union, came to a head in the years that Senator Joseph McCarthy disgraced this country forever with his presence. The beginning of this insanity, though, goes back to World War I.

In early 1919, the Great War had been over for only a few months, and America was in trouble. The country was racked by inflation, unemployment, labor riots, race riots, bombings and disillusionment. The problems were economic and political: economic because there are fundamental flaws in capitalism, and political because the rich elite running the country didn't care; they weren't starving. American leaders were unwilling to admit that the problems were caused by our system. An unrecognized problem cannot be fixed. Americans have always had a superiority complex, and, when the nation has experienced difficult times, this complex has been expressed in the sentiment that since America is perfect there must be some outside cause, someone else to blame. In 1919, it became the communists' fault and this unleashed a new fear — the Red Scare.

The American economic system of *laissez-faire* capitalism that existed in the first part of the 20th Century lived up to its name. Government kept its hands completely off business. The only thing more corrupting than power is money, so when business is allowed to do its own thing, it does. This gave rise to child labor, deadly working conditions, long hours, and low pay. The communist system calls for total control of business by the government to prevent the rich from oppressing the poor in exactly this manner. Certainly this difference does not account for the acute fear of communism that developed, and indeed there was more to it than that. Many in our government saw the threat of communism in a religious context. It was a spiritual battle pitting the atheistic communists against Christian capitalists. This was, of course, an interesting view, as capitalism's most fundamental principle, "Do unto others before they do unto you," would seem to clash with underlying principles of Christianity. But then, religion has never been too disturbed by hypocrisy. Nonetheless, the writings of Karl Marx attacking religion gave support to this view. Marx referred to religion as "the opiate of the masses." His point was that religion acts like a drug, blinding the people to the realities of their miserable lives at the hands of profit-motivated capitalists and other masters. He argued that religion, like a common drug addiction, should be thrown off so that reality may creep in and the people may then attack the sources of the problems causing the misery. He certainly makes a valid point. Religion is always good for bringing irrationality, and viewing the socio-political struggle with communism in that manner helped bring it here, too. Drawing on the fear and ignorance of the suitably "opiated" American masses, the government then, for one can be sure that the American people did not have the faintest idea of what communism was, forced the people to believe it was a threat to our way of life.

At this time, a rise of communism began to occur in America as well. This was due to the hardships on the working classes caused by capitalism. This only supported the government party line that communists were intent on conquering the United States and the world. As the panic spread, it appeared that communists were everywhere subverting our country. In February and March, 1919, a Senate subcommittee led by Senator Lee Overman held hearings on the communist influence in America. The hearings were a circus sideshow, featuring testimony about the rape of women and murdering of priests in Russia. This accomplished nothing more than tabloid-like headlines and more fear. The Red Scare reached its peak on January 2, 1920 when Attorney General Palmer had over 4,000 suspected communists arrested, mostly without warrants or evidence. The American government criticized the Russian government for denying the right to self-determination to its people, and, at the same time, prosecuted Americans who exercised their political right to join a party of their choice, namely the Communist Party USA. The whole episode faded away by late 1920, as America recovered economically and the nation no longer needed to blame anyone. That is, until the next crisis came along.

In 1929, the Great Depression brought massive unemployment, suffering, and starvation on a scale that made the 1919 downturn seem like boom times. Again the communists were blamed, and another congressional panel held hearings on communist subversion in America. This committee, led by Congressman Hamilton Fish, probed throughout the 1930s. In 1937, a member of the House suggested a committee to investigate un-American activities carried out by domestic or foreign groups. In May, 1938, this suggestion was heeded and the House Committee on Un-American Activities, known as HUAC, was born. It was led by Congressman Martin Dies. It developed the techniques and approaches that Joe McCarthy would make infamous a few years later.

HUAC was run by conservatives who used it to attack Roosevelt's New Deal programs by declaring they were "full of communists." These hearings, like those of 1920, were a circus. Testimony was accepted from fascists, assorted union-haters, professional informers, and various malcontents. Even Congressman Dies would later admit that he had used "screwball" witnesses and smeared innocent people. The committee was often to use disreputable tactics such as guilt by association, harassment, and pretending to have evidence when none existed. During this time the committee intimidated the country into a witch-hunt. Even the American Civil Liberties Union was forced to fire suspected communists or face full-scale investigation by HUAC. The American way of life had become equated with living in fear of being accused as a "commie" or "Red." It was a time when an accusation meant an end to career, friends, family and, sometimes life. Eventually, the result was oppressive legislation, fear, and a complete loss of memory concerning the Constitution.

The Smith Act of 1940 was typical of such oppressive legislation. Among other provisions, this law made it a crime to teach and advocate the overthrow of the United States. In the Declaration of Independence Thomas Jefferson pointed out that, "whenever any Form of Government becomes destructive of [certain unalienable rights]... it is the Right of the People to alter or abolish it." Reflecting his great understanding of the nature of power, Jefferson went on to insist that the only way to fully protect the people from the American government was to overthrow it every 20 years. If Jefferson had written the Declaration of Independence in 1940, he would have been locked up as a subversive under the Smith Act. American communists were simply exercising their natural rights; they disagreed with the form of government and they proposed change. Indeed, if ever a government deserved to be overthrown, it was this one! For this they were persecuted and prosecuted. In writing against the Smith Act, Supreme Court Justice William Douglas said, "once we start down that road we enter territory dangerous to the liberties of every citizen." How prophetic! Unfortunately, he was in the minority on the court.

By 1942, the Soviet Union and the United States were allied against Germany. This definitely threw a wrench into the anti-communist propaganda of our government. This replaced America's communist enemy with the Nazis, so the anti-communist paranoia died down temporarily. In fact, during the war, the Smith Act was used as a basis for prosecuting a large group of *anti*-Communists for sedition. Upon the conclusion of the war, however, a chill in relations with the Soviets coupled with the usual economic downturn that accompanies the end of a war, brought a resumption of the anti-communist paranoia. The Truman administration escalated matters with more hearings, laws, and loyalty tests. From 1947-1950, the government investigated two million of its workers at great expense, and found not one single subversive. The fact that the government was investigating proved to the American people that there *must* be subversives, or the government wouldn't be looking for them. Not to be outdone by a Democratic president, the Republican-controlled HUAC hearings resumed, and stumbled across Alger Hiss. The ensuing trial along with several other alleged spying incidents, China going communist in 1949, and the exploding of an atomic bomb by the Soviet Union, dramatically raised the level of paranoia. Cast in the proper light by the government, these events made it appear that communism was closing in on the United States. All that was needed to push the country over the edge was a demagogue. Joe McCarthy was poised and ready.

McCarthy: The American Hitler.
(Reproduced from the Collections of the Library Of Congress.)

McCarthy was a nobody, the junior Republican senator from Wisconsin, who had a history of lying and deceit in his political past. In previous campaigns he seemed to follow the ideas proposed by Adolf Hitler's *Mein Kampf*, and the propaganda techniques of Joseph Goebbels. His early campaigns were marked by lies, innuendo, smear tactics, personal attacks, and distortions. A piece of McCarthy campaign literature portrayed him as a World War II bomber tail-gunner. This earned him the nickname "Tail-gunner Joe." In reality, he rode in the tail-gunner's seat a few times during the war when little Japanese resistance was expected.

By 1950, he had been in the U.S. Senate for three and a half years, during which he had accomplished nothing! Then, one of those little events that change history occurred. One night while at dinner with friends, he solicited ideas on how he could gain some attention. The friends suggested he accuse the State Department of being full of communists. McCarthy agreed to pursue this idea. This was the same man who, in being elected senator, had been assisted by a large number of votes by communist union members in Wisconsin. When asked about that fact soon after the election he replied, "Communists have the same right to vote as everyone else, don't they?" He was not anti-communist, but rather a conniving political opportunist who was to bring his lies and smears to the national scene and the everlasting disgrace of this country.

His rise began on February 9, 1950, while speaking to an audience in Wheeling, West Virginia. During the speech he said, "While I cannot take the time to name all the men in the State Department who have been named as members of the Communist Party and members of a spy ring, I have here in my hand a list of two hundred and five that were known to the Secretary of State as being members of the Communist Party and who nevertheless are still working and shaping policy at the State Department." He had expected to gain some attention with these remarks, but the media jumped on the story and it made national news. Over the next few days, as he made several more speeches and the uproar grew, the number of communists on his list changed from 205, to 57, to 108, to 81, and finally to 66. This revealed two techniques that McCarthy would use consistently. First, the shifty statistic; the practice of throwing out numbers so rapidly and irrelevantly that nobody could follow him. Second, the big lie. McCarthy lied like a rug. Hitler once said, "The masses are more easily victimized by a big lie than a small one... some part of even the boldest lie is sure to stick." This was a philosophy that McCarthy followed. Actually, I hesitate to compare McCarthy to Hitler because that is derogatory to Hitler, but they did share the same sense of politics.

With this national uproar in high gear, a subcommittee of the Senate Foreign Relations Committee began investigating communist infiltration of the State Department. The investigation was headed by Senator Millard Tydings, one of the many senators who were embarrassed by McCarthy's antics. The hearings were characterized by McCarthy's rantings, lying, changing the subject when attacked, and making periodic new and unfounded accusations. The hearings report concluded:

"We have seen the technique of the 'Big Lie' utilized here for the first time on a sustained basis in our history. We have seen how, through repetition and shifting untruths, it is possible to delude great numbers of people.

"We have seen the character of private citizens and government employees virtually destroyed by public condemnation on the basis of gossip, distortion, hearsay, and deliberate untruths.

"We have seen an effort not merely to establish guilt by association but guilt by association alone.

"We have seen an effort to inflame the American people with a wave of hysteria and fear on an unbelievable scale.

"We are constrained fearlessly and frankly to call the charges, and the methods employed to give them ostensible validity, what they truly are: A fraud and a hoax perpetuated on the Senate of the United States and the American people."

The other result of the hearings was, amazingly, that McCarthy became a folk hero to the American people who were duped into believing his act. As it turned out, the public's hostile reaction to the report destroyed the committee's anti-McCarthy chairman Senator Tydings, and intimidated the Senate.

McCarthy was then assisted by the outbreak of the Korean War, which began in June, 1950, with communist North Korea's alleged invasion of U.S.-supported South Korea. Now the U.S. was at war with the communists, and the anti-communist paranoia rapidly got worse.

In September, the McCarran Internal Security Act was passed, which required communists to register with the government and provided for the detention, in concentration camps, of suspected subversives. By this time, the government defined "subversive" as meaning anyone who was accused by someone. This was the age of neighbors turning in other neighbors, in many cases to get even for past grievances. The government then had the power to detain people at will, should it ever choose to do so.

For the next two years, McCarthy was constantly in the headlines attacking the State Department, its secretary, President Truman, General Marshall, anti-McCarthy senators, and just about everyone else. He brought down several senators who had opposed him, including one who opened a hearing on expelling McCarthy from the Senate.

In 1952, the Republicans won the presidency, under Eisenhower, and control of the Congress. This control of Congress gave McCarthy a committee chairmanship. It was a harmless committee dealing with government administration. Even the leaders of his own party hoped to silence McCarthy, and that was the purpose behind the assignment. However, the committee had a subcommittee on investigations. McCarthy made himself the chairman of this subcommittee, and he was off and running again.

McCarthy, in his new position, escalated the attacks to include Eisenhower, began to dictate appointments to the executive branch, interfered in foreign affairs and attacked foreign leaders. He became an international embarrassment. During 1953 his subcommittee launched 445 inquiries and 157 investigations. He discovered not one communist, yet everyone he accused had their lives and careers destroyed. His attacks then spread to the CIA, the Atomic Energy Commission, the Government Printing Office, and the military. Two events then occurred that would lead to his downfall. The Korean War ended, and he attacked the Army.

McCarthy's engagement with the Army began in the fall of 1953, and the hearings started on April 22, 1954. He brutally attacked military officers, used fabricated and stolen documents, refused to answer questions about his evidence, and insulted Army attorney Joseph Welch. The televised hearings lasted until June 17, and gave the American people a chance to see this lunatic in operation. Along with published reports by psychiatrists who watched the hearings and diagnosed McCarthy as paranoid and neurotic, the hearings resulted in a 16-point drop in McCarthy's approval rating.

Senator Ralph Flanders then introduced a resolution to censure McCarthy. In the resulting hearings, McCarthy's vicious attacks on the members of the committee sealed his fate. The Senate voted 67-22 to censure him. His reign was over.

During the next few years he sank into alcoholism, squandered his wealth on bad investments, became ill, and died on May 2, 1957.

There was, rightfully, no big ceremony, and, of course, no real rebirth of concern for civil liberties, but McCarthyism was over. One must wonder whether that piece of paper McCarthy held up in that first speech in Wheeling was actually a copy of the Constitution. The Constitution, with its rights of free speech and press, and its legacy of protection for persons with differing political views, should have kept all this from happening, but after all it is just a piece of paper.

CHAPTER 13
THE CHICAGO DEMOCRATIC
CONVENTION 1968

By 1968, the United States was a nation torn asunder by civil strife. Poverty, racism, and political assassinations had led militant black groups to torch many American cities. The escalating losses of the Vietnam War were showing America to be an impotent giant, an imperialistic nation in decline. Rising protests, originating on the college campuses, and made up primarily of middle-class whites, were bringing the morality of the war into question. Civil disobedience was developing across the nation, as young people burned their draft cards and the American flag, headed north to Canada, marched, staged sit-ins, and protested. The government's "America, love it or leave it" attitude and Red paranoia were reflected in a harsh response to civil unrest. Brutal crackdowns on protesters became the norm, illegal wiretapping and surveillance of citizens the rule. It was the last gasp of a decadent and dying nation, rotten to the core, struggling feebly to protect its power at any cost. All of these forces came together to clash dramatically on the streets of Chicago at the Democratic National Convention in 1968. A national television audience watched as Mayor Richard Daley's stormtroopers viciously attacked citizens exercising their First Amendment rights to free speech, assembly, and protest. The episode represented a great attack on the Constitution, but not nearly as much as the so-called Conspiracy Trial of the Chicago Eight that took place after the riots. The young protesters exemplified by Abbie Hoffman, Bobby Seale, Jerry Rubin and Dave Dellinger were patriotic heroes in the spirit of Washington, Jefferson, Hancock, and Adams. These early revolutionaries helped create a Constitution, the latter ones resisted while the government tried to destroy it.

The 1960s got under way with the high hopes that surrounded the charismatic young President, John Kennedy. These hopes, though, faded in the face of reality as his administration confronted a recession, a hostile Congress, the enforcement of civil rights, the Bay of Pigs fiasco, another Berlin crisis, and the Cuban Missile Crisis. Kennedy also escalated American participation in Vietnam.

America's involvement in Southeast Asia began in 1954. At that time, a communist government took control of the northern part of Vietnam following the defeat of the French at Dien Bien Phu. To keep the rest of Vietnam from turning communist, President Eisenhower sent American military advisers to South Vietnam to assist President Ngo Dinh Diem, a brutal dictator who lacked the support of his people. In 1956, Diem canceled the elections on Vietnamese reunification that had been called for in the 1954 Geneva Agreements. In response, local communists formed guerrilla bands to bring down the Southern government. These guerrillas, the Viet Cong, supplied and aided by the communist North, were strong and well organized. Progressively, Diem needed more and more American assistance to resist them. President Kennedy increased the number of American servicemen from 900 in 1961 to 17,000 by 1963. Kennedy believed that it was important symbolically for the United States to oppose communism and stop the Domino Effect, the domino-like fall of one country after another to communism.

When it became apparent that the war could not be won with Diem in power, the American government approved a coup against him in which he and members of his family were executed. A new government, better able to fight the war, was installed at Kennedy's direction. America was then committed to a war to prevent the spread of communism in Southeast Asia.

The most damaging aspect of the war was the discord it bred at home. The protests of only a few were heard at first, but after My Lai, Tet, the nightly televised casualty lists, and the Kent State Massacre, the nation was ripped by protests against this immoral war. Along the way the government would greatly trample on the Constitution to try to prevent opposition to the war. Fortunately, they failed, though barely.

In November, 1963, John Kennedy was assassinated and Lyndon Johnson assumed the Presidency. Vietnam was not yet out of hand, so Johnson turned to civil rights and poverty. In the early 1960s the United States was a nation split in two. There were the white middle and upper classes who were enjoying the American dream of prosperity. They sported nice houses with white picket fences, cars, appliances, and opportunities in education and employment. On the other hand, there were the poor. They tended to be black and live in the inner city ghettos. They lived in squalor, with little food and no opportunities, among the rats. The American Dream was closed to them, in most cases, by the laws of segregation. Even education was still overwhelmingly separate and unequal. The frustration of hopelessness was building to the boiling point.

From the early 1960s, blacks had pushed to be integrated. Blacks were slowly gaining the rights to eat at white restaurants and sit anywhere on buses. These successes spawned more efforts. In the spring of 1963, a march for civil rights took place in Birmingham, Alabama. The nation watched the televised pictures of the police attacking the marchers. They used dogs, electric cattle prods, and fire hoses to break up the nonviolent demonstration. President Kennedy pushed Congress for new civil rights legislation, but it was defeated. In August, 1963, Martin Luther King led 250,000 demonstrators on a march in Washington D.C. This signaled the beginning of a great wave of civil rights activity across the nation.

By 1965, new legislation barred discrimination in employment and housing. Voting rights were being expanded, and some opportunities were opening up for blacks. For the most part, this only benefited a few. In the ghettos it was the same old thing, and the frustration finally exploded in slum riots. The worst of many examples occurred in the Watts section of Los Angeles. Black mobs burned and looted white-owned businesses in the ghetto, and shot at police and firemen. The National Guard was called in to stop the violence. By the time it was over, 34 people were dead, hundreds were wounded, over 4,000 persons were arrested, and $200 million worth of property was destroyed. In Detroit, in 1967, the rioting lasted for weeks. More than 40 people were killed and 5,000 were left homeless.

A major cause of this disruption was the Black Power movement. There was the feeling on the part of many blacks that the changes were coming too slowly and that the nonviolent means practiced by Martin Luther King would not be successful. This movement of the young preached violence and promoted separatism for blacks. They believed that blacks should form a powerful black nation within the United States, where there would be no economic control by whites. Black leaders such as King denounced these proposals as self-defeating. They also angered the white population. In April, 1968, Martin Luther King was assassinated, and a major voice of reason was gone. Violent black riots immediately broke out in 125 cities.

Added to black protests and violence came the Vietnam protests. By 1968, the Vietnam War was getting out of control. The cost had risen to $25 billion annually, and over 500,000 troops were involved. A draft had been instituted to supply men for the effort. With all of this, we were losing. In January, 1968, the North Vietnamese and their Viet Cong allies launched the Tet offensive. They overran most of South Vietnam's major cities, and many villages in the countryside. They even briefly captured the American Embassy in Saigon. The American military was shocked; their reports that the North was defeated were now regarded with suspicion.

The American people began to question the war. The protests of the young took on a moral slant. A massive peace movement had developed that organized national opposition to the war. They asked, "Why are we fighting for rice in Asia when we don't have rice at home?" This was, of course, a reference to the great poverty that existed in the United States while we spent $25 billion a year on symbolism in Vietnam.

The draft created much opposition, especially among blacks. Blacks were drafted in disproportionate numbers because they could not afford college and the deferment that went with it. White kids hid in college while blacks were sent to Vietnam. It was certainly ironic that they were sent to fight and die for a country that denied them basic human rights. Many men of draft age left for Canada. They were not cowards. They had been given the choice of fight or go to jail. Unwilling to fight for this vile country and unwilling to be persecuted at home, they committed an act of resistance. These were the real heroes who refused to die for Kennedy's symbolic stand against communism. The most unbelievable aspect of the entire episode is that the government was able to indoctrinate so many American youth with the propaganda message that dying for your country is a glorious endeavor. To throw away a life for a country is nothing more than silly and pathetic. My only regret is that I wasn't of draft age so that I, too, could have gone to Canada in a gesture of defiance against the government.

A memorial to 58,000 wasted lives. And for what?
(Southern Cross Publishing)

Symbolism — what an absolutely worthless reason to fight a war! We had no place fighting in Vietnam, and the 58,000 American soldiers who died there were lives thrown away for nothing, like so much garbage. Make no mistake, this waste of valiant American soldiers and the loss of this war was the fault of our ignorant, spineless government, and not the fault of our brave soldiers. They did the best they could under the circumstances, and certainly did not deserve the treatment they received. This nation will be forever disgraced by the scenes of protesters spitting on our soldiers as they returned from fighting for their country. It was all so unnecessary. Red paranoia led us into this stupid war, and then tremendous incompetence administered it. Finally, even our allies deserted us. By 1973, we abandoned South Vietnam and pulled out. Saigon fell to the communists in 1975. We had lost the war. It was not, as Nixon claimed, "peace with honor." It was defeat, dishonor, and disgrace.

In the midst of all this, the Democratic Party met for its national convention in Chicago beginning on August 26, 1968. During the primaries, Robert Kennedy, until assassinated following the California primary on June 5, battled it out with Eugene McCarthy. Both were anti-war candidates. But the nomination of the candidate for President was handled by delegates who were selected by Democratic Party officials across the country. These officials supported pro-war candidate Vice President Hubert Humphrey who had not entered a single primary. With this undemocratic process as the backdrop, the various forces converged on Chicago. The allure of a national television audience made the city a magnet for protests against the war, poverty, racism, and the Democrats. It was a potential powderkeg that was primed to explode.

The national Mobilization Committee to End the War in Viet Nam (MOBE) was the prime organizer of the Chicago protests. Their intention was to draw upwards of 500,000 people to the city and to take advantage of the media that would be present for the convention. One week prior to the start of the convention, an advance contingent of protest organizers arrived in the city. They set up shop in Lincoln Park. During this week they held strategy meetings and recruitment drives, developed protest techniques, and hunted for publicity. As a fitting statement on modern American politics, the Youth International Party (Yippies) nominated Pigasus, a pig, as their presidential candidate.

Chicago was also preparing. Mayor Richard Daley was offended and embarrassed that previous anti-war and black protests had damaged the city and its reputation. It was his stated intention to block any disruption of the convention. Beyond this, it may have been his intention to provoke the protesters into a riot, which could then be crushed by his police force as a warning to future protesters. Part of this provocation was the city's refusal to grant permits. MOBE had requested such permits for marches and protests, as well as for the use of Grant and Lincoln Parks. Permits of this type are rarely refused, due to the First Amendment's right to assembly. In this case, Daley wanted a confrontation, so the city simply stalled on the permits and never did take any action on them. The city then placed an 11 p.m. closing on the city's parks to prevent protesters from sleeping there. They prohibited marches or demonstrations near the Amphitheater, where the convention was to be held. To guard against any trouble, the city organized 25,000 police, National Guard and regular Army troops, and Secret Service agents.

Daley also made threats aimed at protesters. These threats were readily believed by people who had witnessed Chicago police in recent stompings of other protesters. Daley, as a staunch proponent of law and order, and one of the most outspoken supporters of President Johnson's Vietnam policy, was personally opposed to Vietnam protests. His philosophy was, "If the people don't like it they should get out of the country." This was an interesting position for a man with his background. During World War II, while other men his age volunteered to fight, Daley refused to go, and during Vietnam all four of Daley's draft-age sons evaded the draft by joining a safe and cushy reserve unit. Regardless, all these terror tactics helped to greatly reduce the number of people who came to Chicago to protest during the convention.

On Saturday, August 24th, approximately 800 protesters had gathered in Lincoln Park. That night the police moved in and swept them out of the park following the 11 p.m. closing time. These protesters were broken up into small groups and dispersed without any real trouble.

Sunday August 25: The crowds in Lincoln Park grew to about 5,000. They played music, held rallies, and listened to speakers. That night at 11:15 the police again moved in to clear the park. Their tactics this time were not as peaceful as the night before. They attacked with mace and tear gas, clubbing the protesters as they went. They chased the people out of the park and onto the streets, where they continued to assault them. There was a great deal of brutality on the part of the police. It was very ironic that on this same day the Russians were sending their tanks into Prague, Czechoslovakia, also to crush a freedom movement. Ironically, and not a little hypocritically, the United States vigorously protested that Soviet abuse of human rights.

Monday August 26: The convention got under way. During the day there were marches to Grant Park and the Loop, and demonstrations in Grant Park and in front of the Conrad Hilton Hotel where many of the presidential candidates and delegates to the convention were staying. That night the protesters were again in Lincoln Park, and again the police attacked. Violence on the part of the police escalated seriously on this night. They cleared the park with teargas and clubs, and then chased the demonstrators for blocks. Many protesters were brutally beaten with clubs and maced. The gas attacks were so severe and random that gas began to enter nearby homes and the cars of passers-by. Cars stopped, and people ran from their homes, gasping for air, in an attempt to escape the gas. A new twist was police attacks on members of the press who were recording the events. Some Chicago police officers warned friends in the local media to be careful, as the word was out to get the press. City and police leaders did not want the excesses of the police to be reported. Police violence was clearly being increased.

Tuesday August 27: The crowds continued to grow, as did the attention of the world. The day was consumed by marches and protests. During the evening, a group of ministers and priests carried a large wooden cross to Lincoln Park and set it up. Sitting around the cross, the clergymen prayed and sang hymns. They were still doing so when the police attacked at midnight to clear the park. The clergymen were gassed and beaten on the heads with clubs until they fled, bleeding profusely, from the park. The police sank to some new tactics. They threw protesters off bridges and into a nearby lagoon. It was certainly a night to be proud of being an American.

Wednesday August 28: During the morning the crowd had grown to about 10,000 and was assembled in the outside bandshell arena in Lincoln Park. During the afternoon some protesters lowered the American flag and raised a red banner. This set off an unrestrained police charge into the crowd. Using mace, teargas, and their clubs they viciously attacked. They went way beyond what was necessary to disperse the crowd. Cops were seen repeatedly bashing people with their clubs. Their attack was so ruthless that the government-directed inquiry following convention week called it a "police riot." The angry demonstrators then marched off towards the Amphitheater in violation of police orders. The police and National Guard were committed to stopping them before they got to the Convention Hall. They set up a blockade in front of the Hilton Hotel and waited. A massive and violent confrontation resulted at the hotel as the "police riot" continued. In their most vicious attacks yet, the police waded into the huge crowd with clubs and gas, and attacked everyone. At one point they crushed a large number of people, including some convention delegates and bystanders, against the large windows of the hotel lounge. Under the pressure, the windows collapsed, and the people fell into the lounge. The police jumped through after them, indiscriminately beating them and some of the lounge patrons. The media had time to prepare for these anticipated activities and were set up in force. The police attacked them too. Photographers were beaten, their equipment destroyed, film confiscated, and many were arrested for trying to capture on film the acts of the police. Sixty-five members of the press were victimized by the police. After a lengthy and brutal battle, the crowd was dispersed.

News of this atrocity reached the Convention Hall. Senator Abraham Ribicoff was on the podium to nominate George McGovern for president. In a reference to the Chicago police, he declared that "if we had McGovern we wouldn't have the Gestapo in the streets of Chicago." Mayor Daley, sitting up front with the Illinois delegation, according to a news report, stood and yelled at Ribicoff, "Fuck you,

you Jew son-of-a-bitch, you lousy motherfucker, go home." This exchange pretty well says it all about Daley, a classless little power-mad scumbag. Chaos immediately broke out in the hall. Later that night, many delegates participated with demonstrators in a candlelight march of sadness.

Thursday August 29: The demonstrators spent the day licking their wounds. At about 6:30 p.m. they set off on another march, but were stopped and beaten back again. Things began to wind down from this point. As the convention broke up on Friday, so did the rest of the demonstrators. At the conclusion, the police had caused 1,000 injuries, but amazingly no deaths, though this was not from lack of trying. The fact that only about 700 persons were arrested shows that the police had other intentions: that is, to simply hurt people. Most of the Wednesday-night battle had been televised, and the world crucified Daley and the city as neo-Nazis.

As if on the same drugs used by the protesters, Daley claimed the whole thing didn't really happen and that it was all staged by the media. The really frightening thing is that Daley came out of this even more popular in Chicago than before. Most people there seemingly approved of his "bust their heads" response. Nationally, though, these events helped defeat Democratic nominee Hubert Humphrey in November. Unfortunately, this resulted in the election of Richard Nixon, an even bigger constitutional threat than Daley.

Daley was intent on getting the leaders of the protests that had so embarrassed him and the city. His cronies in the local federal district court wanted to use the new federal anti-riot law to prosecute them. They were prevented from doing so by Attorney General Ramsey Clark who was opposed to the law. These forces bided their time, and following Nixon's election and the appointment of a new Attorney General, they proceeded with a grand jury indictment based upon the anti-riot law.

The anti-riot bill had been introduced by Representative Cramer of Florida in early 1967. Under this bill, a person who crossed a state line with the intention to incite a riot, and who later carried out overt acts that led to the incitement of a riot, would be guilty of a federal crime. The push for this law came from the South in response to the growing militancy of the civil rights movement. Following the Newark riots, in July, 1967, an avalanche of legislation appeared to try to stop the increasing violence, and the Cramer bill gathered momentum. The bill, unofficially, became known as the Stokely Carmichael Bill, a reference to the black activist who was touring the country making vicious inflammatory speeches to black communities. The FBI claimed that such elements had stirred up riots in Watts, Harlem, Cleveland and Chicago. This was the type of activity that the government hoped to crack down on. Because rioting or inciting to riot was only a state offense, Congress wanted a strong federal law to help stop persons from traveling across the land fomenting lawlessness.

There were serious First and Fifth Amendment issues involved which caused strong opposition on the part of liberals. Most important was the threat to "due process" under the Fifth Amendment. The bill did not require that the intent to incite a riot and the actual commission of the incitement occur at the same time. Representative Edwards of California, in arguing against the bill, pointed out: "This law makes it a crime to cross a state line with the intent of inciting a riot. Sometime later, even months or years, if an individual after crossing a state line commits an overt act that could be construed as promoting a riot he will have violated the law."

The ACLU argued strongly against the bill on "due process" grounds as well. Their legal brief to the Court argued that the criminal intent and the criminal act must be simultaneous for a true crime to occur. This is one of the fundamental, centuries-old concepts of criminal law. Failure to follow this principle would allow the following hypothetical situation to occur: A man intends to kill his enemy on Monday, but changes his mind on Tuesday, while on Wednesday he is attacked by this very enemy whom he then kills in self-defense. Under the logic that was the basis of the anti-riot bill, the man would be guilty of murder. He had the intent, and at a later date he did indeed kill the other man. This would be contrary to the presumption of innocence on which our law rests.

There was a clear threat to the rights of free speech and assembly inherent in the bill as well. No one, of course, suggested that rioting or inciting a riot was constitutionally protected speech, because it is not. The effect of this law, however, would be to deter the free exchange of ideas and the freedom to freely assemble. A person would have to be very careful about what they said. Provocative language could be construed as showing the necessary intent to incite a riot, and, if after crossing a state line, that person did something that could be construed as incitement, they would have violated the anti-riot law. A major weakness with this law was that, to convict, the government had to prove the mental intentions of a person on different sides of a state line, and then prove that a crowd of people was incited to riot by the overt acts of that person. This required a showing of the crowd's state of mind. A speech, especially to an angry crowd, may have the unintended, and unwanted, result of provoking them to riot. It is not logical to argue that the person who made the speech intentionally caused a riot. The point is that, in light of this scenario, people would have to significantly tone down their remarks in order to make sure the crowd did not then get out of hand. This is a subtle, though unacceptable, limitation on free speech and assembly, but it is exactly what the government wanted.

One of the strongest opponents of the measure was Attorney General Ramsey Clark, who argued against it on constitutional as well as enforcement grounds. He stated that "a law which requires you to prove the state of mind of an individual on one side of a state line or another is very difficult to enforce." The idea of a law based on a person's intentions, or thoughts, smacks dangerously of the "Thought Police" from George Orwell's novel on totalitarianism, *1984*.

These constitutional arguments were not important to Congress. Representative Smith of California replied that "it is not the business of Congress to think about such problems." Representative Sikes of Florida said, "The First Amendment should not interfere in the efforts of Congress to halt black riots. Those who incite to violence should be punished whether or not freedom of speech is impaired." That is an extremely dangerous attitude. Nonetheless, the bill passed the House 347-70, was sent to the Senate, approved, and signed into law in April, 1968.

In March, 1969, a Chicago grand jury indicted eight leaders of the Chicago protests. The indictment read that they did "combine, conspire, confederate, and agree together on or about April 12, 1968, to travel to Chicago in interstate commerce with the intent to incite, organize, promote, encourage, participate in and carry on a riot and thereafter to perform overt acts for the purpose of inciting a riot." There were actually two charges here: first was a conspiracy charge which was aimed at all eight defendants; and, second was the violation of the new federal anti-riot law which was aimed at six of them.

On April 9, 1969, the eight protest leaders, who would become known as the Chicago Eight, were arraigned on the grand jury indictments. They were: Dave Dellinger, Chairman of the National Mobilization Committee to End the War in Viet Nam (MOBE), a loose coalition of more than one hundred antiwar groups; Tom Hayden and Rennie Davis, founders of the radical student organization Students for a Democratic Society (SDS); Jerry Rubin and Abbie Hoffman, leaders of the Youth International Party (Yippies); Bobby Seale, National Chairman of the Black Panther Party; John Froines, and Lee Weiner. Froines and Weiner were not charged with violating the anti-riot law, but with teaching and demonstrating the use of incendiary devices.

These eight individuals represented a whole host of racial, social and political positions. There were extreme differences and disagreements between them. The idea that they all conspired together was contrived. Bobby Seale had never even spoken with any of the other seven defendants until he arrived in Chicago during the convention. At that time he met Rubin, said "Hello," and left. One would think that people would at least have to speak with one another in order to conspire. This was clearly a political trial on trumped-up charges which was aimed at removing a number of the nation's leading protesters in the vain hope of killing the peace movement.

District Chief Judge Campbell, a good friend of Mayor Daley, chose Julius J. Hoffman as presiding judge. Seventy-four years old, five feet four inches tall, a goofy little old man, Hoffman was known for harsh sentences and denial of bail during appeals. He would, throughout the trial, reflect the very essence of injustice that the '60s were a protest against.

One of his first moves during the pre-trial phase involved representation by counsel. The defendants' attorneys were to be Charles Garry, William Kunstler, Leonard Weinglass, and several assistants. Garry had represented Seale in the past and was to do so again, but he had to be hospitalized shortly before the scheduled beginning of the trial. The defense moved for a delay. Generally this is a condition that would warrant a delay until appropriate counsel were available, but Hoffman refused to allow one. He insisted that the defendants had adequate defense attorneys and that Seale would be represented by them. As Seale did not know the other defendants or their attorneys, he insisted on having Garry. He then made a motion to defend himself which, unbelievably, the judge also denied. The 6th Amendment guarantees that the accused "shall have the assistance of counsel for his defense," a right which the courts have traditionally interpreted to mean that if a defendant so chooses he may defend himself. Thus, the United States Code provides that "in all courts of the United States the parties may plead and conduct their own cases." Judge Hoffman knew that this would give Seale the ability to use the court as a political forum, which the government did not want. The denial of this motion amounted to a blatant violation of Seale's constitutional rights. Seale and the other defendants insisted on Garry as an attorney for the defense anyway. Next, Judge Hoffman resorted to blackmail. Four other defense lawyers had filed appearances for the defense to assist in the early preparations. These four withdrew from the case by telegram before the trial began. Judge Hoffman, however, required a personal appearance for withdrawal. Judge Hoffman then held these four lawyers in contempt, issued bench warrants for their arrests and had two of them put in jail. He then told the defendants that these lawyers would be released when they dropped their insistence on Garry. This they refused to do, so the lawyers stayed in jail. An impasse developed which lasted until the third day of the trial. Finally, the judge was forced, by the Court of Appeals, to let them out on bail. Eventually, another federal district court judge ruled that the contempt citations of the two lawyers not yet arrested were invalid because the contempt did not occur in the presence of the judge, as required by law. Having been caught making a fundamental error on such a simple point of law, Judge Hoffman backed down and vacated all four warrants. Still, Seale was denied a delay, and the right to defend himself.

Another controversy arose over the government's intention to use material from illegal wiretaps that had been placed on several of the defendants. The Supreme Court had ruled on March 10, 1969, in the Alderman case, that all illegal wiretaps must be turned over to the defendants, and that evidence tainted by such taps could not be admitted in court. The decision required the transcripts to be turned over so that the defense could object to any evidence introduced at trial that came from them. The defense, upon learning of illegal taps on five of the defendants, moved for the transcripts from them to be turned over. The Justice Department delayed in responding to this request. They finally agreed to turn over some, but not all, of the transcripts. They claimed that to do so would reveal the information-gathering abilities of the United States, and that this would jeopardize national security. As patriotism is the last refuge of a scoundrel, the curtain of national security is the last refuge of an oppressive regime. Since this violated the recent Alderman decision, the defense objected and asked Judge Hoffman to order their release. He decided that he would not rule on this point until after the trial. By then, of course, it would be too late. The prosecution would have already used tainted evidence before the defense even found out about it. This amounted to an intentional violation of the law as declared by the Supreme Court. By this point it was apparent that there was a conspiracy, but that it was on the part of the government.

The next step was jury selection. A panel of 300 prospective jurors was assembled. Judge Hoffman began by reading the indictment with such a vehement tone that it appeared that the charges had already been proven as fact. Both Kunstler and Weinglass objected to the tone, and moved that the entire panel be dismissed. In denying the motion, sounding much like a madman, he screamed at Weinglass for insinuating that he was biased.

In state courts the lawyers question the jurors in a process known as *voir dire*. This process allows both sides to weed out jurors who are not impartial or competent. Jurors can be dismissed by the judge for cause (established legal reasons), and by the attorneys for both sides with several peremptory challenges (which can be for any reason at all). In the federal courts, *voir dire* is left up to the judge, who queries the jurors with questions submitted by both sides. The premise is that he will protect the rights of both sides. Judge Hoffman reduced the normal number of peremptory challenges, and refused to use any of the forty-four questions submitted by the defense. It was clear from the beginning of the trial that these defendants were going to be convicted with the judge's active assistance. It was a page straight out of British colonial legal tactics, which were used to stop protests.

On September 26, 1969, the trial got under way with the opening statements. The defense attempted to bring up the unconstitutionality of the anti-riot law and the First Amendment rights of these protesters to assembly and speech. The judge stopped them every time they began this line of reasoning. He was not going to allow the defense to use the Constitution to attack the law they were indicted under. Nor would he allow the issue of the First Amendment to be brought up. This was a tremendously unfair burden on the defense. Their only chance for an acquittal was in attacking the clearly unconstitutional anti-riot law and claiming that their acts were protected by the First Amendment, but the judge was not going to let them do either.

Bobby Seale then rose to make an opening statement in defense of himself. Judge Hoffman refused to allow this. Then the prosecution proceeded with their first witness. The trial itself was rather anti-climactic. With the use of tainted evidence from illegal wiretaps and unconstitutional laws, the result was never really in doubt. Added to this was a biased judge who gave the prosecution every privilege and denied every right to the defense; he allowed requested breaks and early recesses for the prosecution, but not for the defense; he refused to allow two major defense witnesses to testify, including former Attorney General Ramsey Clark, because the government was afraid his testimony might give the jury the impression that the government was wrong; he yelled at defense attorneys, insulted them, and allowed the prosecution to do the same; he threatened to revoke the bails of the defendants if any more of them made public speeches critical of himself and the trial; he filled the court room with more than 25 armed marshals that gave the jury the impression that the defendants were really that dangerous. These things not only made a fair trial impossible, they violated the law.

Faced with this injustice, the defendants were anything but orderly during the trial. As it became increasingly apparent that they were being railroaded, they resorted to all types of disruptive behavior. They wore loud clothing, brought a North Vietnamese flag into the courtroom, yelled insults at everyone, and called the judge a Nazi, a fascist, a racist, and a pig. Entertaining, yet anticlimactic as it was, one very disturbing incident occurred.

Every time that Bobby Seale was mentioned, he attempted to assert his right to defend himself, which the judge refused. Becoming annoyed at this constant interruption, Judge Hoffman finally threatened to shut Seale up. When Seale continued in this vein, the judge had the marshals take him to another room where they chained him to a chair and put a gag in his mouth. They brought him back into court, but he could still be heard asking for his rights. The marshals removed him again and covered his mouth with adhesive tape, but still he could be heard. Next, they tied another rag up under his chin and tied it on top of his head. He was then strapped with leather at the arms and legs to the chair. The final solution was to completely wrap his head with athletic bandage. When this started to cut off circulation to his head he became unable to respond to inquiries. Defense attorney William Kunstler yelled at the judge that such treatment was an "unholy disgrace." This was backed up by Weinglass, the defendants, and court observers, and developed into a shouting match with the judge and prosecution attorneys. Judge Hoffman then sentenced Seale to three months imprisonment for each of 16 contempt citations, totaling four years! He severed Seale's trial from the other defendants, and had him removed to jail. It was one down, seven to go!

The defense was likewise anti-climactic, as the judge refused to allow their two best arguments. They presented what they could of their defense, the prosecution presented rebuttal evidence, and then after four-and-a-half months, both sides rested. On February 14th, 1970, the jury received their instructions and left to deliberate. By the end of the trial there was very little agreement in the jury as to what had been proven. From the trial transcript it does appear that a few facts were proven. First, these defendants were in Chicago during the convention week. Second, some of them did take part in speeches and assemblies that were constitutionally protected. Third, riots did break out that were caused by the provocation and attacks of the Chicago police.

Following the departure of the jury, Judge Hoffman pulled out a notebook in which he had listed the various incidents of disruptive behavior by the defendants, and announced that they were cited for contempt and would be punished accordingly. It was apparent that the government was afraid they would not get a conviction, so a way was found to send the defendants to prison anyway. The defendants and their lawyers were sentenced to:

Defendant	Counts of Contempt	Sentence
Dellinger	32	29 months & 13 days
Davis	23	25 months & 14 days
Hayden	11	14 months & 14 days
Hoffman	24	8 months & 6 days
Rubin	15	25 months & 23 days
Weiner	7	2 months & 18 days
Froines	10	5 months & 15 days
Attorney		
Kunstler	24	48 months & 13 days
Weinglass	14	20 months & 9 days

Prior to the sentencing for contempt, Kunstler attempted to argue the law on punishment for contempt. He quoted the Supreme Court's recent decision in the Bloom case which stated that "the power of summary judgment contempt should not be exercised after a trial; it is only a method of preventing disturbances during a trial; after the trial a man is entitled to a jury." Judge Hoffman could and should have cited and sentenced a disruptive party at the time of the incident. Once the trial was over, he could not legally send these men to jail without a jury trial on their contempt citations. He responded to Kunstler's legal argument by saying, "I do not share your view." Again, he blatantly disobeyed a ruling of the Supreme Court.

Meanwhile, the jury deliberated. Two factions had developed. Four jurors emphatically supported acquittal. They were appalled at the government's use of infiltrators, and by evidence that the government had placed itself above the law. They felt that the government had provoked the confrontations, and that the defendants did nothing more than exercise their constitutional rights. One of these jurors, after witnessing the government's unlawful and oppressive behavior, later admitted that "for the first time I came to fear our government."

The other eight jurors wanted to fry the defendants. The deliberations led to a hung jury. The judge, when notified, simply ignored them. His intention was to let them stay forever, or until they reached a verdict. Finally, a compromise was presented by one of the pro-prosecution jurors. The jurors who supported acquittal were afraid that a hung jury would result in a new trial where there might be less sympathetic jurors, so they gave in and agreed to the compromise. The verdict that was delivered to the court acquitted all seven of the defendants on the conspiracy charge, acquitted Froines and Weiner on the charges of teaching and demonstrating the use of incendiary devices, and convicted Dellinger, Hayden, Davis, Hoffman, and Rubin under the anti-riot law.

Kunstler was afraid that a compromise had been reached instead of a true verdict, which was a point to be considered on appeal. He demanded, as the law allows, that the jury be polled. Judge Hoffman refused and, raving again like a lunatic, he ordered the defendants and their counsel not to talk to the jury.

Another interesting twist involved one of the jurors. Earlier in the trial, two jurors received threatening notes signed by the Black

Panthers. The judge dismissed one of the jurors who was obviously sympathetic to the defense, and allowed the other who was clearly pro-prosecution to stay. One of the alternate jurors joined the proceedings. This juror, whose husband worked for Chicago City Hall, is the same one who suggested the compromise in the face of the hung jury. It has been suggested that she reported jury deliberations to the prosecution and was instructed as to the compromise.

Finally, Judge Hoffman sentenced the five convicted defendants to the maximum penalty. Each received five years in prison and a fine of $5,000. In addition, they were to pay the costs of prosecution, estimated at $40,000. The defendants went to jail without immediate bail, and the complex appeals process began. Judge Hoffman was celebrated as a hero by the conservative fringe and was even invited to a party at the White House. The following night he attended a Washington banquet that included entertainment. In one of the sketches, an observation was made that it hardly mattered if the country ignored the First Amendment, because there were still twenty-three amendments left. That would be funny if it were not so dangerous an idea!

This whole chapter represents one of the most vile periods in the history of this country. Police brutality against protesters in the face of the First Amendment, unconstitutional laws created to limit protest and free speech, and a trial that violated nearly every principle of criminal and constitutional law as well as justice. Yet this was typical of the government in the 1960s. This is exactly the kind of totalitarianism that Britain practiced against the colonies, and a forewarning of what will happen if we don't enforce the Constitution as it was written. We allowed our government to get away from the Constitution, and the result was the inevitable abuse of power that every government will engage in if not stopped by enforced written laws. We had the necessary written laws in the Constitution, but after all, it is just a piece of paper.

CHAPTER 14
ROE V. WADE 1973

In the Supreme Court case of *County of Riverside v. McLaughlin* (1991), Justice Scalia began his dissent with an amusing anecdote which succinctly sums up the recent history of Supreme Court constitutional interpretation. He stated : "The story is told of the elderly judge who, looking back over a long career, observes with satisfaction that when he was young, he probably let stand some convictions that should have been overturned, and when he was old he probably set aside some convictions that should have stood; so overall, justice was done. I sometimes think that is an appropriate analog to this Court's constitutional jurisprudence, which alternatively creates rights that the Constitution does not contain and denies rights that it does. Compare *Roe v. Wade* (1973) [right to abortion does exist] with *Maryland v. Craig* (1990) [right to be confronted with witnesses, Amend. 6, does not]." How apropos!

As a result of this kind of misguided jurisprudence, abortion has become one of the most controversial and divisive issues facing this country since its legalization by the United States Supreme Court in the landmark *Roe v. Wade* decision in 1973. The debate has pitted the fringe of the religious community against the pro-choice majority of Americans. The issue has become a litmus test for political and judicial candidates, and a source of acrimonious debate in the legislatures. Seen from the pro-choice perspective, this is a question of the limit of governmental authority. Most Americans are reluctant to concede that the government should have a controlling voice in such decisions. In a 1993 NBC News/*Wall Street Journal* poll, 75% agreed that "the government should not interfere with a woman's right to have an abortion," while only 21% disagreed. When asked in a 1991 *Los Angeles Times* poll whether the decision to have an abortion is "a choice that must be made only by the woman herself" or whether "the government has a legitimate right to regulate abortion," 78% said it should be the woman's choice. Allowing a government to dictate what a woman may or may not do with her reproductive organs is a grant of power to the government that violates the very essence of the Founders' fears of abusive government, and exactly what they tried to prohibit with the limited system they established under the Constitution and Bill of Rights.

The Supreme Court: Justice or personal agendas?
(Southern Cross Publishing)

Regardless of the validity of the pro-choice position and the immoral and indefensible tactics of the anti-choice forces (i.e., shootings of doctors, harassment of physicians and their families in their homes, bombings of clinics, and the promotion of lawbreaking by their children), the legalization of abortion that came about as a result of *Roe v. Wade* is fundamentally flawed as constitutional law.

The basis of the *Roe* decision comes from *Griswold v. Connecticut* (1965), though *Griswold* has its roots in some earlier cases. In *Griswold*, Justice William O. Douglas found "that specific guarantees in the Bill of Rights have penumbras, formed by emanations from those guarantees." Once translated into useful language, Douglas was proposing that the specific rights listed in the Bill of Rights create penumbras, or partial shadow zones, which contain other rights. One of these rights was henceforth to be the so-called Right of Privacy. The next step was taken in 1973 in the seminal *Roe v. Wade* decision, which extended the privacy right to include a right to abortion.

The critical issue here is not the morality of abortion. The issue is whether this is a question the Constitution can or should resolve. The word "privacy" is not mentioned in the entire document of the Constitution or Bill of Rights. It was injected in 1965 in a fit of liberal judicial activism. It should also be made clear that this is not a matter of conservative versus liberal ideology, for the conservative judicial activists such as Justice Rehnquist do the same damage to the Constitution when they legislate from the bench in furtherance of their moral philosophies and agendas.

When the Supreme Court acts in this manner, it not only comes close to illegitimacy... it *is* illegitimate. Creating rights not found in the document through the courts, as opposed to the constitutional processes of legislation and amendment, may seem a worthy goal to many in the ivory towers of the law schools and to the anti-majoritarians in the populace, but as anyone can see, this dangerous idea gives the Court the freedom to make whatever they want out of the Bill of Rights. And any court that is allowed to add at its will provides itself with legal precedent for the act, and strengthens its later bid to add or remove at its will. *Maryland v. Craig* (1990), is a good example.

It is this kind of behavior by Supreme Court justices, masking their deceptions in flowery and eloquent legalese intentionally beyond the comprehension of the American people, that threatens the Constitution. It is time to reverse *Roe v. Wade*, reverse the trend of liberal and conservative judicial activism, and return to the only rational, legitimate philosophy of constitutional interpretation — Original Intent.

The case of *Griswold v. Connecticut* (1965), involved the constitutionality of §53-32 and §54-196 of the General Statutes of Connecticut. The former provided: "Any person who uses any drug, medicinal article or instrument for the purpose of preventing conception shall be fined not less than fifty dollars or imprisoned not less than sixty days nor more than one year or be both fined and imprisoned." §54-196 provided: "Any person who assists, abets, counsels, causes, hires or commands another to commit any offense may be prosecuted and punished as if he were the principal offender."

When circus entrepreneur P.T. Barnum said, "There's a sucker born every minute," few people realized he intended to make sure of it by drafting the first American statute criminalizing the use of "any drug, medicine, article, or instrument for the purpose of preventing conception," as chairman of the Connecticut Legislature's Joint Committee on Temperance in 1879. The legacy of that act would continue, in a host of jurisdictions, for more than 80 years.

Appellant Griswold was the Executive Director of the Planned Parenthood League of Connecticut. Appellant Buxton was a licensed physician, and a professor at the Yale Medical School, who served as medical director for the League at its clinic in New Haven. These two, especially Buxton, had long been involved in trying to challenge the Connecticut birth control ban. In 1958, Buxton, Griswold, Yale Law School Professor Fowler Harper, and Catherine Roraback, a Connecticut attorney, began a series of lawsuits to challenge the birth control statutes. They solicited various plaintiffs for these suits in order to conduct the challenge. Indeed, as Judge Robert Bork described it, "This was an attempt by professors at Yale to manipulate the law through the courts." Their repeated attempts to set up this test case are rather ironic in light of the later decision in Griswold. A fake case resulted in an insupportable decision.

In 1959, this Yale gang had managed to get three of their manufactured cases to the Connecticut Supreme Court, requesting declaratory judgments on the birth control statutes. In *Buxton v. Ullman*, the court again rejected this challenge on the grounds that "to overturn the statute would be improper judicial usurpation." In June, 1961, a divided United States Supreme Court dismissed the appeal of these three combined cases. Justice Frankfurter, writing for a four-member plurality, found the case nonjusticiable because there was no realistic threat of prosecution under the statutes.

The birth control activists planned their next step. They decided to open a birth control clinic in New Haven, Connecticut, to see what would happen. If the law was not enforced, then they had achieved their goal; if it was enforced, then they would be able to get into the U.S. Supreme Court again. The Planned Parenthood League Clinic opened on November 1, 1961. Nine days later, the police arrested Griswold and Buxton for violating the birth control statutes. It was found that Griswold and Buxton were involved in giving information, instruction, and medical advice to married persons as to how to prevent conception. They were found guilty as accessories to the prevention of conception, and fined $100 each. Their defense that the statute as applied violated the 14th Amendment of the United States Constitution was rejected in the trial court, the appellate court and the state supreme court. The United States Supreme Court agreed to take the case.

The nine-justice Court released six opinions in *Griswold v. Connecticut*. The majority by Justice Douglas, a concurrence by Justices Goldberg, Warren and Brennan, a concurrence by Justice Harlan, a concurrence by Justice White, a dissent by Justice Black, and a dissent by Justice Stewart.

The majority opinion is brief and to the point. It begins, oddly enough, by stating, "We do not sit as a super-legislature to determine the wisdom, need, and propriety of laws that touch economic problems, business affairs, or social conditions." Amusingly, Douglas pointed out that some have argued that *Lochner v. State of New York* (1905) should guide the Court in this decision. He hastened to reject that invitation. Until 1965, *Lochner v. State of New York*, though a long-dead doctrine, represented the ultimate example of judicial activism in the entire history of the Court. Indeed, the case gave rise to the expression "Lochnerized" as a general term of disparagement for cases in which such activism evidenced itself. And here in *Griswold*, the new benchmark of illegitimate judicial activism, Justice Douglas bothers to include a dismissal of Lochner.

Following these denials, Douglas begins with a survey of cases which established peripheral rights under the First Amendment. The list includes: *Meyer v. State of Nebraska* (1923 — the right to study German in school); *Pierce v. Society of Sisters* (1925 — the right to educate one's children as one chooses); *Martin v. City of Struthers* (1943 — the right to distribute, receive, and read*); Wieman v. Updegraff* (1952 — the freedoms of inquiry and thought, and the freedom to teach). Douglas points out that none of these rights are mentioned in the Constitution nor in the Bill of Rights. He continued, "yet the First Amendment has been construed to include peripheral rights without which the First Amendment would be less secure."

Continuing, Douglas looked at the right of association, and declared, " The right of association is more than the right to attend a meeting; it includes the right to express one's attitudes or philosophies by membership in a group or by affiliation with it or by other lawful means. Association in that context is a form of opinion; and while it is not expressly included in the First Amendment its existence is necessary in making the express guarantees fully meaningful." From this, Douglas deduced that the specific guarantees in the Bill of Rights have penumbras, formed by emanations from those guarantees that help give them life and substance.

In a logical leap of unbelievable dimension, Douglas then cites the First (free speech, press, and assembly), Third (no quartering of soldiers), Fourth (right to be secure from unreasonable searches and seizures), Fifth (Self-Incrimination Clause) and Ninth Amendments (Non-Disparagement Clause) to declare that there are zones of privacy which result from the emanations from these specific guarantees. He concludes this in-depth legal reasoning by stating that, "The present case then concerns a relationship lying within the zone of privacy created by several fundamental constitutional guarantees." And that is it. That is the complete analysis. The right of privacy was born.

It is hard to see how Douglas could make such an erroneous analogy to the cases he cited. In each of the cited cases the Court was dealing with an express provision of the Bill of Rights (i.e., free speech, press, etc.). There is much to be said for Douglas' argument that interpretation must give meaning and protection to these enumerated rights. But that means giving detail to a right, which is appropriate. It is an entirely different matter, however, to fuse some of these details together to create a vaporous new right unsupported by any specific guarantee, which was the case here. One who was more cynical might suggest that Justice Douglas, while standing in one of his penumbral shadow-zones, was momentarily blinded by an emanation.

Douglas, possibly concerned about the lack of depth in his argument, continued the opinion with a burst of oratory, as though the case dealt with "sexual fascism." He asked, "Would we allow the police to search the sacred precincts of marital bedrooms for telltale signs of the use of contraceptives? The very idea is repulsive to the notions of privacy surrounding the marriage relationship." This very statement is repulsive to notions of relevance! This off-the-subject appeal to emotions is a Douglas trademark. In place of critical legal analysis, one is buried under threatening rhetoric. In *Skinner v. State of Oklahoma* (1942), a case dealing with a proposal to sterilize three-time felons, Douglas treated the suggestion as though it raised the specter of racial genocide. As Judge Bork pointed out in his critique of the Griswold opinion, "Courts usually judge statutes by the way in which they are actually enforced, not by imagining horrible events that have never happened, never will happen, and could be stopped by the courts if they ever seemed about to happen."

Justice Goldberg in a concurring opinion sought to find a more concrete basis for this new privacy right. He focused on the Ninth Amendment which reads:

"The enumeration in the Constitution, of certain rights, shall not be construed to deny or disparage others retained by the people."

Goldberg explains in detail the enactment of the Ninth Amendment in the First Congress. He cites James Madison, and Supreme Court Justice Joseph Story, who served on the Court from 1811-1845, in arriving at a conclusion as to the original meaning of this cryptic amendment.

In presenting the proposed amendment, James Madison, who wrote it, said: "It has been objected also against a bill of rights, that, by enumerating particular exceptions to the grant of power, it would disparage those rights which were not placed in that enumeration; and it might follow by implication, that those rights which were not singled out, were intended to be assigned into the hands of the General Government, and were consequently insecure. This is one of the most plausible arguments I have ever heard against the admission of a bill of rights into this system; but I conceive, that it may be guarded against. I have attempted it, as gentlemen may see by turning to the last clause of the fourth resolution [the Ninth Amendment]."

Justice Story also wrote of the meaning of the Ninth Amendment, stating: "This clause was manifestly introduced to prevent any perverse or ingenious misapplication of the well-known maxim, that an affirmation in particular cases implies a negation in all others; and *e converso*, that a negation in particular cases implies an affirmation in all others."

Madison's intent for the Ninth Amendment is clear. To avoid any understanding that the rights of the people were limited to only those stated in the Bill of Rights, the Ninth Amendment makes clear that there are other rights exclusive of those listed in Amendments 1-8, and these are retained by the people, not by the government. The only remaining question was: How are these rights to be obtained?

Justice Goldberg came to this same conclusion as to the meaning of the Ninth Amendment, and then he, like Justice Douglas, launched into a leap of illogic. He concluded that the concept of liberty under the Due Process Clause of the 14th Amendment is not restricted, and that it embraces the right of marital privacy, even though that right is not mentioned explicitly in the Constitution, and claimed this is supported by the language and history of the Ninth Amendment. In other words, the Ninth Amendment stated that there were other constitutional rights, and the Court could use this to create them. He wrapped this up with another appeal to emotionalism by stating, "Although the Constitution does not speak in so many words of the right of privacy in marriage, I cannot believe that it offers no protection. The fact that no particular provision explicitly forbids the State from disrupting the traditional relation of the family surely does not show that the Government was meant to have the power to do so."

This argument turns the Ninth Amendment into a mandate to invent constitutional rights, though that was not its intended purpose. Surely, if such a purpose had been intended, Madison could have used clear language to so indicate, but he did not. To avoid future games of legal construction by potential usurpers of the constitutional system, the Ninth Amendment was included to state simply that the people retained other rights on the same footing as those listed. Those rights could, then, not be denied by the government. When considered in the context of the Amending Process, these new rights could be added to the Bill of Rights through the elected representatives of the people. But that is not a speedy process. Indeed, it is too slow for the social engineers of the left and the right who saw the *Griswold* case as opening up whole new corridors through which to drive the machinery of social change.

The dissent in the *Griswold* case was written by Justice Hugo Black. In the history of the Court, only one justice has served longer than Black's 34 years. Arguably, none have served with more distinction. His criticism of the decision attacks two areas. First, on the topic of a right of privacy, he said, "The Court talks about a constitutional right of privacy as though there is some constitutional provision or provisions forbidding any law ever to be passed which might abridge the privacy of individuals. But there is not."

Second, on a related issue he stated, "I realize that many good and able men have eloquently spoken and written about the duty of this Court to keep the Constitution in tune with the times. The idea is that the Constitution must be changed from time to time and that this Court is charged with a duty to make those changes. For myself, I must reject that philosophy. The Constitution makers knew the need for change and provided for it. Amendments suggested by the people's elected representatives can be submitted to the people or their selected agents for ratification. That method was good enough for our Fathers, and I must add that it is good enough for me."

It is not the right, nor within the constitutional power of the Supreme Court to update, modify, or change the Constitution. Yet its trampling of the document in violation of this fact has been continuous and substantial, and *Griswold v. Connecticut* was a major milestone on that path.

That path continued with *Roe v. Wade* (1973). *Roe* involved Arts. 1191-1194 and 1196 of the Texas Penal Code, which made it a crime to "procure an abortion, as therein defined, or to attempt an abortion, except with respect to an abortion procured or attempted by medical advice for the purpose of saving the life of the mother." Such statutes were in effect in thirty-two states at the time.

In March, 1970, Jane Roe, a pregnant woman who desired an abortion, filed suit in District Court for the Northern District of Texas attacking the constitutionality of the Texas abortion statutes. Dr. James Hallford intervened, and John and Mary Doe filed a companion complaint. Mary Doe, while not pregnant, claimed that she might be in the future, and would be unconstitutionally restricted by the Texas statutes. The three-judge District Court dismissed the Does' complaint for lack of standing, held that Doctor Hallford did have standing, held the statute unconstitutional on the basis of the Ninth and Fourteenth Amendments, but denied the plaintiff's requested injunctive relief.

The three plaintiffs appealed directly to the Supreme Court. The Court began by holding that Plaintiffs James Hallford and John and Mary Doe were without standing. The remainder of the case dealt with Jane Roe and the question of abortion.

Justice Blackmun, writing for a 7-2 majority, in the best spirit of Justice Douglas, begins with 23 pages which trace the history of abortion from ancient Persia to modern times, the relevance of which is not explained.

The opinion goes on to cite three reasons to explain historically the enactment of criminal abortion laws in the 19th Century, and to justify their continued existence. First, a Victorian social concern to discourage illicit sexual conduct. Second, the need to protect women from the perils of a dangerous medical procedure. Third, the State's duty to protect prenatal life. Again, the relevance was not clear.

As he finally gets to the meat of the argument on the right of privacy in Part VIII of the opinion, Blackmun's first sentence states, "The Constitution does not explicitly mention any right of privacy." The remainder of the decision is a rambling justification for having made one up and relying on the *Griswold* case to prove it. The legal analysis begins with the statement: "This right of privacy, whether it be founded in the Fourteenth Amendment's concept of personal liberty, as we feel it is, or, as the District Court determined, in the Ninth Amendment's reservation of rights to the people, is broad enough to encompass a woman's decision whether or not to terminate her pregnancy."

That sentence is the extent of the analysis that leads the Court to this extension of the insupportable right of privacy. This statement reminds me of a crusty old professor in law school who, when students would make such concluding remarks in recitation, would respond, "Come now, even the D- student knows better than that." It is interesting to note the lack of specificity as to where this purported right actually resides — in the 9th or 14th Amendments. Apparently, when one is making up a constitutional right it does not matter where it comes from.

Justice Blackmun does go on, again reminding one of the bedroom fascists conjured up by Justice Douglas in *Griswold*, with a lengthy essay on the consequences of not allowing a pregnant woman this choice. It is a story replete with allusions to forcing a distressful life and future on a woman, psychological harm, mental and physical health problems, unwanted children, potential abuse, and the stigma of unwed mothers. But there is not one word about the Constitution! With that as the basis, Justice Blackmun held that the right of privacy includes the right to make a decision on abortion, and therefore all such abortion statutes which restrict that right are unconstitutional. However, the Court then states, "It is reasonable and appropriate for a State to decide that at some point in time another interest, that of the health of the mother or that of potential life, becomes significantly involved. The woman's privacy is no longer sole and any right of privacy she has must be measured accordingly." The abortion right, then, has limits.

Appellees raised the issue that the fetus is a "person" within the language and meaning of the 14th Amendment, and therefore the fetus' right to life is specifically protected. But the Court looked to the use of the word "person" in the body of the Constitution and in the Bill of Rights (specifically, the 14th Amendment), and held that "person" does not include the unborn.

Appellees' next argument was that, apart from the 14th Amendment, life begins at conception, and therefore the State has a compelling interest in protecting life from and after conception. The Court analyzed the legal protection provided the unborn in other areas of law, primarily in torts, and the views of various religions on this question. They waxed philosophically that the judiciary should not speculate as to when life begins. They did, however, hold that "the unborn have never been recognized in the law as persons in the whole sense." Appellees' argument was rejected.

The Court recognized that the State does have important and legitimate interests in preserving and protecting the health of the pregnant woman, and in protecting the potentiality of human life. As to the State interest in the health of the mother, the end of the first trimester is determined to be the compelling point from which time the State may regulate the abortion procedure to the extent it reasonably relates to the preservation and protection of maternal health. Prior to this compelling point, the abortion decision may be made free of interference by the State. As to the State's interest in protecting potential human life, the compelling point is at viability, since it is at this point that the fetus is capable of living outside the womb. After that point, the State may go so far as to proscribe abortion, except when it is necessary to preserve the life or health of the mother.

Measured against these standards, the Court found the Texas statute to be too broad, and therefore unconstitutional.

In effect, the judicial process made a wrong decision in Griswold and claimed a new right existed, then eight years later used that poor decision as the basis for another decision that created another new right. With the votes of seven men, the *Roe* decision effectively overturned the laws of 32 states containing a population of 121,105,250, laws which were enacted by the people through their elected representatives. Now, about 1.2 million abortions occur each year in the United States, and the political process is embroiled in a divisive and redundant rhetorical merry-go-round of charges, counter charges, and threats. To go along with this, we throw in the acts of assorted religious groups who bomb abortion clinics, trespass, march around with pictures of aborted fetuses, destroy private property, and otherwise break the law while singing their silly hymns. It is all so unnecessary.

Part of the alleged basis for the *Roe* decision is the 14th Amendment to the United States Constitution. Not only is this poor constitutional interpretation, but it is based on an amendment with an extremely sordid and checkered past. As we have seen, this amendment was added to the Constitution in a way that constituted blackmail. It is indeed fitting that an amendment with such an illegitimate birth should be the vehicle to further usurp the original constitutional framework.

The judicial battle over the right of privacy and its lack of boundaries has become a source of significant litigation. This was especially true in the late 1980s as state legislatures, perceiving a Supreme Court shift to the right as a result of Reagan/Bush appointees, began to implement anti-abortion regulations. At the same time there were new attempts to expand the right of privacy into other areas of attempted social engineering. Two cases were critical in changing the direction of the right of privacy. In *Bowers v. Hardwick*, the Court put an end to the expansion of the privacy right, and in *Planned Parenthood v. Casey*, the Court finally modified *Roe v. Wade*.

In June, 1986, the Court handed down its decision in *Bowers v. Hardwick* (1986). After being charged with violating the Georgia statute criminalizing sodomy, by committing that act with another adult male in the bedroom of his home, respondent Hardwick brought suit in Federal District Court, challenging the constitutionality of the statute insofar as it criminalized consensual sodomy. The court granted the state's motion to dismiss for failure to state a claim. The Court of Appeals reversed and remanded. They cited Supreme Court decisions in *Griswold v. Connecticut* (1965) and *Roe v. Wade* (1973). The court went on to hold that the Georgia statute violated respondent's fundamental rights because his homosexual activity is a private and intimate association that is beyond the reach of state regulation, by reason of the Ninth Amendment and the Due Process Clause of the Fourteenth Amendment. The Supreme Court agreed to take the case.

The case presented an inevitable extension of the right of privacy. This right, which had never been defined with any boundaries at all, was bound to be tested eventually with private behavior that a majority of the Justices did not feel was appropriately moral. But if the Court were to be consistent with *Griswold* and *Roe*, it would have to strike down this Georgia statute.

Surprisingly, the Court reversed the Court of Appeals and held the Georgia statute to be constitutional. Justice White, writing for the Court in a 5-4 decision, stated that the Constitution does not confer a fundamental right upon homosexuals to engage in sodomy. This was something of a distortion, as the dissent pointed out. The Georgia Statute provided that "[a] person commits the offense of sodomy when he performs or submits to any sexual act involving the sex organs of one person and the mouth or anus of another." This plainly included homosexual and heterosexual conduct. Yet, this distortion raises a question: did Justice White cast the issue in such a way as to ensure a majority based on purely emotional opposition to homosexuality?

The majority also found that none of the fundamental rights announced in the Court's prior cases involving family relationships, marriage, or procreation bore any resemblance to the right asserted in this case. Apparently, Justice White recognized that the Court had long been performing a questionable function in the area of judicially-created fundamental rights. He stated that: "There should be great resistance to expanding the substantive reach of the Due Process Clause, particularly if it requires redefining the category of rights deemed to be fundamental. Otherwise, the Judiciary necessarily takes to itself further authority to govern the country without express constitutional authority. The claimed right pressed on us today falls far short of overcoming this resistance."

This reflected an attitudinal change, though this is somewhat deceptive. Justice White's analysis did not expressly protest the entire doctrine of privacy, but instead found that homosexual sodomy simply was not "deeply rooted in this Nation's history and traditions." This is the old language of fundamental rights of the Due Process Clause of the 14th Amendment. White's reasoning then agreed with the dissenters on the basic validity of this type of judicial interpretation, but disagreed on whether this conduct should get protection. It became clear that the right of privacy would protect any activity which a majority of the Court found to be acceptable, thus highlighting brilliantly the dangerous potential of judicial legislating.

Justice Blackmun's dissent, which was joined by Justices Brennan, Stevens and Marshall, however, finally outlined the right of privacy. It was defined as "an interest with reference to certain decisions that are properly for the individual to make, and an interest with reference to certain places without regard for the particular activities in which the individuals who occupy them are engaged." He went on to explain that "this case is about the most comprehensive of rights and the right most valued by civilized men, namely, the right to be let alone." The dissent chastised the majority for stating that prior cases had related solely to the protection of the family. Blackmun added "We protect those rights associated with the family not because they contribute in some direct and material way, to the general public welfare, but because they form so central a part of an individual's life. The concept of privacy embodies the moral fact that a person belongs to himself and not others nor to society as a whole." This was his basis for asserting that these protected rights should extend beyond just the protection of family privacy.

As Judge Bork has explained, "If the opinion meant what it said, four members of the Court viewed the state of nature, in which every individual is free to be for himself and no one else, as the moral condition contemplated by the Constitution." This was a position of extreme individualism with far-reaching ramifications. Under this notion there would be no obligation to obey the law. Essentially, this reasoning assumed that society may make no moral judgments at all. But this case was the end of the road for this extreme position. Since *Bowers*, Justices Blackmun, Brennan and Marshall have stepped down. That leaves Justice Stevens as the only current member who supports this view.

In July, 1992, the Supreme Court moved strongly in a modified direction on abortion with its decision in *Planned Parenthood of Southeastern Pennsylvania v. Casey* (1992). At issue were five provisions of the Pennsylvania Abortion Control Act of 1982. These required: a woman seeking an abortion give her informed consent prior to the procedure, and specified that she be provided with certain information at least 24 hours before the abortion was performed; the informed consent of one parent for a minor to obtain an abortion, but provided a judicial bypass procedure; a married woman seeking an abortion to sign a statement indicating that she had notified her husband; a definition of a "medical emergency" that would excuse compliance with the foregoing requirements; certain reporting requirements on facilities providing abortion services.

Before any of the provisions took effect, the petitioners (five abortion clinics and a physician representing himself and a class of doctors who provided abortion services) brought this suit seeking a declaratory judgment that each of the provisions was unconstitutional on its face, as well as injunctive relief. The District Court held all the provisions unconstitutional and permanently enjoined their enforcement. The Court of Appeals affirmed in part and reversed in part, striking down the husband notification provision, but upholding the others.

With a court dominated by Reagan/Bush appointees, the nation anxiously anticipated a ruling that would overturn *Roe v. Wade*. Court watchers indicated that there were five votes to overturn as well as two question marks concerning the newest justices, Souter and Thomas. The decision, though, caused consternation on all sides, and established a group of moderate justices supporting a compromise view.

Justices O'Connor, Kennedy and Souter, all Reagan/Bush appointees, combined to form an apparent moderate coalition on this issue, and jointly wrote the majority opinion. They concluded that consideration of the fundamental constitutional question resolved by *Roe v. Wade*, principles of institutional integrity, and the rule of stare decisis require that *Roe's* essential holding be retained and reaffirmed as to each of its three parts: (1) a recognition of a woman's right to choose to have an abortion before fetal viability, and to obtain it without undue interference from the State, whose pre-viability interests are not strong enough to support an abortion prohibition or the imposition of substantial obstacles to the woman's effective right to elect the procedure; (2) a confirmation of the State's power to restrict abortions after viability, if the law contains exceptions for pregnancies endangering a woman's life or health; and (3) the principle that the State has legitimate interests from the outset of the pregnancy in protecting the health of the woman and the life of the fetus that may become a child.

The Justices continued with a statement of guiding principles that should control assessments of state regulation in this area. First, the rigid trimester framework of *Roe v. Wade* was rejected and replaced with the new "undue burden test." The Court held that "an undue burden exists, and therefore a provision of law is invalid, if its purpose or effect is to place substantial obstacles in the path of a woman seeking an abortion before the fetus attains viability." Second, to promote the State's interest in potential life throughout pregnancy, the State may take measures to ensure that the woman's choice is informed. Measures designed to advance this interest should not be invalidated if their purpose is to persuade the woman to choose childbirth over abortion. Third, as with any medical procedure, the State may enact regulations to further the health or safety of a woman seeking an abortion, but may not impose unnecessary health regulations that present a substantial obstacle to a woman seeking an abortion. Fourth, adoption of the undue burden standard does not disturb *Roe's* holding that regardless of whether exceptions are made for particular circumstances, a State may not prohibit any woman from making the ultimate decision to terminate her pregnancy before viability. Fifth, *Roe's* holding that, subsequent to viability, the State in promoting its interest in the potentiality of human life may, if it chooses, regulate, and even proscribe, abortion except where it is necessary, in appropriate medical judgment, for the preservation of the life or health of the mother is also reaffirmed.

With respect to the various Pennsylvania statutes, the Justices held that all but one of the provisions were constitutional. The Court struck down only the husband notification provision, because it constituted an undue burden and was therefore invalid, since a significant number of women would likely be prevented from obtaining an abortion just as surely as if Pennsylvania had outlawed the procedure entirely.

Casey was clearly a compromise position. While restating the validity of the woman's right to abortion, *Casey* also reasserts the right of the State to regulate in the interests of protecting the life of the mother and the fetus. As a result, the rigid *Roe v. Wade* trimester arrangement was rejected and the new undue burden test established. If the Justices felt that this compromise would help, they were sorely mistaken. Anti-abortionists, anticipating a complete overruling of *Roe*, decried this stabbing in the back by the Reagan/Bush appointees, while abortion rights supporters decried this gutting of the *Roe* decision. Representative Pat Schroeder, D-Col., summed up the abortion rights view when she stated that, "Spotted owls have more rights than American women now."

The greatest evil in the entire debate is the position taken by the right-to-lifers (a.k.a. religious fanatics), who insist that abortion must be illegal in all cases, including rape and incest. Of course, their real fear is that each aborted baby is one less donor to money-grubbing church services. These "community morals monitors," it seems, are never happy unless they are dictating how we must run our lives, and this is another of their motivations. This reflects the absolute moral bankruptcy of organized religion.

In 1989, a New York woman was hospitalized on the verge of death. She was pregnant, and this condition threatened her life. The husband sought to have the baby aborted to save the life of his wife. Two religious fanatics associated with the right-to-life movement, yet total strangers to this family, sued for an injunction to prevent it. The ensuing legal battle led to several different courts, and finally resulted in the husband's victory and the eventual abortion of the baby. But at what cost in terms of money and pain to a family already reeling from tragedy? How dare these people interfere in this family's time of anguish!

In 1990, convicted criminal and self-proclaimed protector of the nation's morals, Randall Terry, founder of Operation Rescue, interfered in a similar matter which became a national news story. Nancy Cruzan, 33 years old, had been in a vegetative state since a 1983 car accident. Her parents had pursued a legal battle to the U.S. Supreme Court to have the hospital terminate her treatment and allow her to die with dignity. In a landmark decision, the Court granted them this right, and treatment was suspended. The Supreme Court had decided correctly that the choice of continuing life is not one for the government to regulate.

The decision drew the kooks out of the woodwork. Another stranger filed suit, taking it to the Missouri Supreme Court, requesting an order to continue the treatment. Joining in this quest was Terry, who showed up at the hospital with his tiny band of nuts, and demanded a meeting with the parents. What a sickening thing to do! What goddamn right do these religious kooks think they have to interfere in a family crisis? Randall Terry and his followers are the best argument going in favor of abortion.

The extent and scope of civil disobedience by anti-choice groups has reached staggering proportions. It is, as was the case with forced busing, the inevitable and natural outcome of attempted social engineering. But that is not to excuse the tactics of the religious fanatics. Their unlawful behavior is the most disgusting element of this entire debacle. Between 1977 and 1990, there were 829 acts of anti-choice violence, including 34 clinic bombings, 52 clinic arsons, 266 clinic invasions, 64 assaults and batteries, 2 kidnappings, 22 burglaries, 77 death threats and 269 incidents of vandalism. In 1992 alone there were 116 cases of clinic vandalism, 12 reported cases of arson, 9 cases of attempted arson, 5 burglaries and a bombing.

Property damage, though, is now not the only concern of those providing abortion services. Across the country, doctors and their staffs have become the targets of stalking, harassment, and death threats. Protesters have even set up shop in front of their homes to broadcast their message of "baby killer" throughout the neighborhood. Unbelievably, these groups have even gone after the children of the doctors and clinic workers. In Florida, in 1993, the 13-year-old son of a clinic worker was approached by two women seeking information on an apartment. They lured him into a car and took him to a restaurant where they confronted him saying that he and his mother were going to "burn in hell." They identified themselves as members of Operation Rescue, and demanded names of patients at the clinic. In many other locations these groups have confronted children of doctors and staff with pictures of aborted babies and accusations that their parents are baby-killers.

Anti-choice groups have recently resorted to new lows in their attempts to close abortion clinics in Milwaukee, Wichita, Houston and Florida. The Milwaukee case revealed a new tactic. In a shabby and obvious attempt to gain publicity, the anti-choice groups sank to forcing their children to run the police lines and be arrested. Sickening scenes of eight- & nine-year-olds being carried off to jail while screaming scripted propaganda lines and sounding rather like brainwashed parrots showed up on the nightly news. Have these people no decency at all?

In July, 1991, Operation Rescue launched an all-out attack on the three clinics in Wichita, Kansas. It became a summer-long siege. The anti-choice groups came up against a determined foe in Wichita — Federal District Judge Patrick F. Kelly. As the protests grew violent the protesters physically tried to prevent employees and patients from entering the clinics. Finally, on July 23, using the Ku Klux Klan Act of 1871, Judge Kelly enjoined Operation Rescue from blocking entrances to the clinics. As a result, Judge Kelly was forced to accept federal marshal protection due to death threats.

But the protesters were not the only ones promoting lawlessness. The Justice Department of the anti-choice Bush Administration stepped in and asked the Court of Appeals for the 10th Circuit to vacate Kelly's order. Kelly angrily charged that "the Justice Department was giving its imprimatur to a license for mayhem." Meanwhile, Kelly's hard-line stance resulted in 2,600 arrests. The protests cost the city $800,000. Things were clearly getting out of hand.

Wichita may have been the highwater mark of the anti-choice movement. Jurisdictions across the country prepared hard-line preventative measures, and met protests with strong counterprotests and unbending enforcement of the law. Legal actions against the national anti-choice leadership put the protesters on the defensive.

The winning side in the abortion debate.
(Southern Cross Publishing)

Mass rallies were planned for Houston, Texas, during the Republican National Convention in August, 1992. Their goal was to close all the abortion clinics in the city. Local abortion-rights groups mobilized to combat them when they arrived, and two extremist homosexual-rights groups announced that they were going to violently attack the fundamentalists at the clinics. Pro-choice groups overwhelmed the anti-choice groups, and not a single clinic was closed. The only result was the arrest of a number of anti-choicers who violated an injunction not to approach within 100 feet of the clinics. It seemed that the rising tide of legal maneuvers by the pro-choice side was wearing the protesters down. Attendance in Houston was light, but pro-choice groups fielded masses to defend the clinics. Two years later the protesters were still embroiled in legal controversy stemming from their arrests.

Finally, in March, 1993, a member of a pro-life group took the ultimate step in Pensacola, Florida. It was probably an inevitable step, due to the frustration of the protesters, who were on the defensive in every area. Their forces were dwindling, and desperation set in. Abortion provider Doctor David Gunn was approached and shot three times in the back at point-blank range by a pro-life advocate. He died hours later. Across the country, pro-life groups celebrated. Reverend Joseph Foreman of Missionaries to the Preborn said, "We will not be outraged over the one death and not the other 4,000 precious human beings that were killed today by abortion." Randall Terry, founder of Operation Rescue said, "After all, Dr. Gunn was a murderer of babies." Don Treshman, national director of Rescue America stated, with a logic long familiar among extortionists, "This will have a chilling effect on the abortion business." When the murder of this doctor was announced to pro-life forces conducting a month-long protest at a clinic in Melbourne, Florida, the protesters took up a chant: "One down! How many more?" Another doctor was shot in Wichita, Kansas, in August, 1993. And another doctor and his bodyguard were shot to death by a pro-lifer in Florida in 1994.

These tactics of terror finally drew a reaction, though it was not the one desired by the anti-choice movement. In 1991, the National Organization For Women and several abortion providers sued the Pro-

Life Action Network (PLAN), a coalition of anti-abortion groups, and other national anti-abortion leaders, in the Federal District Court for the Northern District of Illinois. The suit alleged violations of the Racketeer Influenced and Corrupt Organizations (RICO) chapter of the Organized Crime Control Act of 1970.

In 1994, this case reached the Supreme Court as *National Organization For Women v. Scheidler*. It was the attempted use of RICO which made this action notable. With civil and criminal penalties (including treble damages), RICO is the kiss of death for organized crime. Its effective use against anti-choice groups could destroy their movement. The plaintiffs' case alleged that the defendants were members of a nationwide conspiracy to shut down abortion clinics through a pattern of racketeering activity, including extortion.

NOW alleged that the defendants conspired to use threatened or actual force, violence or fear to induce clinic employees, doctors and patients to give up their jobs, give up their economic rights to practice medicine, and give up their rights to obtain medical services at the clinics. It was further alleged that this conspiracy had harmed the plaintiff's business and/or property interests, and that PLAN constituted a racketeering enterprise.

The District Court dismissed the case. It concluded that the petitioners failed to state a claim, since "an economic motive requirement exists to the extent that some profit-generating motive must be alleged in order to state a RICO claim." The Court of Appeals affirmed.

The Supreme Court granted *certiorari* due to a conflict on this point in the Courts of Appeals. The Court did not face the merits of the claims, but simply had to decide if petitioners had stated a claim upon which relief could be granted. Specifically, the issue concerned whether a racketeering enterprise or predicate acts must be accompanied by an underlying economic motive in order to sustain a RICO claim.

Justice Rehnquist, writing for a unanimous Court, held RICO does not contain an economic motive requirement, and therefore a valid claim had been stated. The Court's decision simply means that

NOW can go back to District Court and try to prove their RICO case, which is not a simple matter. Pro-choice forces across the country now have use of a very dangerous statute which can easily destroy the financial resources of anti-choice groups. And while successful use of these statutes may help to prevent the terror tactics, it has a potential downside. The use of RICO against groups involved in protest on political issues raises First Amendment concerns. Will this have the effect of chilling free speech and assembly rights?

Besides the societal cost of *Roe*, it has had severe political implications as well. Supreme Court nomination hearings, such as those conducted on Judge Robert Bork in 1989, have become a circus of special-interest litmus tests, with a nominee's position on abortion playing in the center ring. Instead of providing their constitutional role of ensuring qualified candidates for the Court, the Senate now acts as a censor of political views. The legitimate questions for a nominee should focus on qualifications, ability, intellect and willingness to support the Constitution, without judicial legislating. Democrats and Republicans both, however, insist that candidates express views on cases and issues to make sure they have the proper views. That is not what the Founders intended for the Court.

At the Constitutional Convention in 1787, there were four attempts to give judges a political role. Each was rejected. The intention of the Convention was clearly described by Alexander Hamilton in *The Federalist* No. 78: "The judiciary, from the nature of its function, will always be the least dangerous to the political rights in the Constitution; because it will be least in a capacity to annoy or injure them." To this statement Hamilton appended a quotation from Baron de la Brède et de Montesquieu (1689-1755), the celebrated French philosopher, writer and jurist: "Of the three powers above mentioned [the others being the legislative and the executive], the Judiciary is next to nothing."

This is true because judges were, as Rufus King, delegate to the Constitutional Convention from Massachusetts, explained, "merely to expound law made by others." Expounding law made by others, not creating law on their own whims, was the design of the Founders. From that we have strayed, and for that we pay.

State legislatures are also increasingly consumed by pitched battles over abortion. Pennsylvania and Louisiana are two examples of states which became involved in repeated time-consuming attempts to draft anti-abortion limitations which would satisfy the Court. Years of expensive litigation followed.

Congress has also become bogged-down in addressing the issue. The *Casey* case immediately spawned efforts to establish a right to an abortion through the Freedom of Choice Act of 1992 (FOCA). The Act would codify the decision of *Roe v. Wade*, making freedom of choice a fundamental right and, thus, terminating the debate concerning the appropriate level of judicial scrutiny.

Even with the support of the Clinton administration, the Freedom of Choice Act stalled in Congress. Should it pass eventually, the state legislatures may be caught between a judicial rock and a statutory hard place. This act could have a substantial impact on the states. The Act provides that a state may not restrict a woman's right to choose abortion before viability, or restrict an abortion that becomes medically necessary to protect her life or health at any time during the pregnancy. The state may impose restrictions only if they are medically necessary to protect the woman's life or her health. Thus, if the Freedom of Choice Act is passed, a possible conflict may arise, testing the boundaries of the right enunciated in *Casey*, the power of the state to pass restrictive laws, and the provisions of the Act.

In another legislative area, the increasingly violent tactics resorted to by the anti-choice forces to prevent access to clinics have led to a movement for federal legislation. The Freedom of Access to Clinics Entrances Act, which was signed into law by Clinton in May, 1994, with all of its First Amendment implications, is a troublesome example.

Of course, new legislation and judicial action led to more litigation. In May, 1994, Planned Parenthood won a huge judgment including $1.01 million in punitive damages against protesters who disrupted a Houston clinic in 1992.

Another clinic, in Melbourne, Florida, had been for some time a regular battleground, as protesters committed vandalism, stalked and threatened staff members, their children, and their neighbors, and physically harassed patients attempting to enter the facility. A judge placed a series of restrictions on protesters. These established a 36-ft. zone around the clinic from which protesters were forbidden. Protesters were also forbidden to enter a 300-ft. zone placed around patients, staff members, and staff members' houses. Ironically, the religious fanatics, who constantly fight the free-speech rights of others, sued, claiming their free-speech rights had been violated. The case of *Madsen v. Women's Health Center* was decided by the U.S. Supreme Court in July, 1994. The Court upheld the 36-ft. zone, stating that, "It burdens no more speech than necessary to accomplish the governmental interest at stake." The other larger zones were struck down. Still, it was a major defeat for protesters. The real issue was the fact that a constitutional right to abortion existed, and these violent protests were designed to prevent women from reaching the clinics and exercising that right. It was probably an inevitable outcome. The decision reflects an old principle in free speech law: time, place and manner restrictions may be placed on the exercise of free speech in order to protect the rights of other people. Immediately thereafter, another fanatic in Florida approached a clinic doctor and his two bodyguards, and using a shotgun killed the doctor and one bodyguard. A leader of a radical anti-abortion group, he had long advocated that killing abortion doctors was justifiable homicide. The government disagreed, filing state murder charges in Florida and violations of the FACE Act at the federal level. If not executed, he will never leave jail, and rightly so.

The final question is: What to do about a beneficial decision that violates the Constitution? Our history since the inception of the Constitution shows a consistent trampling involving the government taking rights away from the people and progressively narrowing our liberties. But the *Griswold* and *Roe* decisions actually limit the power of government by adding a right for the people. Some would make the argument that the 9th Amendment allows the courts to create new rights for the people, or that the Due Process Clause allows the same. Certainly one can argue that a right of privacy makes sense, and is indeed a requirement for the people in an age of an ever-intrusive government and new snooping technologies. However, any Court that can freely add to the Constitution, no matter how appropriate that addition might be, is also further strengthened in attempts to interpret the Constitution based on the personal whims of Justices. It may even limit the Constitution. And the Constitution provides a procedure for amendments which could be used to add a valid right of privacy, if that is the wish of the people. *Roe v. Wade* and its underlying foundational decisions are clear examples of the abuse of power by the Supreme Court. They should be overturned.

In the larger scheme of things, pro-choice is consistent with views against strong abusive government. No government should have the power to tell a woman what she can or cannot do with her body and her reproductive system. In a system of law where precedent is the building block to future laws, allowing a government the authority to tell a woman she can't have an abortion must eventually lead to the question: can the government tell a woman she must have an abortion? Is this a future argument which may become necessary someday due to an important social need? Could these recent decisions act as precedents for future abuse of the Constitution? Critics of this reasoning naively respond by declaring that our government would never abuse its power like this. But unfortunately, government never fails to use the power it takes. It would be better if the government had no such authority in the first place.

Of course, the overturning of *Roe v. Wade* will not make abortion illegal. It will simply put the issue back in the hands of the state legislatures where it should be. The anti-choice forces may regret their current agitation because, once the issue is back in the legislatures, the pro-choice majority is going to end it by maintaining the legality of abortion, with the exception of a few states. Fortunately, all of these states will be surrounded by states where abortion is legal, so women will simply cross state lines to get an abortion. The pro-lifers will have won nothing!

The *Casey* decision illustrates a problem of the Supreme Court. The authority of this Court rests on the assumption that the people see it as an impartial arbiter of the Constitution and laws of the United States. But the debate over *Roe* shows otherwise. Since 1973, the only change in the Constitution has been the addition of the 27th Amendment, which restricts congressional pay raises. Otherwise, not one single word has been added to or subtracted from the Constitution, but *Roe v Wade* is inevitably, albeit slowly, being chipped away. Its demise cannot be far off. In other words, the public notes that the document is being read to mean something different only 21 years after the *Roe* decision. If the language has remained the same, how is it possible to get two different decisions? There either is a right of privacy or there is not.

To the common man, this exposes the depth of political influence that has pervaded the Court. Nominees to the Supreme Court now have positions on the issues. Recent debates over the nominations to the Court have become circus side-shows as candidates are attacked and supported by various special-interest groups. Lost in the shuffle is the important question: what is his view on the Constitution? That is not what was intended. The Founders wanted a non-political court whose members were granted a life-long tenure in order to guarantee this. They foresaw these Justices ruling on the Constitution and its principles, not on their various positions on the issues. The decision of a Supreme Court Justice on abortion should be based on one question: does the wording of the Constitution include a right that protects abortion? Their decisions should not be made, as they are now, on whether they are a Democrat or Republican, liberal or conservative, pro-choice or anti-choice!

Possibly a reawakening of the Reserved Powers Clause of the 10th Amendment will be forthcoming. Returning to the theory of a central government with limited powers, while all other authority is vested in the states and the people, would help return balance to our constitutional structure. Strict Construction was the view of constitutional interpretation of most of the Founders, and it is worthwhile to re-examine. In forgetting the lessons of our constitutional beginnings, we are in danger of repeating the mistakes of the past, hard lessons the Founders learned so well from their experiences with the tyranny of the British government during the colonial period. The Founders learned irrefutable lessons concerning the true nature of government and power, and their system was designed to control it, but that great experiment in democracy now lies battered along the shores of the Styx. Its resurrection lies in rejecting the theories of social engineering through the courts, and returning to the Original Intent of the Founders. To do otherwise leaves the future uncertain.

All of this is really so unnecessary. This divisive issue could have been avoided if the Supreme Court had stayed within its constitutional boundaries in the first place. Instead, it embarked upon another example of constitutional trampling. Well, after all, the Constitution is just a piece of paper.

CHAPTER 15
BUSING IN BOSTON 1974

The 1950s saw the legal end of racially separate schools in America. The battle to integrate is still going on today, but reached its heyday in the 1960s in the South and the 1970s in the North. The method consistently used to integrate the schools was busing, whereby white children were moved into predominantly black neighborhood schools, and blacks were bused into predominantly white neighborhood schools. This was a plan created by liberals, who envisioned a way to bring the races together, and with this exposure to each other, it was hoped, the races would develop understanding, cooperation, and an end to bigotry. What they got instead was massive violence and protests, racial animosity, "white flight," a heavy financial burden on schools, the destruction of quality education for everyone, and serious abuses of constitutional rights.

The American people, white and black, did not respond well at all to this "brotherhood at the point of a bayonet." Busing was one of the most patently offensive and obnoxious ideas ever conceived — not to mention a complete failure in achieving its stated goals. While not being a violation of any language of the Constitution, its implementation by the federal courts was clearly the act of an abusive government, the very thing the Constitution was intended to prevent. When a government dictates who one associates with, all freedom is lost. The implementation of busing created numerous incidents of chaos throughout the country. Boston was but one typical example. Subjected to the abuse of federal court-ordered busing, the city and its people suffered through all the traumas that were caused in other cities by this outrage, but it was made all the more offensive by the city's past. Boston, the cradle of American liberty, was the center of rebellion that created this country in the 1770s, but in 1974 the city's citizens' independence was stolen by the federal court dictatorship.

In 1896, the Supreme Court decided *Plessy v. Ferguson*, a case dealing with a negro who violated Louisiana law by refusing to vacate a seat in a white-only railroad car. The state law dictated that "all railway companies carrying passengers in their coaches shall provide separate but equal accommodations for the white and colored races." It also included a fine and jail sentence for sitting in the wrong compartment. The court held that "the negro is not denied the equal protection of the laws under the 14th Amendment by compelling him to accept separate but equal accommodations." This standard was applied across the board to separate whites and blacks until 1954. It applied vigorously to education, especially in the South, where, in most cases, it was against the law for whites and blacks to attend the same school. But with prejudice so rampant, what developed was "separate and unequal." White schools had better buildings, facilities, teachers and equipment. Black schools were clearly inferior. By the 1950s, it was apparent that blacks were being denied equal protection in education, and since education prepares a person for their future, this denial also limited the ability of blacks to move into the economic mainstream and improve their lives. In effect, it locked them into a cycle of poverty.

In 1954, the Supreme Court ruled in *Brown v. Board of Education of Topeka* that "separate but equal was no longer valid in the realm of public education." The decision was aimed at segregation intentionally created by state governments and local school boards, which was the case in the South. The decision set off more than a decade of struggles in the South, where integration was massively and violently resisted.

The Court's decision technically applied only to the five school districts, in four states and the District of Columbia, whose cases had been combined into this one suit. The great difficulty that developed in getting these schools to obey the law was an omen of things to come. One of the five school districts was the Prince Edward County Schools, Virginia. The Virginia legislature responded to the Court's decision by closing integrated schools, cutting off their funds, paying tuition grants to students in private nonsectarian schools, and providing state and local aid for such schools. In 1959, the Virginia Supreme Court held these actions to be in violation of the state constitution. The legislature then repealed the law and enacted a program under which school attendance was a matter of local option. With that power, and faced with a desegregation order, Prince Edwards County closed all its public schools and provided financial support for private segregated schools. In 1964, another suit against the county, *Griffin v. School Board of Prince Edward County*, reached the U.S. Supreme Court which agreed "that a state could have wide discretion in allowing local control over schools, but that the closure of the county schools was done for one reason and one reason only: to ensure, through measures taken by the county and state, that white and colored children would not, under any circumstances, go to the same school." After trying in vain to find out what the penalties for refusal would be, the county supervisors reopened the schools on an integrated basis in 1964.

This was minor in comparison to the integration battles with some school districts in the Deep South. The battle over the Little Rock, Arkansas, schools was probably the worst. Massive riots and violence led to the call for the U.S. Army to intervene. As Army troops escorted blacks into school and guarded them in class, one would think that someone might have questioned the wisdom of forcing the races together in such a manner. Integration was not only to be forced on the Southerners though, and in the 1960s it began to affect the North. There was, however, a big difference in the North. Their schools were segregated, but not because any government agency had caused them to be. It was because whites and blacks simply lived in different neighborhoods, so the neighborhood schools reflected the community and were not mixed.

In 1965, Massachusetts passed the Elimination of Racial Imbalance Act, the nation's first state law banning de facto segregation in the schools. This meant segregation which is inadvertent and without assistance of school authorities, and not caused by any state action, but rather by social, economic and other determinants. The law declared that any school with a minority population above 50% was racially imbalanced. Integration with white schools within the system was then required to achieve balance.

Little Rock: The beginning of brotherhood at the point of a bayonet.
(Reproduced from the Collection of the Library Of Congress.)

In Boston, a system with 94,000 students, 80 of the 200 schools exceeded this limit. The city schools were run by an all-white School Committee (school board) that was absolutely opposed to integration. It, along with the city's white politicians, refused to implement the law, which enmeshed the school system in protracted legal battles that lasted until federal court intervention in 1974.

Resistance by the city government certainly represented the views of a large percentage of the people, who were overwhelmingly white. The 1970 census showed only 17% of Boston was black. The city was traditionally an immigrant town. Over its rich history of three centuries, Boston was one of the major East Coast ports of entry for Europeans escaping economic turmoil and political oppression in their homelands. Each ethnic group established itself in a different neighborhood. When new people arrived, they moved into the neighborhood of their group. By the 1960s, the city was clearly divided into tight ethnic communities. They were mixing with the American "melting pot," but also maintaining the cultures of their ethnic heritages, of which they were immensely proud. Boston was a lower-middle-class workingman's town as well. With little hope for upward mobility, the people of these neighborhoods tended to focus their lives on their church and their neighborhood school. High school sports were an opportunity for success for the young and a social gathering point for the adults. Most were so loyal to their local community that they never left. In many cases, even the unemployed preferred to stay and wait for better times, rather than flee the neighborhood.

These ethnic neighborhoods were not, as liberals ignorantly suggested, the result of racism. As new immigrants entered the city, it only made sense for them to join with others of their ethnic group. They could join with people who spoke the same language and had similar customs, and could count on assistance in being assimilated into the new country. South Boston, known as the Southie District, and its Irish Catholics, was typical of these ethnic neighborhoods and, like the others, the residents were fiercely protective of their neighborhood and its institutions: the church and school. So when the state ordered desegregation, Boston balked. The people, especially in

Southie, angrily refused to cooperate. When the federal court ordered Phase I busing to mix the white schools of South Boston with the predominantly black schools of Roxbury, it was seen as a threat to all the neighborhoods represented. Whites worried that strangers were to be bused in while residents were bused out of the neighborhood, and feared that white girls were to be bused into dangerous high-crime black areas. The ensuing riots were then the acts of those defending their families and communities. These people would have reacted in a similar manner if it was any group that they were being forcibly integrated with, though in this case it was blacks. This doesn't mean that racist attitudes did not exist, because they did on the part of both whites and blacks. Most Bostonians were not racists when this crisis began, but many were when it ended.

In 1972, the NAACP filed a class-action suit against the Boston School Committee and the State Board of Education. The case, *Morgan v. Hennigan*, went before the federal district court of Judge Wendell Arthur Garrity in Boston. The NAACP claimed that Boston's schools violated the 14th Amendment's "equal protection clause." The case dragged on for two years.

Throughout the early 1970s, the state and the federal government attempted to push Boston schools into desegregating through busing. In 1973, the School Committee willingly gave up $65 million in federal funds rather than desegregate. By this point in the national school integration battle, the Department of Health, Education and Welfare (HEW) was spearheading the federal approach by withholding aid to segregated schools, under the 1964 Civil Rights Act. In the spring of 1974, reflecting popular opposition to busing, Louise Day Hicks led a protest march of over 20,000 whites to the Massachusetts Statehouse. Hicks, a member of the Boston City Council and former member of Congress, became an outspoken leader of the anti-busing forces. Faced with this pressure, Governor Francis Sargent proposed a compromise plan to integrate the schools through transfers and voluntary busing. The legislature approved the plan as a modification to the original 1965 law.

On June 21, 1974, Judge Garrity issued his decision in *Morgan v. Hennigan*. The court held that Boston maintained racially segregated schools. The city was ordered to eliminate segregation immediately. Garrity's plan, Phase I, affecting only the 80 racially-imbalanced schools, required the transfers of 45,000 of the city's students, including 18,000 that were to be bused. The plan was to be implemented for the 1974 school year. Phase II, though undefined, would be implemented in the fall of 1975. The people of Boston were outraged, as were their leaders who, faced with a federal court order, griped and complied. The school district proceeded with plans to implement the order. The logistical planning and training that was needed required a two-week delay in opening the schools. The schools did open on September 12, and then all hell broke loose.

On this first day back to school, angry crowds were everywhere. The police surrounded the buses carrying blacks into the white neighborhoods. The crowds chanted racial epithets, threw bottles and rocks at the buses and police, marched around the schools, and threatened violence. Inside the schools police lined the halls, creating a police-state atmosphere. Attendance was down sharply. In South Boston, only 13% of the students showed up for school as the anti-busing forces had called for a boycott. Not only whites stayed at home. Black parents, fearing the violence, kept their children at home. They were not any happier about this forced integration than the whites were. It was abundantly clear that the only person supporting this absurd race-mixing was Judge Garrity. This city-wide disruption continued at this level for several weeks and then escalated wildly.

During the week of October 14 -21, riot-equipped police were drawn into running battles with crowds all over town. Roving mobs of whites attacked and beat blacks who came into their neighborhoods, continued the rock- and bottle-throwing at blacks and police, set fires, and wrote "Kill Niggers" on numerous walls. Blacks responded, as gangs of youths attacked whites and police in South Boston and in Roxbury. White passersby were stopped and dragged from their cars and beaten, stores were looted, and racial fights broke out at several high schools. This continued through December and intermittently for another year-and-a-half.

The city government had the 2,000 members of the Boston Police to protect the bused students and deal with the violent riots. Even with this significant force the city began to lose control. Mayor White declared that things were out of hand and that the city could no longer guarantee safety. He then appealed to Judge Garrity for federal marshals. Garrity denied the request and suggested White get state and local assistance. This was done, and more forces were drawn together. They included 500 State and specially-trained riot police, 450 members of the National Guard, and even the Army's 82nd Airborne Unit, which was placed on alert just in case. The liberal notion of bringing the races together by force wasn't working out too well.

With the city in turmoil, the educational process was seriously affected as well. Violence in and around the schools, animosity in the classrooms, and fights and stabbings among students completely disrupted the schools, where teaching essentially came to a halt. In December, a white student was stabbed by a black during the day at a South Boston high school. The news spread immediately throughout the neighborhood. An angry mob of whites then converged and surrounded the school, trapping the black students inside. The police were barely able to sneak the blacks out the back way. The school was closed for four weeks in order to let tempers cool. Seven other schools were also closed due to violence.

Racial animosity flared out of control. The busing caused hatred on both sides. A white youth told reporters, "If I see a black guy on the street I'll hit him. It's not an argument about busing anymore. It's a race war." Another white youth was seen dancing on a street corner in front of a white crowd. He sang, in attempted jive, "Got to show my rhythm. I'm a nigger, man — where's my welfare, honkies?" The crowd roared with laughter. But these scenes were not funny. They were part of a social disaster caused by this federal judge with his ordered busing. Any sensible person could have predicted these results, but we were dealing with the federal courts!

During this school year, Judge Garrity exacerbated the situation when he issued his order for Phase II, which was to be implemented in September, 1975. Under this plan, busing would be expanded to the entire city and apply to all grade levels. The Boston School Committee again resisted. Mayor Kevin White, an opponent of busing but a realist when it came to federal court orders, stated that he would refuse to allow city resources to be used to comply with Phase II if the federal government did not provide assistance in dealing with the riots and violence. When the school committee voted 3-2 to reject the city-wide integration plan, Judge Garrity held the three opposing members in civil contempt. So much for democracy! The plan was finally instituted in September, 1975. The protests, problems and boycotts continued. Four weeks into the 1975 school year, the student population had dropped to 76,000, and 27% percent of them had not yet attended a single day of classes.

At this time the continuing and escalating protests against busing were organized by members of the Save Boston Committee, which included numerous school, neighborhood and government leaders. As their rights continued to be trampled, they decided to take the anti-busing movement to a national forum. The committee changed its name to ROAR (Restore Our Alienated Rights), and then began to do as the name suggested. Their feelings were clearly set out in their pledge which stated, "I don't pledge allegiance to the U.S district court and the dictatorship for which it stands, one nation, under Garrity, with liberty and justice for none."

ROAR organized an anti-busing conference that was attended by representatives from eight states and the District of Columbia. They moved to open chapters across the country and a lobbying group in Washington to push a constitutional amendment banning busing. Busing had indeed outraged the nation.

It seemed unconscionable to many people that a constitutional amendment would be required to prevent the government from forcing people to mix with other races. The government did have an interest in making sure that no government institution created segregation, as in the South, because this did violate the 14th Amendment. The approach there should have been to repeal all segregation laws in education and institute voluntary transfers and busing. But in the Northern states, segregation was simply the result of people choosing to live where they wanted. There was no violation of the equal protection clause, and here the government had no rightful recourse to any action.

The Constitution does not include specific rights to live where one wants or to go to the school of one's choice. Neither can these rights be legitimately construed from the document. But if the Constitution embodies anything, it is freedom from the abuses of government. It is the inherent spirit of the Constitution that is violated by busing. I certainly am not suggesting that government action should be based on the unwritten spirit of the Constitution, for if I did, I would be no better than the social-activist government officials and jurists who, in continually doing just that, have led us to such a desperate condition. But there is no freedom when a government can order its citizens to live in a particular place or to associate with certain individuals or groups. This is an intrusion into the private choices of the people, and is an area that should be absolutely off-limits to government. To do otherwise would dictate that government is more able than individual sentient beings to make such personal choices. Man has the free will to do as he pleases within commonly accepted boundaries. It certainly is within his right to make associations as he wishes without government intrusion. Allowing the government to have this authority is the prelude to true totalitarianism.

Maybe the most dramatic result of the court-ordered busing was the ensuing "white flight." In the first year of integration (1974-75 school year), 10,000 whites withdrew from the school district. In the second year 9,000 more left. These whites, for the most part, moved to the suburbs or to parochial schools. Many of them, however, stayed and went to private academies. Of these, some were lucky enough to get into existing private schools, but most went to hastily-set-up institutions. This was a trick the Bostonians learned from the Southern states in their battles against forced integration. In the South, more than 4,000 private white academies were established for whites fleeing integrated schools. This was civil disobedience at its best, and there wasn't a damn thing the impotent federal government could do about it. (Though they did make a feeble attempt, however, when they sicced the IRS on these schools and revoked their tax exempt status, which affected them not at all. In Boston nine such academies popped up in the white neighborhoods and enrolled several thousand white students.)

White flight occurred wherever forced integration was imposed. Besides removing whites from these poor city schools, it also greatly damaged the cities. Whites tended to be the company owners and skilled workers, and when they fled, they took their companies and skills to the suburbs and set up shop. This, of course, lowered the tax base of the cities, which then were forced to raise taxes in order to maintain the same level of services. This caused more people to leave, and the tax base continued to decline. Many Northern cities are now reaping this harvest. The only people who stay in these crime-ridden sewers are the ones who cannot afford to leave. They cannot support the city with their few tax dollars, so the city must cut services and fall into bankruptcy. These cities are in a vicious circle that will lead to their financial inability to function. Philadelphia and New York in 1991 are classic examples of the dying city.

Nonetheless, busing continued, and the protests tapered off. The people grudgingly accepted it as a *fait accompli*. Almost twenty years later, what impact has busing had on Boston? Did it achieve all its liberal goals? The obvious violence and hatred that were sparked drove a wedge between whites and blacks that is still felt today; white flight removed the whites to the suburbs, causing a huge disparity between the cities and their suburbs; great economic damage was done to the cities; and the people continue to be disillusioned over a government that would so blatantly abuse its power by forcing integration. There was also great damage done to the educational system. Boston schools now have a majority of minority students, and most of the schools are racially imbalanced. A huge sum of money was spent to implement the busing, money that could have been spent on the educational process. Instead of putting blacks into better schools, it caused the decline of the schools for everyone. Boston schools today are unsafe and ineffective, a part of the national collapse that can be directly attributed, in part, to busing. All in all, this attempt at liberal social engineering was a complete and resounding failure. Unfortunately, this failure was applied to many other Northern cities, all of which had the same results. For all the liberal propaganda today about the benefits of cultural diversity, it is very clear that the only thing which results from forced diversity is divisiveness.

By the mid-1970s, white flight had rendered impossible the task of fully integrating most big-city schools. There simply were too few whites to do the job. At that point, the federal courts looked to busing between city schools and suburban districts. It was required by the district courts in Richmond, Virginia and Detroit, Michigan. In order to avoid admitting defeat, the courts were willing to order students to ride buses for hours each day. One can only imagine the disaster that this obscenity against the people would have caused. Fortunately, on appeal, both cases were reversed. The Supreme Court, which steadfastly approved of busing to remedy past discrimination refused to extend it to the suburbs, though barely. Four Justices voted to allow this stupidity. Really, how do so many mental defectives end up on this Court?

It is interesting to speculate on the eventual course of events if the Court had approved of this practice. Assuming that the same or a higher level of violence and protests would occur, it must also be assumed that whites would again flee, this time to the countryside, leaving the suburban schools unable to be integrated. The courts, with the precedent of having expanded to the suburbs, would be empowered to expand again to the schools of the countryside. Then students could be bused several hours each way. This would mean the time a student spent in school would then rank third behind watching television and riding buses.

The only other solution to integration would be to somehow limit whites from fleeing due to integration, or ordering them to move back. Drawing the logic out this far brings one to a ridiculous and unlikely position, but in light of past government practices, I would not be at all sure that it couldn't happen. Once government embarks down the road to totalitarianism it does not turn back, but rather takes increasingly abusive steps.

Freedom demands that the people have a right to live where they want and to associate with whom they want. For the government to force citizens to do otherwise is an example of totalitarianism at its worst. Forced busing never should have been allowed in this country, and once started it should have been stopped when its disastrous consequences were revealed. This was exactly the kind of government abuse that the Founders fought against. Obeying the principles for which the Constitution stands would have prevented busing from happening, but after all, it is just a piece of paper.

CHAPTER 16
GUN CONTROL 1989

In recent years the government and courts have decided that achieving appropriate public policy is more important than following the Constitution. They see a social problem, and then with actions that violate the spirit and the letter of their constitutionally-assigned roles, they attempt to solve it. One of the greatest lessons learned from our war for independence was that liberty can only be protected when there are written laws, so that a government is not run by the whims of men. We are now in an era of judge-made law. The Constitution has become whatever they say it is. We have reached a point where the judiciary threatens the existence of the entire system. The people must put a stop to this before these bastions of stupidity put an end to our liberties.

Gun control is such a social issue. The courts have weighed the social ills of guns versus the Constitution, and found the document lacking. The Second Amendment guarantees the right to keep and bear arms. It doesn't take a Rhodes Scholar to read the words and the historical context of this amendment and see that it means the government may not interfere in the people's right to own guns, even machine guns or semi-automatics.

The American Revolution had numerous causes which occurred over many years. The last straw, which brought on the actual fighting, occurred in April, 1775. On the 18th, British forces marched out of Boston towards Concord, Massachusetts. Their goal was to capture the arsenal of weapons that the Americans had stockpiled there in case of hostilities with Britain. As tensions had increased, the Americans were preparing to defend themselves. The British solution

The Rape Of The American Constitution

was to deprive the Americans of their weapons and therefore make a revolution impossible. It was the usual approach followed by abusive governments.

The patriots who met the British on Lexington Green during the morning of April 19 knew that our liberties depended upon maintaining our ability to take and enforce them if necessary. Captain John Parker and his 70 men were drawn up to slow the British march on Concord, thus allowing the relocation of the American weapons. A short, confused engagement followed. The Americans suffered eight dead and ten wounded. As news of the attack spread, local militia soldiers rushed to Concord and defeated the British regulars, forcing them to retreat under constant attack to Boston. These first battles of the American Revolution were fought to protect our weapons. This accounts for the right to bear arms in the Second Amendment, second only in importance to our religious and political rights listed in the First Amendment.

The idea of gun control is a relatively recent phenomenon. The meaning of the Second Amendment has always been clearly understood and agreed upon until the last few years. Gun-control proponents generally have employed typical propaganda techniques, but they have increasingly turned to the wording of the Second Amendment to try to prove that the people do not have a right to bear arms. Their misinterpretation revolves around the phrase "well-regulated militia." They argue that this guarantees the right to bear arms only to the well-regulated militia, which in modern times is the National Guard. So, their argument goes, the only Americans who may bear arms are in the National Guard. This is nothing more than an attempt to confuse the issue before the illiterate American public. There are two arguments against such an interpretation, and both are obvious to anyone who analyzes the historical record. First, as the states came out of the American Revolution, they all established written constitutions, and every one forbade permanent standing armies. The modern National Guard is exactly the kind of standing army that was prohibited under these constitutions. The Americans had a serious and justified fear of standing armies which gave the government the ability to enforce its oppressive will, just as the

British had done. These prohibitions in the laws of the states lasted through the Articles of Confederation period, and had not changed when the Constitution was written in 1787. It is not logical to argue that these same persons, who were so fearful of a military enforcement power in the hands of the government, would write an amendment allowing just that.

The second argument focuses on the historical context of the term "militia." In the vernacular of the late 1700s, the "militia" referred to an armed group of citizen soldiers ready at a moment's notice to spring forth from their beds with their weapons to defend against whatever perils threatened their liberty. In 1791, Samuel Adams, a major revolutionary leader, said the Second Amendment meant "that every peaceable citizen could have a gun, because every citizen belonged to the militia." The group that confronted the British on Lexington Green and at Concord was at that time considered a well-regulated militia, though this in reality meant only slightly organized and hardly trained. Clearly, the original intent of the Second Amendment was to guarantee the right to bear arms to every citizen who, as a part of the militia, would then be able to defend his liberty when necessary. The Founders held the view that guns in the hands of the people are truly required to maintain a free state. That fact has not changed since 1791.

"There is no right, under the Second Amendment, to keep and bear arms pertaining to the individual." — Caroline Kennedy, a member of the nation's most renowned political family

2nd Amendment to the U.S Constitution
A well regulated militia being necessary to the security of a free state, the right of the people to keep and bear arms shall not be infringed.

"We did come away with a very good and patriotic feeling about how lucky we are to have a Bill of Rights and to live in this country and be as free as we are." — Caroline Kennedy

These quotes come from an interview with attorneys Kennedy and co-author Ellen Alderman in *USA Today,* Wednesday, April 17, 1991. The interview concerned their recent book *In Our Defense, the Bill of Rights.*

Frankly, if this is the level of knowledge possessed by a member of the nation's leading political family, even after researching the subject of the Bill of Rights, one must wonder if they read the American Bill of Rights. The only other explanation, that they believe this garbage, leaves one fearful for the future of America.

The question becomes: who did they fear as a threat to the freedom of the state? Was it outside influences? Was it our government? The answer is that they were, to some degree, afraid of both. In exploring the historical context, one notes that the Bill of Rights was passed in 1791, just eight years after the Treaty of Paris that ended the American Revolution against Britain. That was a war against our ruling government which had abused its power, as is so clearly shown in the Declaration of Independence. The Founders knew that strong government was bad and would have to be kept in line through the use of force, if necessary. If we had possessed no guns, our revolution would have been as unsuccessful as that carried out by the Chinese students during the summer of 1989.

The Founders were concerned about an outside threat, but their main fear was our own government. This was a fear that lies at the very heart of our entire Constitution. The whole system reflects the realization that strong government will attempt to abuse its power. The final solution to this is for the people to overthrow a despotic government, and for that the people will need guns. Guns, then, are the guarantors of our liberty; their need is clear. A government that abuses its power cannot be overthrown if the oppressed possess no weapons.

The Declaration of Independence states, "But when a long train of abuses and usurpations, pursuing invariably the same Object evinces a design to reduce them [the people] under absolute Despotism, it is their right, it is their duty, to throw off such Government, and to provide new Guards for their future security." We will irreversibly lose this right if we give up our guns, and we will be at the mercy of totalitarianism in no time at all.

The historical record, and indeed our future freedom, translates into the necessity of maintaining an absolute right to keep and bear arms. Left-wing elements recoil in horror at this idea, but they desire total government control and realize they cannot have it when the people are armed to the teeth. However, an absolute right to keep and bear arms does not mean a totally uncontrolled right. There are certain reforms that must be applied to gun ownership. They reflect the practical needs of our time, and do not violate the meaning of the Second Amendment. The following are steps that need to be taken:

1. A computerized background check on purchasers of guns. This must be a system that can operate within a few minutes and does not require a waiting period. This does not restrict the people's legitimate right to own guns. It would allow authorities to determine if any criminal or mental problems exist. Persons with such conditions should obviously be excluded from gun purchases.

2. Severe minimum penalties should be established for crimes committed with guns. Some states have already moved forward in this area with a five-year automatic sentence for these offenders.

3. Education programs that teach responsible gun ownership should be added to the school curriculum. The number of accidental deaths, especially among children, requires that this step be taken.

During the last 60 years, the government and left-wing elements have developed a variety of convenient excuses to claim that guns must be banned. It started with bans on machine guns, then sawed-off shotguns, various handguns, and more recently spread to semi-automatic assault weapons. The removal of guns in most countries has been done quickly, but our country has the Second Amendment to get around. With this in mind, gun-control advocates must follow a slow path to their goal. Attack one type of gun, use assorted horror stories to show the need for banning it, and get rid of one gun at a time.

James Brady, after taking a bullet in the 1981 assassination attempt on President Reagan, has become a voice committed to the removal of handguns. In 1991, Congress and the nation debated the merits of the so-called Brady Bill, which proposed a 7-day waiting period for the purchase of a handgun. Ironically, this bill was killed during the 1980s by none other than President Reagan, who was also shot in the same incident which wounded Brady.

Brady's crippled act, resulting from a head wound, plays well in the legislative halls and on television. The American people see a life shattered by a handgun, so they jump on the bandwagon of gun control. What these people need to remember is that guns don't kill people, people kill people. I hesitate to sound like another bumper-sticker, but this really is a truism. A waiting period is not the solution to the problem, as Brady and his wife claim. Going after the guns is not the solution to crime, as the criminal will resort to other means. What will we ban next? Knives, bats, clubs, cars, axes, hammers, ice picks, rope, bricks, screwdrivers?

The last line of defense against an abusive government.
(Southern Cross Publishing)

The 1980s, however, saw a more serious threat to gun rights, as several cities moved to prohibit handgun sales. In some cases, cities prohibited handgun ownership. Morton Grove, Illinois, has the infamous distinction of starting this trend. Similarly, New York City and Washington, D.C. passed the strictest gun laws in the nation. These have turned out to be utterly useless. The two cities have some of the worst gun problems in the world. Washington, D.C. was officially declared the murder capital of the world in the early 1990s. A fine reputation for the center of gun control. Yet liberals just don't seem to get it — banning guns simply does not work. The only successful approach would be harsh punishments for criminals using guns. Of course, liberals don't like punishment; they want to try to humanely rehabilitate all these poor criminals.

The most recent attack has been on semi-automatic rifles. In 1989, a lunatic, using such a gun, attacked a schoolyard in Stockton, California, killing and wounding several elementary-school students. This set off a national move to ban these guns. If it weren't so dangerous, the debate on this issue would be humorous. California responded with a law that banned the sale and manufacture of 55 types of military-style semi-automatic weapons in the state. People who lawfully owned them prior to June 1, 1989, were allowed to keep them, provided they registered them with the state. During the ensuing 18-month grace period for the registration, fewer than 7,000 of the estimated 300,000 such guns in California were registered. This amounts to 2% of the guns. Californians were afraid that this registration was the first step towards confiscation, and they might have been right. They are to be congratulated for this feat of civil disobedience. In another brilliant move, Los Angeles instituted a week-long ban on the sale of ammunition prior to New Year's Eve. It was designed to reduce random shooting into the air by revelers. Partyers simply went to neighboring communities or used their stockpiles, and fired away.

During the summer of 1994, Clinton and Congress finally managed to take their attack on semi-automatic rifles, by then referred to by the more ominous moniker of "assault weapons," to the federal level, with the passage of the Crime Bill of 1994. This utter charade included a ban on the sales of 19 types of assault weapons. These included the TEC-9, the AK-47, and the MAC-10. Interestingly, several American-made assault weapons were left off the ban list because the congressmen from the states where these guns were manufactured refused to support the bill. The bill barely passed, as Clinton gave away the farm in order to bribe congressmen with anything they wanted. I guess this reflects the sincerity of their concern about all assault weapons. This was a giant defeat for the Second Amendment and the American people. Unfortunately, this ban acts only as a precedent for future gun bans. It has no other effect. Law enforcement agencies report that less than 1% of all crimes involve an assault weapon, so the ban is certainly useless in affecting crime.

Time and time again the gun control proponents rely on two basic propaganda scripts. First, they point to all the innocent children mowed down by semi-automatic guns. When rhetoric is added to pictures of these scenes, this becomes convincing to many Americans. Second, they argue that these guns are not needed for hunting and they are therefore not entitled to constitutional protection. The amazing thing is that the anti-gun-control forces respond by claiming that they are valid hunting and sports weapons. The NRA does itself, and the Second Amendment, a great disservice when they take this position. What is lost in all of this is the fact that the Second Amendment does not say, "the right to keep and bear *hunting* Arms." Nor does the historical context have anything to do with hunting weapons. The amendment was to protect the people's right to own all weapons so that they could safeguard themselves from abusive governments.

In a December, 1991, CNN interview with former Supreme Court Chief Justice Warren Burger, celebrating the anniversary of the Bill of Rights, Burger claimed that "there is no right for the individual to bear arms." He went on to say that this was a fraud on the American people carried out by special-interest groups. There certainly is a fraud here; it is the fraud that was committed in giving this person a law degree with no understanding of constitutional law, and a fraud in allowing such an unqualified person onto the Court! For a Supreme Court Justice to come to this conclusion can only be the result of either a conspiracy to destroy the Constitution, illiteracy, or stupidity. Or maybe all three in Burger's case.

Frankly, gun control is not going to stop crime, and we can risk a few deaths like Stockton to maintain our absolute right to bear all arms. In the words of another famous bumpersticker, "They will take my gun away when they pry it from my cold dead fingers." That is a serious message which the government had better understand. The people will never give up their guns, and their right to use them to overthrow the government, should that become necessary. An attempt to remove the people's guns will justifiably lead to another revolution in this nation. These recent incidents add meaning to the warning of Thomas Jefferson that the only way the people can protect themselves from government is to overthrow it violently every 20 years. The language of the Second Amendment is so clear that it is amazing that we have this debate at all, but after all, the Constitution is just a piece of paper.

CHAPTER 17
THE DRUG WAR 1989

Today our country faces a dire threat related to drugs, but it is the government's response to them, and not the drugs themselves, that is the cause for alarm. The common folk have been led to believe any approach is worth the price if it is used to get rid of the drug menace. With such attitudes, it is no wonder that the drug prevention effort has led to some incredible trampling of the Constitution. Drug tests, denial of bail, Zero Tolerance, pre-trial seizure of assets, and unreasonable searches have been perpetrated on the American people and, just like Prohibition before it, the result is and will be failure, unless the Constitution is done away with completely. Continuation of the current policy could do just that, and be the end of our liberties, unless we accept the only sensible and logical alternative: drug legalization.

In 1919, the government, led by the forces of the temperance movement, began a "noble experiment" in dictating their view of moral behavior with the ratification of the 18th Amendment. This amendment outlawed the "manufacture, sale, or transportation of intoxicating liquors." It was the beginning of Prohibition. The push towards Prohibition had been building for many years. A great many social problems — including broken families and crime — were being blamed on alcohol. The temperance movement made it a political question of national import. The steamroller of moral activism swept the country and led to the proposal of the amendment in 1917. It was ratified by the states and added to the Constitution in 1919. This really was a misuse of the Constitution, which was designed as a

204

governmental system, not as a vehicle for promoting the moralizing of assorted fringe elements.

Prohibition lasted just thirteen years, until the 18th Amendment was repealed by the 21st Amendment in 1933. It was an absolute and complete failure. Its results were an increase in drinking, increased death from poisoned bootleg booze, prison-overcrowding problems from the huge numbers of people arrested for this minor crime, large numbers of law-enforcement agents accepting bribes or being involved in the trade itself, the creation of violent organized crime, and serious abuses of the people's constitutional rights. Does that sound at all like the results of the war on drugs? It should, because these conditions show Prohibition to be an exact parallel to the drug war. Any attempt to argue otherwise is the result of wishful thinking, or possibly excessive drug use.

Drugs, like alcohol, are addictive, and have created modern societal problems. Millions of Americans, including kids, are using; many die from drugs primarily due to uncontrolled quality; police are regularly arrested for involvement with drugs; levels of drug related crimes are dangerously high and rising; and we have resumed the serious threats to constitutional rights. We have indeed returned to Prohibition.

During Prohibition, state and federal authorities gave it their best effort for thirteen years and failed. Speakeasies popped up everywhere, bootlegging ran rampant, and prices rose sharply, causing thousands of honest people to become involved in the illicit production and distribution of alcohol. In their attempts to stamp out the illegal trade, the government resorted to a number of techniques that violated the letter and the spirit of the Bill of Rights. We owe wiretapping, warrantless searches of private homes, and other civil-rights abuses to the Prohibition period.

By 1933, the government had realized that the cause was lost. Huge numbers of people were openly disregarding the law. A government cannot afford to be recognized by its people as unable to enforce the law, because that promotes disregard of other laws. A strategic retreat was needed before disobedience of the laws got out of hand. In February, 1933, the 21st Amendment, repealing the 18th

Amendment, sailed easily through Congress and on to the states. Ratification was accomplished in a brief ten months. The "noble experiment," doomed from the start to be an ignoble failure, was over.

In the 1990s, our nation is on the same path and achieving the same results. The history of attempts to halt drug use began with the Harrison Act of 1914, which outlawed the use of several drugs. Immediately afterwards, drug prices skyrocketed, and a black market was created to satisfy the demand, a basic rule of capitalism. Since that time, drug use has continued at a constant level. Studies show that the same percentage of the population is using drugs now as in 1890. Apparently, a certain number will use drugs and alcohol whether they are illegal or not. One would get a different idea from listening to the government. It would seem that illegal drug use is affecting everyone. They would have us believe that all the problems this country faces are caused by such drug use. But this is nothing more than the usual deception aimed at blinding the people to the real problems our government cannot fix.

The government takes a peculiar view of certain drugs. In 1993, tobacco products killed more than 1,000 Americans a day, for a total of over 434,000 people; alcohol killed 125,000; while hard drugs killed an estimated 5,000 (estimates from the U.S. government). This reflects a set of misplaced priorities, especially since government subsidies keep the price of cigarettes low and affordable, and tax money flows in large amounts from cigarettes and alcohol. It is a fact that more Columbian children are killed each year as a result of the export of American cigarettes than American children are killed by Columbian cocaine. Our government hypocritically allows and promotes the use of drugs which bring in tax revenues, while attacking those that do not. Further, the supposed drug epidemic is only in the minds of those who have been brainwashed by the propaganda, those who see an opportunity to make political points, and those who wish to greatly increase government power at the expense of our liberties.

As during Prohibition, law enforcement has come up with some new methods to abuse our rights, along with a few of the old ones. The most offensive is drug testing. Government has led the way by claiming a need to test people in "sensitive" jobs, and this has been upheld by the courts. That led to a safety concern, which required testing for people entrusted with public safety: pilots, bus drivers, police officers, etc. The private sector jumped on the bandwagon and began testing employees and job applicants. Even many local convenience stores now test all applicants. The associated propaganda line ran that anyone who was not using drugs would not have anything to hide and would gladly submit to a drug test. So now we humiliate and inconvenience people until they prove themselves innocent.

Many people have sued their employers for violating the 4th Amendment prohibition against unreasonable searches and seizures. They have consistently been defeated. The courts have held that the Constitution limits governmental actions, not those of private companies. Well, isn't that ironic! The government has steadfastly prevented employers from discriminatory practices in the workplace in order to prevent violations of other constitutional rights, and with federal legislation based on the 4th Amendment they could prohibit drug testing. They don't, because it lends support to government testing and the expansion of intrusive government power that goes with it.

The 4th Amendment says, in part, that, "the right of the people to be secure in their persons, houses, papers, and effects, against unreasonable searches and seizures, shall not be violated." Blood and urine samples necessary for testing are unquestionably a part of the "person" and therefore protected, supposedly, under this amendment. Testing proponents, when confronted with this argument, reiterate that no honest citizen will mind a drug test — the basic "guilty-until-proven-innocent" approach. By inference, they are saying that the opponents of testing are on drugs. This is readily accepted by the people, and the whole constitutional issue is skirted. On a higher plane, testing proponents attempt to claim that these tests are not unreasonable searches and seizures, and so do not violate the 4th Amendment. But there are two facts that *do* make them unreasonable. First, when someone is told to urinate in a bottle while being watched, that crosses the line into unreasonableness. A witness has become a part of the process, as many people found ways to falsify the test sample with untainted urine. The solution from the government results in a humiliating exposure to a bureaucrat. The second problem is the fact that there is a violation of a fundamental principle of law here. English common law has given us the tradition of "probable cause." In other words, before an action like a search can take place, there must be some proof, some reason to believe a law has been broken. However, for the overwhelming majority of those tested, there is no cause at all. This reminds one of the old pirate who severely beat a crewman who had committed no error. When questioned as to why, he responded that this was preventative discipline.

The motivation behind drug testing is that people will stop using drugs if they know they may face random testing, with their jobs on the line. That is logical, but not constitutional. The final argument from testing proponents asserts that testing may indeed violate the 4th Amendment, but getting rid of drugs is in society's best interest, and therefore more important. There is, unbelievably, popular support for such a position. In a December, 1991, American Bar Association survey, it was found that 50% of the people were willing to give up some or all of their constitutional rights in order to win the war on drugs. The survey also found that 41% would allow police searches of homes without a warrant. This stupidity, which is reflective of the Supreme Court as well, would not even warrant a response if it weren't so dangerous. Preventing drug use is not worth destroying the Bill of Rights. One can only hope that the people figure this out before the nation is turned into an irreversible police state.

Related to drug testing are other 4th Amendment violations. Searches of homes and cars without warrants are increasing to alarming proportions. This has been made possible as the Rehnquist court continues to expand exceptions to the Exclusionary Rule. This rule prohibits the introduction, at trial, of evidence that was illegally obtained. Consistent and defiant police abuse of 4th Amendment rights led the courts to develop this appropriate response. In the 1991 Crime Bill, Congress and the President debated over language that would allow courts to use illegally obtained evidence, thus contravening the Exclusionary Rule.

We have also seen the use of "drug smuggler profiles" at airports and other points of entry. A series of characteristics that appear to be common to those smuggling drugs make up these profiles. Persons fitting these descriptions are then detained and searched. The government officially denies their use, but anyone who doubts their existence should grow long hair, wear ratty clothes, tightly clasp their carry-on bag, and look shifty and nervous while disembarking last from a plane arriving from Columbia and see how long it takes to be introduced to the joys of a body-cavity search. If even one innocent person is harassed in this manner, it is one too many.

In a June, 1991 case, the Supreme Court ruled on the mass search of passengers on buses, trains and planes. In this case from Broward County, Florida, heavily armed police had been regularly boarding interstate buses and trains at station stops, where they moved down the aisles asking passengers for their tickets and identification. They also asked to look in passengers' bags. Now, the only thing missing from this throwback to the Gestapo is the leather trench coat. The Florida Supreme Court declared the searches an illegal violation of the 4th Amendment and called them better suited to "totalitarian states." The court added that "this is not Hitler's Berlin, nor Stalin's Moscow, nor is it white supremacist South Africa where badge-wielding police can stop travelers at will." Apparently it is, because the U.S. Supreme Court overruled this decision in *Florida v. Bostick* (1991). Justice O'Connor, writing for a 6-3 majority, declared that such searches were constitutional so long as "a reasonable passenger would feel free to say 'no' to the police." As if one would! Unbelievably, O'Connor added that these searches do not violate the 4th Amendment because they do not involve the use of force by the police. This is exactly the kind of harassment by police that this amendment was designed to prevent. Maybe she should try reading the amendment, because it says no searches without a warrant based upon probable cause. It does not mention anything about searches being okay as long as no force is used.

Three recent abuses by the government include Zero Tolerance, pre-trial seizure of assets, and denial of bail. The Zero Tolerance policy led to the immediate seizure of any and all property where drugs were found. In one example, the owner of a large yacht had given control to a crew for delivery to a new port. The Coast Guard, for no particular reason, boarded the ship and searched it. They found a few tiny fragments of marijuana in a trashcan. The owner was not present, apparently the substance belonged to one of the hired sailors. The ship was seized and sold by the government at auction. There was no court action taken against the owner, his property was simply sold. The government, of course, kept the proceeds. This is deprivation of property without due process of law in violation of the 5th Amendment, on top of the unreasonable search and seizure violations of the 4th Amendment.

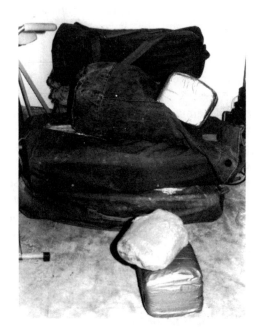

350 pounds of marijuana: Preventing this is not more
important than the Constitution.
(Southern Cross Publishing)

The government has also begun to seize assets of persons, arrested for drug possession, before their trials, before they are proven guilty! Besides being a clear violation of the 5th Amendment, it is also an obscene trampling of most of the principles of American law. The intent of the program is to deprive people of their ill-gotten gains from the drug trade. In many instances it is intended to harass. An intended side-effect is that once relieved of assets, it is hard to pay for the services of a lawyer good enough to get an acquittal.

Judges have increasingly, at government prosecutors' requests, denied bail to drug defendants. The claim is that this prevents them from skipping the country, but it also severely impairs their ability to assist in the preparation of their defense. The 8th Amendment prohibits excessive bail, meaning bail that is so high that it can not possibly be met. This would obviously apply to denying bail as well. These three practices have in common provisions which punish for an arrest, not a conviction, and that is another dangerous trend. This situation really is quite amazing. It seems that we have turned back the hands of time to 1775, the only difference being that the abuses of the British government are now being carried out by the American government.

Other avenues being explored by the government currently include giving permission to the military to shoot down suspicious planes nearing this country. The military is already taking an active part in interdictions along the borders. There has been discussion of using the military as a national police force. Police state, here we come! This is a situation that deserves serious attention from the American people. Anyone who has read the Supreme Court's decision in *Korematsu v. United States* (1944) should understand the implications of this. There is precedent from this Japanese-American internment case that gives the military the power to ignore the Constitution when they see the urgent need to do so, even in areas not under martial law. Obviously, the country is threatened by these abuses. A new direction is needed.

The only solution to the drug problem is legalization. The war on drugs is already lost. The effort in Washington, D.C., during 1989-90, is absolute and final proof of this fact. Our nation's capital city, also known as the murder capital of the world, was targeted for a maximum effort by the federal government to stop drugs. This attack was led by then-Drug Czar William Bennett. The District of Columbia program involved billions of dollars and a great influx of manpower — the best they could give in a one-year effort. At the end of that period, the government studied the results and found that they had not affected drug use by even one percent. Nationally the picture is much the same, as marijuana has become the largest cash crop in some regions. It should be clear that the current methods are a failure. This drug war never had a chance to be won in a country that still has some protection from the Bill of Rights. A police state could end the use of drugs and, even though our government has tried to turn this country into one, they have failed, so far.

Drugs should be made legal, but within a framework similar to that which controls alcohol. Government regulations covering quality will solve one of the real killers in the current drug world: death from overdose or poisoned drugs. The danger element and limited supply have always kept the price high, but legalized drugs will remove this condition, and the price will drop. A major benefit of this policy would be a drastic drop in drug related crime. A significant percentage of crimes, especially home burglaries, are committed by people attempting to get money for drugs. It is only logical that a cut in price would mean that addicts would not need such huge sums of money to maintain their habits. Legalization would also take control of this trade away from the highly-violent organized-crime groups. Government taxes, like those on alcohol, could net a large sum. This money could then be used to sponsor drug education programs and rehabilitation facilities.

The greatest protest against legalization comes from the religious community. They realize that drugs are, for many people, an escape from the drudgery of their lives. The church wants everyone to be miserable so that they will be susceptible to the nonsense spewed forth in pulpits every Sunday morning. They also realize that money spent on drugs leaves little for the money grubbing that is a major part of every church service. As Marx said, religion is the opium of the masses, and the religionists don't want any competition from real opium. With these motivations in mind, their objections should be dismissed.

There are two basic arguments against drug legalization: that the use of drugs will go up dramatically, and that our children will all be doing drugs. Both arguments are flawed. Now alcohol is legal, and it is estimated that only about 10% of the population has a problem with it. In other words, alcohol is legal, and not everyone is an alcoholic. Granted, 10% means a lot of lives ruined by alcohol, but as in the Prohibition days, banning it would only make the problem worse. In the modern era of media glorification and lack of drug-education programs, it is amazing that things aren't worse. The post-Prohibition period also proves that drug use would not rise. As far as the children go, the same kind of laws that control availability to alcohol should apply to kids. A uniform minimum age of 18 should be the rule for drugs and alcohol. If a person is old enough to vote and be drafted to go to war, then they are old enough to drink or take legalized drugs. There must be strict penalties for violating this and for anyone who sells to a minor. A first offense should cause a store to lose their license to sell, and pay significant fines. Another required reform is the end to all promotion and advertising for alcohol on television, and in all other media sources that kids are exposed to. Every week I deal with 6th- and 7th-grade students in our school district anti-drug program, and every week these 11- &12-year-old kids tell me they think drinking is cool because that's what the commercials say. This has to be stopped!

Support for legalization should in no way be construed as support for drugs. The end of drug use is a desirable goal. Legalization is just a response to the current failed approach. Once the huge profit incentive is removed, along with the "forbidden fruit" phenomenon, we can direct our efforts to attending to the underlying causes of drug use. Through self-esteem based education programs beginning in the early elementary years, and running through high-school graduation, we can achieve that goal.

One can only hope that this new direction is the course we set, for the failure to do so leads down the road to a police state. The outlook is not bright. In the words of Ludwig von Mises, "No paternal government whether ancient or modern, ever shrank from regimenting its subjects' minds, beliefs, and opinions. If one abolishes man's freedom to determine his own consumption, one takes all freedom away." The Constitution was designed to preserve freedom, but after all, it is just a piece of paper.

CHAPTER 18
FLAG BURNING 1989-90

The U.S. Supreme Court has made two rulings on flag burning in recent years, both of them correct constitutional decisions. It seemed, momentarily, that we might be actually heading back to following the Constitution as it was intended. That was, until a patriotic President (remember patriotism is always the last refuge of a scoundrel), a politically motivated Congress, and the typically ignorant American people got involved.

The whole affair began in Dallas at the 1984 Republican National Convention when Gregory Lee Johnson, a member of the Communist Youth Brigade, burned an American flag outside the convention hall. He was making a political protest about the sorry state of affairs in this country, and demanding change. The burning of a flag violated a Texas statute, and he was arrested. The case came before the federal courts, challenging the Texas law as a violation of First Amendment free speech. In *Texas v. Johnson* (1989), the Supreme Court ruled that such a political protest was protected by the First Amendment, and his conviction was overturned.

For a change, the Court made a correct ruling, for this is exactly the kind of thing that the First Amendment was designed to protect. One of the most important principles underlying this country is protection for political dissent. Great latitude must be given those who oppose the government, no matter how offensive their protests might be. Former Supreme Court Justice Robert Jackson once noted in a free speech case that, "If the First Amendment were only designed to protect inoffensive speech it would be pointless." Some argue that free speech means only that which is spoken, a typical argument from those who do not understand the Constitution. In the context of the Bill of Rights, the meaning of Free Speech is closer to freedom of expression, especially expression in a political sense. All the methods of protest used by the colonists were to be protected by the First Amendment. These included speeches, marches, demonstrations, flag burnings, or the burning of effigies of British political leaders. The Johnson protest was a political protest and, as such, was protected by the First Amendment. The Supreme Court agreed.

This is protected free speech.
(Southern Cross Publishing)

Of course it did not stop there. The country panicked over the decision. Polls showed 86% of the American people disagreed and wanted flag burning outlawed. This gave rise to a move to amend the Constitution and overrule the Supreme Court. With poll numbers like these, it was inevitable that some members of Congress would see this as a chance to grandstand and grab some credit for trying to protect the symbol of our country. The political speeches began immediately. The rhetoric reminded one of the old "America — love it or leave it" nonsense of a previous era.

The Republicans, to no one's surprise, proposed a constitutional amendment to prohibit the desecration of the American Flag. In the July, 1990, edition of The *Nation* magazine, an amusing editorial really outlined the stupidity of this idea. Paraphrased somewhat, it went like this:

This law will ban the desecration of the American Flag, but what is the American Flag? What if someone burns an old flag with 48 stars, should they go to jail? Or what about burning a photograph of the American Flag? How about a person who makes a photocopy of it, faxes it to a friend who burns the copy? And if someone wrote the words "The American Flag" on a white piece of paper and burned it, would they go to jail? What if you burn a book that includes instructions on how to make an American Flag? After all a lot of people believe that life begins at conception. What of the man who conjures up an image of the American Flag and mentally torches it? Finally what of the little kid whose birthday cake has those little American flags on it and he puts a candle to one of them, will he go to jail?

The thing that is not funny about this is that some of the patriotic fanatics out there *would* put all these people in jail.

President George "Read my lips, I lied" Bush also jumped on the political-glory bandwagon. Bush specialized in cheap demagoguery, so this was a tailor-made situation to garner some headlines. Bush and the majority claimed that the flag must not be burned because it is our sacred symbol which, during our history, many Americans have died to protect.

George "Read my lips, I lied" Bush
(Reproduced from the Collections of the Library Of Congress.)

What have Americans actually died for in America's wars?

WAR	AMERICAN REASON FOR FIGHTING
War of 1812 (1812-1814)	American desire to take Canada and Florida, British seizure of American ships, Indian trouble stirred up by British. (2,000 Americans killed)
Mexican War (1846-1848)	When American attempt to buy Mexican land in New Mexico and California failed, the U.S. invaded Mexico and took the land. (13,000 killed)
Spanish-American War (1898)	American imperialism desired Spanish lands in Cuba, Puerto Rico, and the Philippines. (2,000 killed)
World War I (1917-1918)	American need to protect capitalist trading partners in Europe. (112,000 killed)
World War II (1941-1945)	American need to protect capitalist trading partners in Europe. Response to Japanese sneak attack which was provoked by the United States. (405,000 killed)
Korean War (1950-1953)	Needless paranoia over communism. (54,000 killed)
Vietnam War (1965-1974)	American imperialism. Needless paranoia over communism. (58,000 killed)
Gulf War (1990)	A President who wanted to break his reputation as a wimp and to improve his re-election chances. (200 killed)

If we look closely at the foreign wars in which America has taken part since its independence, we see just how many have been fought to protect America and our liberty. It must be said that America has not, on even one occasion, entered a war to protect this country. Even the attack on Pearl Harbor which brought us into World War II was provoked by the United States. We interfered in Japanese affairs, threatened her, caused damage to her economy with a peacetime economic embargo, and forced her to defend herself. And, while some would debate that point, it is without question that during World War II there was never even a remote possibility of defeat at the hands of the Japanese. That nation simply wanted to prevent us from continuing our aggressions aimed at her. It is interesting to note that as soon as the U.S. joined that war, our leaders sent all of our resources against Germany first.

There is still much debate about Roosevelt's involvement in the disaster at Pearl Harbor. In the best case scenario, Roosevelt knew of the impending attack and allowed it to take place in order to shake the American people out of their isolationism and to get America into the European war to save Britain. In the worst-case scenario, he assisted in the arrangement of mass destruction at Pearl Harbor so as to guarantee serious loss of life. Nonetheless, we entered the war with our fullest might against Germany in order to protect our capitalist trading partners in Western Europe.

So the argument that we must protect our flag in reverence for all those who died defending it must fall. Our military personnel died for imperialist economic reasons, as well as paranoia. It must also be pointed out that it is the Constitution, not the flag, that is and should be the symbol of this nation. Presidents and soldiers take an oath, swearing allegiance to the Constitution, not the flag. The Constitution has given us our liberties and allowed this country to achieve greatness. It is much more important than a piece of cloth.

Logic and history notwithstanding, the debate continued and the battle to amend the Constitution moved into Congress. The Republicans supported this unwarranted defilement of the Bill of Rights, while many Democrats were opposed. The bottom line was that in more than 200 years the Constitution has only been amended eighteen times (the first ten amendments were ratified together, followed by 17 others), and none of them have affected the Bill of

Rights. Democrats showed real courage by standing against the amendment and the Republican threats to develop 30-second attack commercials against anyone who opposed them. The entire episode began to sound like the McCarthy Era all over again. Surprisingly, the Democrats ignored the flag-burning amendment, and passed a bill to ban flag burning that supposedly got around the constitutional issues involved. On the day this new law went into effect, protesters across the country lit up their flags, were arrested, and the legal challenges began anew. The Supreme Court ruled that this law also violated the First Amendment, and back to Congress it went. This time it was different. The American people had gone back to their soaps and sitcoms. They weren't interested. Maybe they had realized this was all a game being played out by a lying President and the incompetent members of Congress who want to keep the people's attention from the real problems, such as the S&L scandal, the deficit, the education crisis, and so on. Nonetheless, the constitutional amendment was reintroduced into Congress, and it began to work its way through the process. It was finally defeated in both houses by the Democrats.

The battle may not yet be over. The Republicans threatened to use the other method of amending the Constitution described in Article V, having the states call a new Constitutional Convention. A new convention, like the one held in 1787, would have the power to change any part of the Constitution or throw the whole thing out and start again. That's a terrifying thought — a Constitutional Convention made up of Hillbilly Clinton, Henry Cisneros, Jimmy Carter, George "Read my lips, I lied" Bush, Ronald Reagan, Mario Cuomo, Joe Biden, Ted Kennedy, Howard Metzenbaum, Tom Foley, Jim Wright, Pat Robertson, Jerry Falwell, Randall Terry, Jesse Jackson and other distinguished career politicians. The Founders would turn in their graves at the thought of these "persons" messing with the Constitution. Fortunately, the people don't seem to have any real interest in this, at this time. Maybe they realize the absolute nightmare that would result. Let's hope this continues to be the case. This whole affair would not have occurred if people simply understood and followed the Constitution, but after all, it is just a piece of paper.

William "dumbass incompetent hillbilly" Clinton
(Reproduced from the Collections of the Library Of Congress.)

CHAPTER 19
THE INCOME TAX
AND THE IRS 1990

A steep progressive income tax was one of the ideas advanced by Karl Marx for destroying the bourgeoisie. Never would one have thought that this principle of communism would be established in the United States, let alone added to the Constitution. The Founders originally added a constitutional provision prohibiting the government from levying direct taxes, unless based proportionately on population, and they had strong reasons for so doing. It took the 16th Amendment to change that fact in 1913. Since the addition of this amendment, the conditions feared by the Founders have arisen; we have returned to "taxation without representation" carried out by the IRS. Better known as the American Gestapo, this most feared and despised institution, along with the offensive tax system that has developed, is a good example of unchecked power. The time has come to correct the Constitution, repeal the 16th Amendment, and abolish the IRS.

The Founders had a profound fear of the taxing power. They had witnessed its abusive nature for many years while under British colonial rule. As a result of numerous tax acts, hard-earned colonial wages were siphoned off to British fat-cat businessmen who profited from laws passed by a Parliament completely lacking American representatives. This tax burden had robbed the American economy and slowed growth, so that the mother country could get rich. As Supreme Court Chief Justice John Marshall would later say, "the power to tax involves the power to destroy." With these sentiments in mind, the Second Continental Congress, when approving the Articles of Confederation in 1781, totally denied the taxing power to our new national government. However, the Articles failed, for largely economic reasons, and it became clear, in the words of Alexander Hamilton, that "money is one of the essential agencies of government."

During the Constitutional Convention, the solution, as was so often sought by the Founders in their attempts to correct the weaknesses in the Articles of Confederation, was to allow the government to possess a power within certain controls. The taxing power was put in the hands of the legislative branch, with the requirement that revenue bills start in the House of Representatives. This meant that the house with the closest contact to the people would control revenue raising. Presumably, then, the people could exercise control through their representatives. Direct taxes were discussed at the Constitutional Convention, and they were expressly forbidden (Article I, Section 9, Clause 4) unless they were based proportionately upon population. Such taxes were forbidden because they had the potential to become abusive, unfair, and generally gave more power to the government than the Founders were prepared to give following their experiences with Britain. A definition of "direct taxes" was requested at the convention, but as James Madison's notes reported, "no one answered." The traditional belief has been that the Founders understood this to be a tax placed directly upon the people, which would then include income taxes. The Supreme Court has at times disagreed with that view, but the definition has found wide acceptance since 1895.

In two early cases, the Supreme Court held a very narrow definition of direct taxes that left open several possibilities that the Founders had not intended. In *Hylton v. United States* (1796), the Court held that taxes on expenses or consumption were indirect taxes. Other language in the opinion showed that the Justices considered direct taxes to include only taxes on land and poll taxes. In 1861, to meet the financial needs of the Civil War, the government passed its first income tax. Its constitutionality was tested in *Springer v. United States* (1881), where the Court supported the narrow position of the *Hylton* case and decided that an income tax was not a direct tax and therefore escaped the constitutional proportionality requirement in Article I. In 1894, the government again taxed income, and this was tested in the courts. In *Pollock v. Farmer's Loan and Trust Company* (1895), the Court held the law unconstitutional, as it violated the proportionality requirement. This decision has been widely construed to mean that income taxes were direct taxes which must be proportional. The Court had finally interpreted the term by its correct original meaning. Possibly the best indicator of original intent is the opinion of Justice Paterson in the *Hylton* case. William Paterson, a delegate to the Constitutional Convention, was the only member of the Court deciding this case to have had that distinction. As such, his views must carry great weight. His opinion in the case stated that "indirect taxes are circuitous modes of reaching the revenue of individuals. This would include all taxes on expenses or consumption." The inverse of this definition would explain direct taxes as those with direct modes of reaching an individual, and this would include an income tax which is taken directly from an individual's wages which have been exchanged for the use of his labor. If Paterson had provided this definition at the Constitutional Convention, the Founders' intent would have been clearer.

This was clearly the definition in 1909, because the government was forced to propose a constitutional amendment to get around the question of direct taxes. The 16th Amendment gave Congress the power to collect income taxes without being based upon population. This amendment then was placed in the rare position of overturning an express and fundamental desire of the Founders.

The amendment process was designed to allow correction of deficiencies in the Constitution as time progressed. The Founders' fears of the taxing power are as valid now as they were in 1909 and 1787. The amendment process should not be used to change a major underlying principle that was expressly written into the Constitution. Our generation has not faced totalitarian abusive government on the scale of the British during the colonial period. Not yet, at least. Nor have we been forced to endure the hardships of an eight-year war on our shores in a fight to preserve our liberty. The Founders learned first-hand the lessons of abusive government, and we should not change these principles.

The amendment process, though, has always been dominated by the elitist power structures that run this country. An income tax was seen, during the Progressive years (early 1900s), as a way to raise large amounts of revenue, and to increase government spending and power in many areas. More revenue means more administration, more control, more power. Congress and the states easily passed a measure that was to benefit the very levels of government that were entrusted with its passage. There was also a feeling that the law would allow taxing of the rich to provide assistance to lower classes, a desirable goal for the Progressives. The result was ratification of the 16th Amendment in 1913.

The 1913 income tax amounted to 1% for incomes in excess of $3,000 ($4,000 for married couples), with surtaxes up to 6% on incomes from $20,000 to $500,000. In 1950, an average U.S. family of four sent 2% of its income to the federal government. By 1990 the figure was up to 24%. Taxes now account for the largest single item of a family's budget. In 1991, the average taxpayer had to work a record 128 days — January 1 through May 8 — to earn enough to pay his taxes. The so-called Tax Freedom Day falls later every year, as the government steals a larger share of the people's hard-earned salaries. Personal income for 1991 rose by only 3.7%, while the tax take rose 6.6%. For every dollar sent to Washington, 14 cents goes to pay interest on the national debt, now approaching $5 trillion, a problem that the incompetent Congress seems totally incapable of handling. This is, of course, only one example of government waste that creates the need for these high taxes.

The current system does not tax the lower classes, and the rich are able to avoid their share. The result is an oppressive and intolerable burden on the middle class. The continuation of such a system brings into question whether representative government really works. Since the overwhelming majority of the people are outraged at the tax system and their representatives do nothing, the answer must be an unequivocal "NO!"

And what about the bureaucratic nightmare that was established to collect the income tax? The IRS is as feared by Americans as the Gestapo was by the German people during World War II. A condition such as this that causes the people to live in fear is unfortunate and unacceptable in this country. Like the colonists before us, it is time for today's Americans to resist abuse and tyranny from our government. Patriot Samuel Adams, in the face of this current tyranny, would argue that it is the responsibility of every American to cheat on taxes, to hold them up as long as possible, to stall, to take every waiver or extension, to sue, and to violently protest until we destroy this perversion of our system.

The IRS is now unchecked by any branch of government. They have the power to confiscate any and all of a person's property, to seize bank accounts, to harass and to intimidate. If a person takes on the IRS in court they are bound to come out the loser. Even if the IRS is wrong, the lawyer's fees are destructive to most people.

In 1973 the Congressional Joint Committee on Internal Revenue Taxation issued a report entitled "Investigation into Certain Charges of the Use of the Internal Revenue Service for Political Purposes," which revealed two lists of hundreds of celebrities and politicians viewed as "enemies" by the IRS. These lists included John Wayne, Bill Cosby, Gregory Peck, Paul Newman, Barbara Streisand, Joe Namath and Walter Mondale. Other lists since discovered included Sammy Davis, Jr., Lucille Ball, Frank Sinatra and Ronald Reagan. The IRS purpose in attacking celebrities was to ensure maximum exposure to the nation. This "free publicity" was designed to scare the American people into voluntary compliance with the tax laws. It has worked only too well.

The IRS also uses domestic terrorism to further intimidate the people. On February 20, 1980, more than 30 heavily-armed IRS Special Agents burst into a peaceful home in an Amish community in Oakland, Maryland, bearing M-16 rifles, shotguns, and tear gas.

On November 28, 1984, IRS agents entered a Detroit, Michigan, day-care center and herded approximately 30 young children into a room. The parents were not allowed to take their children home until they turned over cash, checks, or promissory notes to handle taxes allegedly owed by the day-care center.

On April 10, 1986, a pack of IRS agents swarmed into the home of a family in Idaho Falls, Idaho, and assaulted a man. His pregnant wife went into premature labor immediately following the incident, resulting in the death of one of her twins. The IRS agents had no warrant, and the couple's taxes were not in question.

In May, 1990, a Minnesota couple received a $6,601 refund check from the IRS. This was a godsend to this couple who were unemployed with three children and bills amounting to about $7,000. As they had already received their refund for the year, the couple checked with the IRS to see if a mistake had been made. After numerous calls and two letters from the IRS assuring the couple that the check was theirs, they cashed it and paid their bills. Then in January, 1991, the IRS said that the refund had been a mistake, and that the couple owed the entire amount within 10 days, and that they would be responsible for penalties and interest. At this same time, two more letters arrived from the IRS saying the refund was correct and the money was theirs to keep. Then other letters came warning them that their house, car, and other property assets would be seized if they didn't pay up. A costly nine-month battle in the media and in court then ensued before the IRS admitted a mistake and backed down.

In another 1990 incident, a California man was involved in a fight with the IRS. The agency claimed that a large amount of additional tax, interest, and penalties were due. The individual took the case to court, and after several legal rounds was bankrupted by the legal fees. His family's life in shambles, he finally committed suicide to allow his wife to have some money from insurance to prevent her from suffering through poverty. Further review in court noted that the IRS had been in error. The man had owed nothing.

In 1993, the IRS went after a Louisiana woman for $120,000 in back taxes. However, it was her employer's taxes she was being held liable for. The IRS used a new law against her, under which employees can be stuck with the employer's federal payroll tax bill if they have any responsibility for company finances. The woman involved here performed clerical duties such as signing company checks. The irony is that this woman is the one who tipped off the IRS that the company owners were dodging the payroll taxes. These are just a few examples of the everyday kind of abuse that is carried out by the American Gestapo. In a fitting end to these matters, the law does not allow one to sue the IRS in such cases. Is this justice? Does this give anyone the right to be proud of this country?

In a recent Congressional investigation, it was discovered that the IRS information lines gave out wrong tax information to approximately one out of every five people who called for assistance. The survey showed an accurate reply rate of 80% in 1991, up from 77% for 1990. It is comment enough that the government has created a system that is so complicated that it cannot even be understood by the very agency empowered to administer it. Ironically, if one receives incorrect information from the IRS and files a return based on that information, that person is liable for penalties and interest for the mistake. An IRS spokesman nonchalantly responded to the survey results by saying, "We're getting better."

As if the abuses against the people are not enough, recent Congressional investigations have found a pattern of improper and unlawful conduct by a significant number of senior IRS officials. In a Cleveland case, the head of the criminal investigation division was the subject of several probes for spending government money on alcohol and drunken excursions in IRS vehicles, including a DeLorean and a speedboat. In a Los Angeles case, an IRS investigator allegedly launched harassing IRS investigations on numerous competitors of Guess Jeans. Apparently he was associated with officers of this company. This agent also, it seems, tried to discourage an IRS investigation into Guess finances, because his friends at Guess had offered him a job after he retired. Interestingly, a recent IRS survey of its top executives and managers revealed that only 47% feel the need to be honest when testifying before a Congressional committee. With ethics such as these it is no wonder that the organization is hopelessly abusive, corrupt and incompetent.

The federal government is not the only government entity that has a taxation problem. Living in Harris County, Texas, I am burdened with direct taxation by the City of Friendswood, Harris County, the Harris County Hospital District, the Harris County Flood Control District, the Harris County Department of Education, the Port of Houston Authority, the Galveston County Education District, the Clear Creek Independent School District, the State of Texas and the federal government. These are just the taxes I get a bill for. There are, of course, endless hidden taxes as well on utilities, clothes, food, entertainment and everything else. Every one of these tax entities is run by a different governing body. It was a typical year in 1992 when every single one of them raised taxes. They did so because every single one of them was faced by a deficit due to their inability to work within a budget.

As the American people become increasingly angry over these schemes, government has been forced to use deception to gain new revenues. Aware that the people may revolt over taxes, as occurred with California's Proposition 13 in the 1970s, taxing authorities are reluctant to raise taxes directly. Their new approach is to use an appraisal district and indirectly raise taxes. In Texas counties, the members of the Commissioner's Court are the elected county representatives. Each year they trumpet their success in keeping the tax rate low. However, it is common knowledge that the Commissioners secretly order their appraisal district to raise the appraised value of property in the county each year. In most years this increase averages 15%. This amounts to an indirect increase in the property taxes paid by every individual. If the elected representatives voted for a 15% tax increase, they would be rightfully booted out of office, but when the appraisal district with its appointed members does it, the common man generally does not even know it happened. According to officials in a local appraisal district, only 3% of property owners protest the appraised values. When this occurs, the appraisal district concedes, and reduces the increase. This is done so as to avoid legal action, which might alert the rest of the public to this scam. This is the true nature of the taxing power. And the worst part of this fraud is the increasing tendency of government at all levels to spend this money on useless wastes of skin such as the homeless.

Across the nation, several cities and states are on the verge of bankruptcy. Some have even had to shut down for periods of time due to a lack of funds. Sooner or later the people have to stand up and ask why every level of government in this country is incapable of efficient spending and taxing. The government has perpetrated a divide-and-conquer policy upon the American people. There are so many taxing authorities run by unknown persons in unknown places that the people cannot possibly get mobilized to protest against all of them. Safe from reproach by the people, the various government institutions go about business as usual in their typically incompetent fashion. They know they can waste and steal billions, and no one will find out. Anyone who does find out is blocked by the maze of bureaucracy that every government sets up to confuse the people and make sure that no one can be held responsible. This certainly is not the future picture of America that the Founders imagined.

In 1990, Texas passed a school funding scheme known as the "Robin Hood Plan." It was pure and simple a share-the-wealth plan right out of Marxism. No one in the 1990s thought that Texas would join the ranks of socialist states, but it happened, as usual, under the leadership of the Democrats. In each county an Education District was established. Its purpose was to take property tax money from wealthy school districts and share it with the poor districts. Trumpeted by liberals as basic fairness, what it really amounted to was taking resources away from the rich districts, the only ones in Texas that were not dismal failures in the education business, and wasting it on the poor districts. Instead of finding a way to boost poor districts, the braindead state legislature, after years of study, came up with a plan to destroy the few good districts left. However, in 1991, the Texas Supreme Court struck down the law as an unconstitutional imposition of a state property tax. The court opinion then took a bizarre turn. The court held that since striking down the law would cause much confusion in school funding, the state could keep using it for two more years. Even though it was unconstitutional? It was a clear example of what judges have been doing for years — ignoring the law. But it was another crystal clear exposé of the taxing power.

The solution to abusive and corrupt federal income taxation is to return to the original intent of the Constitution and repeal the 16th Amendment. That, of course, brings budgetary questions into play. What will the government do without these revenues? For one thing, they may increase other taxes. For another, they will be forced to develop a responsible monetary policy for a change. The income tax in 1991 provided approximately 38% of the revenue taken in by the federal government. The loss of that money would have to be partially offset by a corresponding cut in outlays. These cuts must come in four areas: corporate welfare, social welfare, military welfare, and foreign-aid welfare. Government subsidies to businesses are a socialistic tactic that the collapse of Eastern Europe and the Soviet Union have discredited. A welfare system that allows people to make more from the system than from working, and encourages people to live off the government, will no longer be tolerated. Welfare mothers with excessive numbers of children need to get a job or suffer the consequences of their actions. There will be no "free lunches." Military aid to countries like Japan must end. So, too, must foreign aid to countries which continually seem to turn their backs on us. The world can stand on its own feet. The United States needs to return to the foreign policy of Washington and Jefferson: peace and commerce with all who want them, no entangling alliances, no foreign meddling, and a strong defense for our shores.

Repeal has many advantages: it would force these fiscally responsible measures on our inept Congress and reduce the deficit; it would allow the people to keep the fruits of their labors, which could then be stored in savings, thus producing new capital, or used to make purchases of goods which would spur the economy; and it would also end the approximately 5.3 billion man-hours wasted yearly as the people fight their way through the maze of these ridiculously complex tax forms. Repeal is, however, unlikely. The liberals who believe the federal tax code should be used to redistribute the wealth will stand in the way, as will the bureaucrats who are reluctant to give up their power over the citizenry. The biggest problem is the American people and their timidity. The people must take a large part of the blame for this situation, as they have allowed it to happen and to continue. Had today's Americans lived in 1776, we would still be a British colony. The bottom line with the 16th Amendment and the IRS is a daily reminder that, after all, the Constitution is just a piece of paper.

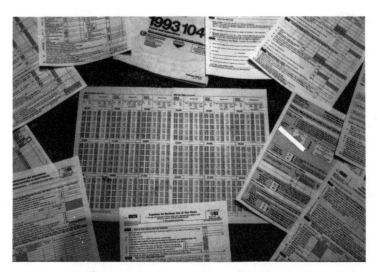

The paperwork of an abusive bureaucracy.
(Southern Cross Publishing)

CHAPTER 20

FEDERAL JUDGES

RAISING TAXES 1990

On Wednesday, April 18, 1990, the Supreme Court rendered one of the truly worst decisions in its history. In reviewing a school desegregation case from Missouri, the Court upheld the actions of a federal district court judge who had ordered the doubling of Kansas City's property taxes to finance his court-ordered desegregation plan for that city's schools. In doing so, the Court expanded the power of the federal judiciary beyond all precedent, and completely beyond the authority of the Constitution.

In 1977, the Kansas City, Missouri, schoolboard and a group of students sued the State of Missouri for operating a segregated school system in the Kansas City metropolitan area. By that time the previously-desegregated city schools had become racially imbalanced again due to white flight. In a phenomenon that has occurred in every case of forced integration, whites left the cities for the suburbs, leaving too few whites to fully integrate the schools. The suit sought to somehow rectify this situation.

In 1984, Federal District Court Judge Russell Clark delivered his decision. He agreed that the state was operating a segregated school system. He also ordered a sweeping plan of construction and student assignments that would make the city school system comparable to those in the suburbs. His goal was to improve the schools to such a point that whites would be lured back to the city system, thus allowing full desegregation. In this endeavor he ordered massive changes for the city schools. His order included a 25-acre farm, a 25-acre wildlife area, animal rooms, a planetarium, 15 computers per classroom, a model United Nations equipped with language translation capabilities, greenhouses and vivariums, movie editing and screening rooms, radio and television studios, a diesel mechanics lab, instruction in cosmetology and robotics, and an art gallery. Total cost, to be shared by the district and the state, was estimated in excess of $700 million. The final insult was that this figure also included $30,000 per year for a "public information specialist" to promote the court's plan.

The funding for the project required city property taxes to be doubled. However, the state constitution placed a cap on property tax increases that could only be exceeded with the approval of the voters. Exercising their constitutional rights, the people of the city repeatedly refused to approve this outrageous tax hike. Of course, the city's blacks claimed that this showed racism on the part of the people. Apparently it never occurred to them that the people couldn't afford such a huge tax increase and therefore correctly voted against it. Judge Clark then took a step that had never been done before. Indeed, the idea was so far-fetched and unconstitutional that it had never even been discussed before. He ordered the city's property taxes doubled immediately. In so doing, he violated the state constitutional cap on tax increases, and violated the U.S. Constitution, not to mention the very essence of democracy.

Judge Clark's reasoning stated that "the power of the court to determine unconstitutional behavior entails the power to decree sufficient remedies and this includes raising taxes to further desegregation." Well, he is unequivocally wrong! Taxation in the federal system, and in every state, is granted constitutionally to the legislative branch. The U.S. Constitution lists the powers to be held by each branch. In Article I, Section 8, the Legislature (Congress) is granted the *sole* power to lay and collect taxes. Article III, which delineates the Judicial Branch, lists the powers of the federal courts, and does *not* include the power to tax.

Original intent on the subject is clear as well. During the Constitutional Convention no discussion arose about a prohibition against taxation by the federal courts. No discussion was necessary, as all the Founders would have agreed that this was an absurd and tyrannical idea. *The Federalist Papers*, which were written to encourage ratification of the Constitution, frankly spell out the positions of the Founders. Alexander Hamilton in *The Federalist* 78 stated that "the judiciary has no influence over the purse!" (The purse being the traditional nickname for the power to tax and spend.) James Madison in *The Federalist* 48 said that "the legislative department alone has access to the pockets of the people." These positions are in keeping with the Founders' fear of abuse and tendency towards republican government. It was felt that the taxation power must be held by the people's representatives, who could be immediately voted out of office if they abused this power. It is totally inconceivable that the Founders would have approved of giving the taxing power to judges who hold their offices for life and cannot be removed by the voters for abuse. It must then be accepted that for federal courts to raise federal taxes is totally out of the question.

Federalism would then dictate that the federal courts cannot order a state to raise its taxes. The 10th Amendment is supportive of this argument. It says that "the powers not delegated to the United States by the Constitution, nor prohibited by it to the States, are reserved to the States respectively, or to the people." Taxation by the federal courts to support schools is not a power granted to the federal government (United States). It is not possible to even imply this authority! Taxation by the states to support schools is not prohibited to the states by the Constitution; therefore, this power is reserved to the states *only!* It may be noted that the federal government does provide a huge sum of money annually for education, but this money goes to the states and individual school districts to be used as they see fit. There is no federal school system using federal tax money.

The decision was ripe for appeal, and by April, 1990, it had made its way to the Supreme Court. All constitutional scholars were sure the decision would be reversed. In a shock to the entire nation, the Court revealed its decision in *Missouri v. Jenkins* (1990) and upheld this unconstitutional action. Actually, the Court held that the district judge overstepped his authority by increasing the taxes himself, but held that he could order local government officials to raise taxes. A semantic difference at best. The four liberal judges combined with Justice Byron White, a moderate who becomes a liberal in civil rights cases, to form a 5-4 majority. Justice White, writing for the majority, held that "this is plainly a judicial act within the power of a federal court." The Constitution says it is not, the writings of the Founders say it is not, the entire history of the federal judiciary says it is not, but these five decided that it is.

Make no mistake about the error-making capacity of the Supreme Court. Throughout the history of the Court it has overruled 260 of its previous decisions. The justices are frequently wrong in their constitutional interpretations. In an ironic twist to the *Missouri* case, the typically Constitution-destroying, ultraconservative Antonin Scalia, dissenting, predicted that "this begins a process that over time could threaten fundamental alteration of the form of government our Constitution embodies." He is right on that score.

This decision represents the most dangerous abuse our system has ever seen. Politicians who know it is political suicide to raise taxes now have an out. They can take no action on, or make cuts in, constitutionally mandated programs like prisons and schools, wait for the federal judiciary to intervene and dictate tax hikes, then blame the judges while avoiding all political liability. Taxes can now be raised by federal judges for whatever purpose they want, even if it runs against state constitutions, laws, or the votes of the people. We the people have no recourse, because we cannot touch a federal judge with the democratic process. This has returned us again to taxation without representation. The people responded to this situation once before. It is time they do it again!

Frankly, this decision is totally unfathomable. The doctrine of "separation of powers," which lies at the very heart of the Constitution, placed the power to tax solely in the legislative branch. This Court decision takes that primary authority away from the representatives of the people and puts it into the hands of non-elected life-term judges who now have the authority to forcibly raise the people's taxes for whatever purpose they desire. The clear language and intent of the Constitution prohibit a federal judge from raising taxes, but Judge Clark did it anyway, and the Supreme Court approved. This decision never should have been made. This type of tyrannical government is absolutely forbidden by the Constitution, but after all, it is just a piece of paper.

CHAPTER 21

ROADBLOCKS AND

FACING WITNESSES 1990

For many Americans, concern about the Supreme Court arose in the 1960s in response to decisions of the Court under Chief Justice Earl Warren. That Court did, for the first time, in numerous cases, interpret constitutional rights as they were intended. By the 1980s, William Rehnquist was Chief Justice, and he, along with several conservative Republican appointments to the Court, began issuing decisions that narrowed constitutional civil liberties. The damage was especially severe to the 4th and 6th Amendments.

During the 1960s, decisions regarding the rights of the accused continually faced the Court. One of the most important was *Gideon v. Wainwright* (1963). This case established the right of an accused person to have an attorney in state court as well as federal court in a criminal prosecution. This was part of a process called "incorporation." Using the 14th Amendment's "due process" clause, the Court had begun over a period of years to incorporate the rights in the Bill of Rights to the states as well. Critics of this process argued that the Bill of Rights only applies to the federal government, and under the original intent of the document they are right. In fact, it is quite disingenuous to argue that the 14th Amendment supports incorporation. If it was the intent of the authors of this amendment to incorporate the Bill of Rights to the states, they could have said so with simple language. But they did not. The purpose of this amendment was solely to attempt to protect the unconstitutional congressional grab for power committed in the Civil Rights Act of 1866.

On the other hand, the states presently hold more power than the Founders ever imagined the federal government would have. There is, of course, a valid concern over protecting the people from abusive state laws. It seems illogical for the states to have created a national government that was to be supreme over them, that was constrained by a list of rights for the people and limits on its power, that the states could avoid. So it would seem that incorporation is a natural course to follow in order to protect the people from the states. Yet incorporation is an unwarranted intrusion into the power of the states and is unconstitutional. Applying these specific rights to the states should have been accomplished through the amendment process, and not with the vague language and questionable legality of the 14th Amendment. Nonetheless, the Warren Court did move the country significantly to a point where our federal constitutional rights applied to the state governments.

Discontent with Supreme Court decisions in the 1960s even led to a movement to impeach Chief Justice Earl Warren. This would have been another constitutional travesty, as the impeachment process was established to remove officials who violated the law, not to get rid of judges whose decisions were unpopular yet constitutional. Nonetheless, the Warren Court has become known as the great liberal court that legislated social policy in total violation of the Constitution. Some of that criticism is deserved, but most of it is not. Admittedly, many of the Justices on the court in the 1960s were followers of the legal philosophy preached by the gurus in the ivory towers of Yale University Law School. Arthur Schlesinger, Jr., explained this philosophy. "Any judge chooses his results and reasons backwards," Schlesinger reasoned. "The resources of legal artifice, the ambiguities of precedents, the range of applicable doctrine; are all so extensive that in most cases in which there is a reasonable difference of opinion a judge can come out on either side without straining the fabric of legal logic. A wise judge knows that political choice is inevitable; he makes no false pretenses of objectivity and consciously exercises the judicial power with an eye to social results." This liberal view of the fundamental principles of legal interpretation actually means there is no law; there are only social results desired by judges which are brought about through litigation. This dangerous doctrine renders absolutely void one of the major underlying principles for which the American Revolution was fought: that this was to be a nation of written laws.

Following this doctrine, some very questionable decisions came down from the Court in the 1960s. Many seemed wholly unrelated to the Constitution, and added new provisions. A classic example was the right to privacy as expressed in the flowery nonsense of the opinion written by Justice Douglas in the 1965 case of *Griswold v. Connecticut*. In many other cases, however, it can be said that the Warren Court simply interpreted the old constitutional provisions correctly for the first time, or began to enforce them correctly. For example, the Court applied the "Exclusionary Rule" as a way to enforce 4th-Amendment protections. This rule prohibits the introduction of illegally obtained evidence at trial, and thus acts as a deterrent to police who are tempted to carry out illegal searches and seizures. Some saw this as a liberal attempt to let all the criminals go free. It wasn't, of course; it was following the Constitution.

A Court that is well on its way to outdoing the Warren Court as social legislators (and this time the label is entirely deserved) is the current Court under Chief Justice William Rehnquist, a Justice who has time and time again proved that his right-wing political agenda is what determines his vote. This court has made two recent decisions that are quintessential examples of raping the Constitution. These cases dealt with drunk-driving roadblocks and the right of an accused to face witnesses in child-abuse cases. As 1990 wore on, these types of decisions were coming down at such an accelerated pace that it became difficult to keep them straight.

Drunk driving is without question a severe national problem that demands a solution. Each year more than 25,000 Americans die in alcohol-related traffic accidents. Enforcement is not really the problem as much as the lenient punishments handed out by spineless judges. I had an occasion to witness this kind of judicial irresponsibility up close. A former girlfriend's father was killed by a drunk driver in Illinois. The drunk had three prior convictions for this offense, yet he received probation for the accident that killed her father. Of course, Cook County, Illinois, is known for corruption in the judiciary. When the criminal justice system fails to this extent, the people have a duty to take matters into their own hands. Unfortunately, this kind of sentence is more the rule than the exception in the United States. In Norway, a drunk driver's license is revoked for life on the first conviction. Other countries have similar penalties, and some even levy the death penalty. Suffice it to say they do not have a drunk driving problem.

The American approach is, as usual, to find some way that does not work, and yet tramples on our constitutional rights. Drunk-driving roadblocks and checkpoints are such a system. Maryland seems to have the dishonor of beginning this police-state tactic. It spread to other states including Michigan, where the practice was challenged in federal court as a violation of 4th-Amendment freedom from unreasonable searches and seizures.

The 4th Amendment states that: "the right of the people to be secure in their persons, houses, papers, and effects, against unreasonable searches and seizures, shall not be violated, and no warrants shall issue, but upon probable cause..." Analysis in 4th-Amendment cases involves several steps: was there a search or seizure involved which requires a warrant; is there an exception to the warrant requirement; if a warrant was required, was it properly obtained; what is the remedy if an illegal search or seizure took place?

During the 1960's the Supreme Court was faced with technological advances which made new types of searches possible. Many cases came up involving the use of wire tapping, binoculars that could see into a home, helicopters that could fly over a home, and numerous others. In *Katz v. United States* (1967), the Court established a major new principle in search-and-seizure law. It was held that 4th-Amendment protection would extend to all areas where a person had a reasonable expectation of privacy. This was an expansive view of the words of the amendment, and it certainly worked to protect individual liberties as intended by the Founders. Unfortunately, this rule was based on the use of the word "unreasonable" in the 4th Amendment. The Court assumed that the amendment prohibited only unreasonable searches and seizures without a warrant. There were then, according to this logic, some searches which were reasonable and thus did not require a warrant. The actual meaning of the language in the amendment is that all searches and seizures are *per se* unreasonable without a warrant. By misplacing the emphasis on the word "unreasonable," the Court opened up the amendment to interpretation over what is and what is not unreasonable. This did not pose a problem while liberals dominated the Court, but as conservatives assumed control the outcome was predictable.

Nonetheless, the Katz Rule created a very wide circle of protection, as warrants were required in more cases. Unfortunately, in the 1980s, conservatives began to dominate the Court and the view of *Katz* changed. Under Rehnquist and his cronies, the Katz Rule was used to limit the warrant requirement by increasingly holding that the people do not have a reasonable expectation of privacy anywhere. In later cases, defendants were held to have no reasonable expectation of privacy when: the police searched a barn in the middle of 200 acres of private property; the police searched the bags of garbage in front of a person's home; the federal government required banks to report banking transactions, such as large deposits, to the government; the police used devices to record phone numbers dialed from a person's house; and the police used a plane to fly over a private residence in order to observe activities. In all of these cases the defendant was found to have no reasonable expectation of privacy, so a warrant did not even have to be considered.

The next step in the conservative destruction of the 4th Amendment came in the area of exceptions to the warrant requirement. Even if it was found that there was a reasonable expectation of privacy, thus requiring a warrant, there have developed eleven exceptions. They are:
1. Stop & Frisk
2. Searches Incident to Arrest
3. Protective Sweeps
4. Plain View Searches
5. The Carroll Doctrine for Automobile Searches
6. Exigent Circumstances

7. Administrative Searches
8. Special Needs Searches
9. Roadblocks
10. Inventory Searches
11. Border Searches

Each exception is a large and complex area of law. Suffice it to say that these exceptions carve out huge areas where the police may search people, homes, papers and effects without warrants. Then the conservatives found new ways to gut the 4th Amendment.

The Exclusionary Rule, which requires that illegally obtained evidence not be admitted at trial, has also been narrowed. This doctrine has its roots in *Weeks v. United States* (1914). It reappeared in *Mapp v. Ohio* (1961) as police across the country consistently and continually executed illegal searches. The Supreme Court warned that they would, and finally did, enforce this rule. In *United States v. Leon* (1984), the conservatives on the Court held that the Exclusionary Rule does not apply when the police in good faith use a warrant which later turns out to be defective. Prior to this rule the police had to take great care in obtaining a valid search warrant so that the evidence they collected would not be thrown out in court. Now, there is no such need. This gives the police the same power as possessed by the royal tax collectors of the 1760s with their Writs of Assistance.

At the same time the courts, when faced by illegal searches and seizures, held that the violation was really harmless and that no remedy was necessary. These cases signaled the death of the 4th Amendment.

A major exception to the warrant requirement involves the use of roadblocks and checkpoints. Michigan began to use drunk-driving checkpoints in 1986. The police would monitor a section of highway and stop all cars for questioning. If a driver showed signs of intoxication, he was held for more questioning and sobriety tests. At one such checkpoint, the Michigan State Police stopped 126 cars and arrested one driver for intoxication. Soon thereafter, a federal district court struck down the practice, citing "the potential for an unreasonable subjective intrusion on individual liberty interests in violation of the 4th Amendment." In *Michigan Police v. Sitz* (1990), the Supreme Court disagreed, ruling 6-3 in favor of the checkpoints. They claimed that this tactic is an acceptable violation of the 4th Amendment. Chief Justice Rehnquist, writing for the majority stated, "The balance of the state's interest in preventing drunk driving, and the degree of intrusion upon motorists who are briefly stopped weighs in favor of the state program." After reading this one must wonder, how does a person get to be Chief Justice without understanding or even knowing what the Constitution says? This decision goes totally against the letter and the spirit of the 4th Amendment, which disallows searches without warrants lawfully obtained from a judge according to the prescribed process.

Rehnquist's opinion really says that preventing drunk driving outweighs the violation of the 4th Amendment that is inherent in these roadblocks and checkpoints. Of course, a logical continuation of this dangerous precedent would lead the state to: expand these kinds of roadside searches in attempts to enforce other laws; to search people's homes to prevent drug use, or to prevent certain sex acts (see Supreme Court ruling in *Bowers v. Hardwick* [1986] upholding Georgia's anti-sodomy law) or any other social ills. That is the problem with constitutional rights: you either have them or you do not. There is no middle ground. Once a right has been intruded upon it becomes easier to repeat that action, and eventually that right will cease to exist.

There has been a trend to allow a lesser degree of protection from unlawful search and seizure in cars as several exceptions to the warrant requirement developed. This is troubling because the 4th Amendment includes "effects" as one of the areas to be protected. *Black's Law Dictionary* defines "effects" as "movable personal property," and expressly includes "cars" in a list of examples. This definition can be applied to 1791 law even if they did not have cars at that time. They did have coaches and buggies which are essentially the same as a car in that they are movable personal property. The irrefutable conclusion is that allowing lesser protection for cars is not in line with the Constitution.

A few of the exceptions to the warrant requirement are necessary and were established practices at the time of the adoption of the Bill of Rights. Police should certainly have the ability to briefly search the immediate area in which a person is arrested so as to find weapons. Also, in emergency situations where the safety of the public is threatened, police should have the ability to search a limited area to prevent harm. Unfortunately, today the numerous court-created exceptions have swallowed the rule.

About a year after the *Michigan Police* case a new kind of checkpoint appeared. In July, 1992, the North Carolina Highway Patrol set up a flashing sign along a stretch of interstate highway warning "Slow Down, Drug Check Point Ahead," but it was just a prop. The signs were located just before recently opened exit ramps outside a small town in a deserted area. During a six-hour operation, law officers stopped and searched only the cars which chose the exit ramps, some 200 cars. A patrol spokesman declared that "unless you lived there, anyone who exited had only one reason to exit — to avoid the drug checkpoint." On the other hand, I can think of other reasons to exit, such as to avoid an unlawful search which absolutely violates my 4th Amendment rights. Since police often joke about their ability to find something wrong with any car they stop, could it be that people just don't want to be harassed in such a manner? This is, however, a good illustration of the expansive tendency of abusive government building, in this case, on the Supreme Court's approval of drunk-driving checkpoints. People may be stopped for no other reason than their use of a highway exit.

The 4th Amendment was intended to be absolute, but it's not anymore. The right wing crowd of Justices White, O'Connor, Scalia and Kennedy joined Rehnquist and liberal Blackmun on the checkpoint decision. The dissenters, Brennan, Marshall and Stevens, wrote: "This decision sacrifices individual liberty in favor of a police state tactic that might not make any difference in the fight against drunk driving." With the retirement of Brennan in 1990 and the confirmation of David Souter to the Court, things could only get worse. Souter, while on the New Hampshire Supreme Court, was the only dissenting voice in an otherwise unanimous decision to strike down that state's drunk-driving checkpoint program.

Now we can all expect, as we drive down the highways, to be pulled over by the police for no reason, to be questioned, and to be hindered from going on our way because the Supreme Court thought it would be better than having drunk drivers on the road. It is a wrong decision. The ironic thing is that the American people applaud and say "good job" as the government easily removes another of our constitutional rights. Just like sheep being led to the slaughter. One day, when we have a totalitarian system, the people will ask, "What happened to our rights?" Some of us will reply, "We had a Constitution, but after all, it was only a piece of paper."

In a similar vein, the Supreme Court also ruled recently in *Maryland v. Craig* (1990), a case that involved the 6th Amendment right of the accused to face their accusers in court. The question before the Court concerned whether or not an accused child abuser should have the right to face the child witness against him.

The background for this case, as with the checkpoint case, comes from Maryland. Ironically, at the Constitutional Convention, Maryland was one of the loudest opponents of strong abusive government. Now they seem to be a leader in bringing about that very condition. The owner of a Clarksville day-care center was convicted on molestation charges. At trial, the four young witnesses were allowed to testify out of the defendant's presence. They were interviewed over a one-way closed-circuit television system. The defendant appealed the conviction with a challenge based on the 6th Amendment, which says, "in all criminal prosecutions, the accused shall enjoy the right... to be confronted with the witnesses against him." Confronting a witness is a basic component of a fair trial. Many a witness has broken under face-to-face cross examination and recanted previously told falsehoods. There must be a right to face accusers and question their accusations.

The Court, however, disagreed. Justice O'Connor, writing for a 5-4 majority, stated that "a state's interest in the physical and psychological well-being of child abuse victims may be sufficiently important to outweigh, at least in some cases, a defendant's right to face his or her accusers in court." In plain English, the Court decided that a defendant has no right to face his young accusers if the children would suffer emotional trauma as a result. The decision allows states to use measures that include videotaped testimony, testimony by one-

250

way television, and even testimony on behalf of a victim by a physician or other person who has interviewed them.

A witness on the stand confronts a defendant.
(Southern Cross Publishing)

Child abuse, like drunk driving, is a terrible social problem that seems to be growing. Again: strict laws, immediate enforcement, and harsh penalties are the solution, for any civilized culture must be judged by the way it treats its children. The Supreme Court shares this feeling, but goes one step further in saying that preventing children from being traumatized at trial is more important than the 6th Amendment. It is not — and one day when the government is abusing all of our rights, after having destroyed the Constitution, maybe we will figure that out.

How much clearer must it be for these justices? The Constitution says an accused person must be allowed to face his accusers in all criminal prosecutions, and it prohibits unreasonable searches and seizures, but the Supreme Court ignores it. They simply are not following the Constitution! And really, why should they? It is, after all, just a piece of paper.

CHAPTER 22

CRIME, FEDERAL JUDGES, AND

PRISON REFORM 1990s

The Preamble to the Constitution sets out several goals for the government. Two of these were to ensure domestic tranquillity and to promote the general welfare. These refer to the most crucial responsibility of government: the protection of its citizens. As this relates to protection from crime, our federal and state governments are a dismal failure. The government's inability to protect the people from crime, federal judges who have misinterpreted the 8th Amendment, and liberal prison reform brought on by them are further examples of constitution trampling.

On April 28, 1991, the FBI released their annual crime report indicating, to no one's surprise, that criminals had a banner year in 1990. Such increases have occurred each year in the 1990s. Apparently crime does pay, and pays well. These statistics result from reported crime and are criticized as understating the real level of crime, as many incidents go unreported.

- Violent crime up 10 %, to 1,810,000 incidents
- Murder up 10%, to 23,600
- Rape up 9%, to 103,000
- Robbery up 11%, to 642,000
- Aggravated assault up 10%, to 1,050,000
- Burglary down 4%, to 3,040,000
- Theft unchanged at 7,872,000

Add these statistics to the fact that juvenile crime is up 23%, and an intolerable situation is created. The people are no longer safe on the streets, in their homes, or anywhere else, and the blame for this lies squarely on the government. This nation is being victimized by crime like no society has experienced in modern times. We are awash in criminality. A recent study shows that one in seven Americans carry a gun or has one in their car for protection. Florida passed (and other states are debating) laws that would allow the people to carry concealed weapons for this purpose. What a sad state of affairs it is when the people must arm themselves for protection due to the government's inability to do its job.

The causes of the ever-increasing crime problem are numerous and complex, but there are two basic sides to the equation: first, the societal causes of crime; and second, the government policies aimed at dealing with it.

The primary cause of crime is the capitalist socioeconomic system. Crime has existed ever since humans first came together in primitive groups. It is a sociological factor inherent in group relationships where property ownership is the basis. It also results from emotional responses to stimuli, mind-altering substances, and mental illness, but the root of most crime is property. It is those who perceive themselves as "have-nots" desiring the property of the "haves." Our capitalistic economy aggravates this desire. Essentially, capitalism dictates that one must do whatever is necessary to gather and hold wealth. As there is a limited supply of the resources that produce wealth, people are forced to be competitive as each struggles to get his share. We are all raised in this environment. It should not, then, be surprising that so many resort to unscrupulous means in order to achieve this goal. So, then, a crime problem is bred into our society.

If capitalism promotes crime, maybe the inquiry as to solutions of crime should center on alternative socioeconomic systems. What effect has communism had on crime? Karl Marx's plan was, in part, to create a society where everyone was equal and no one privately owned property. This was more or less instituted in the Soviet Union and in other nations, and the results were hardly surprising. There was a significantly reduced crime problem. Of course, authoritarian rule played a role in this reduction. This has, however, changed with the break-up of the Soviet Union, the freeing of economic controls, and the advent of capitalist free-market influences. Now the former Soviet states are experiencing the good and bad of capitalism which, of course, includes increased crime. They are still an authoritarian nation, which proves this is a secondary factor. If, then, the cure is to have a society devoid of property ownership (and the demise of world communism has proven that is unrealistic and unworkable), then the root cause of crime might have no solution

The other causes of crime are equally without solution. Society cannot easily change a person's behavior, especially in reaction to disturbing stimuli. A man who discovers his wife in bed with another man, reacts violently, and kills them both is a classic example.

Nor can society stem man's desire to ingest mind-altering substances. Due to the despondency that results from life, man has always sought to escape from it, with alcohol and other drugs being the most common modern forms of escape. Historically, man has sought other escapes such as religion. Karl Marx said that "religion is the opiate of the masses." He recognized man's need to escape the futility of his own existence by relying on nonsensical mind-altering philosophies which offer the carrot of eternal paradise in the hereafter. This escapist mentality can be extended to substance abuse as well.

Society is also limited in its ability to control mental illness. This field is not fully within our understanding at this time. We cannot predict the person who goes off the deep end and commits a crime, nor can we make much progress in resolving his mental problems afterwards.

The fact that crime is increasing suggests that we were doing something right traditionally, and that we are no longer doing those things. Crime has always been held in check by authority which undertook severe steps to punish it appropriately. Two break-downs have occurred in this area: the people's respect for authority has diminished, and the government's movement towards liberal views of rehabilitation and protection of criminals' rights have amounted to a lessening of authority.

The attitude of the people has changed towards authority. The first part of the break-down in attitudes was caused by the government's misuse of power that was so evident in the 1950s. At that time, we were experiencing the oppression and repression of the anti-thought, anti-freedom forces of the Cold Warriors, men like

Senator McCarthy who violated the very spirit of this nation. Oppression always breeds rebellion, and it surely did with the generation that came of age in the 1960s. The youth of that period were quite logically and correctly rebelling against authority they saw as abusive. The government reacted to the social rebellion of the 1960s by further abusing its authority (Vietnam, Trial of the Chicago Eight, illegal FBI investigations of citizens, Kent State, Watergate), which only cemented the anti-authority attitude for the next several generations.

At the same time, society changed as a result of the feminist movement. The traditional family concept broke down as women left the home and entered the workplace. This left the children of the next generation in a vacuum. Dumped into child-care facilities, often run by persons of questionable value as parents, authority figures and role models, children were increasingly left to their own devices. Children began to be brought up under either the excess authority of rigid child-care programs, or no authority at all in weaker programs. In both cases, the children grew up without a respect for authority, in a society that had become anti-authority.

The second major problem was the government's reaction to crime. The authorities reduced their level of control and allowed crime to escalate. Along with the "free-for-all" that was the 1960s-80s came the desire to treat criminals humanely. This tack was taken by social-activist federal judges. It was the eternal argument of rehabilitation versus punishment. The rights of criminals expanded under the Warren Court until they were more important than the victims'. Conditions in the prisons were made almost pleasant by the federal courts, and the judicial system began to be perceived as a joke. Now no criminal is afraid of prison; it has lost its deterrent value. Even if criminals are sent to prison, they know it is like a country club and that they will be out on early release in a very short period of time. The bottom line is that crime is out of hand, the government is failing to protect its citizens, and no one is safe.

The experience of Texas is typical of what has happened across the nation. Traditionally, Texas prisons were a sort of "hell on earth." Inmates were prohibited from decorating their cells. The dormitories had no partitions, and convicts often slept next to urinals in tiny cells that held three convicts. All inmate mail was censored. Medical and dental care were almost unheard of, as was psychological and psychiatric counseling. Senseless brutality was the rule among the inmates. Under this old system, wardens delegated special duties to chosen inmates, known as "building tenders." They were, in a sense, inmate guards. They penetrated the jail cells, solved disputes, and kept inmates in tow through threats and violence. They accumulated great power in the prisons, and of course many abused this power. Prison life was not a pretty picture, but this was necessary to prevent crime.

In 1972, a prisoner's hand-written complaint (I'll leave his name out because useless scumbags like this petty criminal don't deserve to be known for anything) got the ball rolling on a legal battle that would transform Texas prisons. This battle dragged on until 1980, when the inappropriately-named U.S. District Judge William Wayne Justice declared the state's prison system to be unconstitutional, based on the 8th Amendment's prohibition against "cruel and unusual punishment." The state viciously attacked Judge Justice and refused to implement the desired changes for two years, but were finally forced into federal court control over the state's prisons.

The courts have indeed changed the prisons. A tour of Hightower Unit and Ellis Unit 1 reveals a comfortable environment. These units include gymnasiums with full-length basketball courts, weight-lifting and exercise equipment, volleyball and handball courts, open-air courts, picnic tables, benches and barbecue pits.

Vocational programs offer inmates a chance to become trained in textile weaving, welding, woodworking, painting, upholstery and mechanics. At taxpayer expense they are provided with the materials for these endeavors and are allowed to sell their work. All sales proceeds are kept by the inmates.

Both units contain educational facilities for elementary levels through college. They also provide instruction in computers, foreign languages, Braille and law. It surely comforts one to know that tax dollars are being used to teach inmates the law so they can circumvent it in the future.

Prisoners may now decorate their cells with pictures and calendars; the inmates must be given clean clothes and linens each day; no more than two inmates can be placed in a cell; they are given time for recreation; they have television lounges and libraries; mail is inspected, not censored; medical care has improved; the number of doctors has been increased by 2300%; drug and alcohol abuse programs have been established, as have programs to help convicts find jobs after prison; convicts are given $200 release money when they get out; and the building-tender system has been dismantled. These reforms have pushed prison costs up dramatically. It now costs $35,000 a year to take care of each criminal. This has helped worsen an already serious state budget crisis.

While the pleasantries have been established for the inmates, the deterrent value of the prisons has been lost. Control over them has been sacrificed as well. Sexual molestation and thievery have increased; women guards are sexually harassed; inmates throw urine and feces at officers; and the rules are generally ignored. When faced with these violations, guards are limited to filing charges and removing privileges, which everyone admits fails to deter most inmates. The prisons have become country clubs, and the inmates are clearly running the asylum.

Judge Justice has also placed a cap on prison capacity in order to reduce overcrowding. The Texas prisons must shut their doors to new inmates when they reach 95% of capacity. This, of course, has placed serious burdens on the county jails, causing them to be overcrowded. Then, because of violations of prisoners' rights, the county jails too have been placed under federal court supervision. To comply with the prison population cap, the state and counties have been forced to resort to early-release programs in order to make room for other criminals.

The overcrowding problem has forced the state to adopt the practice of early release. The state's revolving doors to justice now swing open daily to release an average of 150 convicts long before the end of their sentences, in order to make room for other criminals. Parole rules, passed by the state legislature in 1987, required inmates to serve one-fourth of their sentences, but in reality few served even that long. In 1992, a criminal served 23 days for each year of his sentence. This nightmare unleashed thousands of criminals onto the streets. All because a federal judge, who has absolutely no concept of the real meaning of the 8th Amendment, didn't want the poor criminals mistreated.

A life sentence handed down by a Texas jury conjures up visions of decades behind bars, but it often can be reduced to just a few years by various good time and parole rules. A criminal sentenced to "life" is eligible for parole after 15 years calendar time. This time can be made up of actual calendar days served plus time earned through good conduct. The highest good behavior status earns 30 days for every 30 served. On top of this, diligent participation in work or school programs earns 15 days for each 30 served. A convict who behaves well and works hard in a school program for a month earns credit for the 30 days actually served as well as 45 days for good behavior and work. This amounts to two and a half years for every year served. The lifer can then be eligible for parole in 6 years. Early release has risen by 500% since 1982, and its effects have become painfully clear. Some illustrations are appropriate.

Criminal #1 had served slightly more than four years of two concurrent 15-year sentences for aggravated sexual abuse before being released early. While on parole he was charged and convicted in the rape and strangulation of an 18-year-old girl.

Criminal #2 was sentenced to 123 years in 1977 for burglarizing women's homes and then choking and raping them. He was paroled after nine years. Within a year of his release he was charged with two attempted capital murders.

Criminal #3 had served only 13 months of a 15-year sentence when he was paroled. Within two months he shot and killed a Houston police officer who had stopped the car in which he was a passenger.

Criminal #4 had been out on parole for three weeks. During this time he had been arrested for a new string of crimes and was out on bond when he shot a 22-year-old woman to death at a stoplight. It seems his car was almost out of gas and he wanted hers as a replacement.

Criminal #5 was released early after serving only four years of a 13-year sentence for trying to kill two policemen who chased him after a holdup. After being out on parole for only two months he was indicted for five capital murders, two attempted capital murders, and five armed robberies.

Unfortunately, this depressing list could go on and on. Crime has doubled in Texas in the last 20 years, and much of it is committed by criminals in early release programs forced on the state by Judge Justice. This is another case where a federal judge has completely missed the point of original intent. His view of the 8th Amendment is fundamentally flawed. It is skewed to this incorrect view by his desire to be a social activist. The Founders never imagined a federal judge with the power to so harm the people of a state.

Texas is not the only state suffering these experiences. In a 1990 decision, another federal judge struck down a prison rule banning inmate subscriptions to pornographic magazines, ruling that this violated the First Amendment rights of inmates.

Frankly, it is time to tell so-called judges like William Wayne Justice to go to hell. A federal judge should have absolutely no enforcement power, and it is time the people pointed this out to them. The American people will no longer be abused by the misguided and unconstitutional rulings of these black-robed morons. If we can't force them to follow the Constitution, then term limitation should be implemented, and impeachment should be used based on their gross violations of the Constitution.

Amusingly, in June, 1990, the federal judges demanded an additional appropriation from Congress to provide for their protection. They wanted $11 million of taxpayer money for home-security systems, remote car-starters, and other measures. Over the last 12 years, three of the nation's 1,900 federal judges have been killed. All sides agree that these recently-requested measures would not have prevented any of those deaths. The whole thing is rather ironic; these federal judges are the single most important factor in the rise of crime in America, and now they want money to protect themselves because a few of their colleagues have been killed. Too bad these federal judges don't have that kind of concern for the Americans murdered in 1990 whose blood is on their hands.

The Arab world has very little problem with crime. For the act of theft, a criminal's hand is cut off. A criminal there knows he will pay a serious penalty for his acts. This is the approach that must be used with crime in America. If Simon Wiesenthal, on his silly and misguided half-century-late quest to track down Nazi war criminals, hasn't gotten them all, what we need is a few ex-concentration camp guards hiding in Argentina to come and run our prisons properly. The 8th Amendment was designed to prevent the torture of prisoners, and it should be obeyed. It was not designed to prevent prisons from being places of harsh punishment for criminal acts.

Modern prisons should allow absolutely no rights for the inmates. Their rights will be rigorously enforced until that jury says "Guilty," and then their rights end. That is the penalty they must pay for choosing to commit crime. Inmates should be locked in their cells 24 hours a day with no social or recreational privileges at all. Nor should the prisons be made to spend taxpayer money on these vermin except for the bare minimum of food. These steps will reduce crime drastically in this country. There is no constitutional prohibition against this kind of treatment, if one follows Original Intent. The 8th Amendment was not designed to protect inmates lawfully convicted by their peers from facing severe consequences for their acts.

Another step that is required is reform of the death-penalty appeals process. The Constitution absolutely does not prohibit the death penalty. The only limitation is that it cannot be carried out in a cruel and unusual manner. This reflects the desires of the Founders. The death penalty was a common sentence in colonial times. If the Founders had wanted to prevent all capital punishment they would have written a prohibition against it into the Constitution. But that is not what they wanted, so no prohibition was included. They simply wanted a restriction against torture and inhumane punishments. Now the liberal establishment, and for a while the Supreme Court, claimed that the death penalty was cruel and unusual punishment. This was nothing more than misguided weakness on their part. Many states have begun to execute by using lethal injection, and this has taken the cruel and unusual punishment argument away from the liberals, as it is a quick, painless way to kill someone. Certain people are such a threat to society that their crimes deserve to be repaid with death. The death penalty is a deterrent to crime if it is used consistently, quickly and regularly. No amount of statistical manipulation by liberals will ever change this fact. The death penalty should be invoked for any serious violent crime, and the stupidity of excessive appeals that drag on for years must stop. An accused must be allowed one run through the appeals process and then be executed (unless the conviction is overturned, of course).

Many critics of prison overcrowding claim that there are too many small-time criminals in jail. They would suggest that anything short of a felony should not require prison time, but in this they are mistaken. Anyone who commits a crime must go to jail and serve their time.

There is one exception. In recent years our jails have become clogged by persons having committed minor drug offenses. As the nation has become paranoid about drugs, the people have pushed for the incarceration of every small-time drug user. In 1991, 60% of all court cases at the state and federal level were drug-related. This is one area which requires change. As previously discussed, drug legalization is the only appropriate answer to drug use and crime related to it. Once done, the prisons will be relieved of this unnecessary burden and there will be more room for real criminals.

Another change that must take place is the end of all early-release programs. When the court decides on a sentence, it must be served. To avoid bleeding-heart judges who wish to issue short sentences, there must be strict and heavy sentencing guidelines that a judge must follow. When this was attempted recently, outraged federal judges declared it unconstitutional. Well, if Congress can establish the Rules of Civil Procedure, (and these rules were upheld) they can constitutionally establish sentencing guidelines.

Of course, abolishing early release will result in more prison overcrowding. Two things must be done to avoid this. First, remove the restrictions on the number of inmates held in one cell. If they don't do the crime, they won't have to do the time. Second, the state legislatures, which are very much to blame for the prison-overcrowding mess, must build more prisons. Not the expensive recreational country clubs that Judge Justice would warrant, but real, serious prisons.

During the summer of 1994, Congress and that dumbass, incompetent Clinton got fed up with rampant crime, or rather they got fed up with the American people castigating them for not doing anything about the problem. And an election was fast approaching. The easily predictable result was Clinton's Crime Bill. Cast by the politicos as the solution to the crime problem, it barely passed Congress as Republicans declared it to be what it actually was: a charade. Its provisions included: $20 billion promised to cities over five years to hire more police; a ban on the sales of certain assault weapons; an expansion of the federal death penalty; and a three-strikes provision requiring life in prison for repeat offenders.

There were several problems with this alleged solution. First, the money promised to the cities was just that: a promise. The money was not actually appropriated, which means that in the coming years each successive Congress must authorize the actual expenditure of this money. It is a truism that no Congress is bound by the actions of a previous Congress. Even if this money was actually spent, it would only cover the short term, and in a few years the cities would take the entire burden of paying for all these new police. This is a burden they cannot afford. The truth here is that Congress and Clinton found a brilliant way to gain political favor with the people for very little, if any, money being spent. In addition, the crime problem is not due to lack of police, but the lack of courage on the part of the President, Congress and especially the cowards in the judges' robes who refuse to take a hard stand on crime.

Second, the ban on assault weapons is another joke. The day this bill was signed into law I joined a group at the gun range. As we peppered our Bill Clinton silhouette targets with 32-round clips from our TEC-9s and MAC-10s, I contemplated the reality of this gun ban. Besides being a total contravention of the 2nd Amendment, it is also quite useless. Law-enforcement agencies report that less than 1% of crimes involve assault weapons. We all feel much safer now. This ban is nothing more than the first major step towards rendering the law-abiding citizens defenseless in the face of an ever-increasingly abusive federal government and the criminals which it coddles.

Third, the expansion of the federal death penalty. When was the last time the federal government executed someone for criminal conduct? It simply does not happen, and this expansion of the federal penalty will not bring it about either. Basically, the effect of this change is to multiple zero by three. The result is still zero. The fact of the matter is that 98% of crimes committed are within the jurisdiction of the state criminal systems where the federal government cannot touch them. This expansion, while designed to make the Feds look tough, is a complete charade.

Fourth, the three-strikes provision for federal crimes. Like most Americans I ask rhetorically: why should criminal get three chances before being locked up for life? And this provision only applies to serious violent crimes. It also applies only to federal crimes which, as we have seen, make up only a tiny percentage of all crimes committed.

A population barricaded behind bars: Is this freedom?
(Southern Cross Publishing)

While Congress and Clinton excel at creative deceptions such as this Crime Bill, the people put bars on their windows and cower in fear. The fortress mentality spreads. Is this freedom? Today's judicial system is a complete failure, as are the federal government and states they represent. These institutions are violating the most sacred right of the people and the constitutional duty of government, the duty to protect its citizens. These federal judges who have misinterpreted the Constitution and enslaved the people with a revolving-door justice system that allows criminals to go free to terrorize the populace are a disgrace to the constitutional principles they are sworn to uphold. Wouldn't it be ironic, and amusing, if some convict on early release murdered Judge Justice? That would certainly be justifiable homicide. All of this would not be happening if we resorted to following the Constitution, but after all, it is just a piece of paper.

CHAPTER 23
CENSORSHIP 1990s

Society swings like a pendulum between the restrictiveness of conservatism and the openness of liberalism. As the pendulum swings to the extreme of one side there tends to be a backlash against it. When society becomes too liberal, a conservative reaction sets in and vice versa. The 1960s-80s saw a very liberal period, and finally in the late '80s the pendulum began to swing back. A march to the repression and oppression of the 1950s began. In one area, that of censorship, this process has been alarmingly rapid.

In the last few years the nation has seen: literature affected as school libraries have been forced to pull classics; the operators of a Cincinnati art museum arrested for displaying works by Robert Mapplethorpe; a cut of National Endowment for the Arts (NEA) funding for art that Senator Jesse Helms finds offensive; the arrest, trial and banning of musical groups; albums and books banned, and record store owners arrested for selling albums. All of these are the offspring of conservatism. Music is the area where we have seen the most intense attack on free expression. Censorship, a highly inflammatory issue, always brings the First Amendment to the forefront of the eternal battle over what is, and what is not, constitutionally protected free speech.

The people are to have an almost uncontrolled right to expression, even that which is deemed offensive by the majority. This debate has raged, of course, in the Supreme Court. The positions of the Justices have ranged from strict regulation of speech to no regulation. In *Miller v. California* (1973), Chief Justice Burger, writing for the majority in an obscenity case, defined the First Amendment, saying that it "protects works which, taken as a whole, have serious literary, artistic, political, or scientific value, regardless of whether the government or a majority of the people approve of the ideas these works represent." He also argued that an expansion of First-Amendment free speech to cover obscenity was "a misuse of the great guarantees of free speech and free press." Burger pointed out the historical background of free speech under the First Amendment was designed only to protect political speech. This is not correct. The Founders, in writing this amendment, were intent on preventing our government from prohibiting the various forms of political protest that Britain had attempted to crush. However, the amendment does not say "freedom of political speech" it says "freedom of speech." This deletion amounts to the Founders intent to protect all speech. It is interesting to note that Burger claims the original intent was to protect political speech only, yet his definition of constitutionally-protected speech includes that which is literary, artistic and scientific. He has himself approved of the expansion of free speech to cover a wider area.

A line must be drawn, though, on speech that violates the rights of others. At the time of the adoption of the Bill of Rights, defamation (slander and libel) was a violation of laws dating back to early English history. As defamation falsely destroys a person's reputation, it invades the rights of others and is not constitutionally-protected free speech. But that is a rare clear exception. In *Schenck v. United States* (1919), Justice Holmes presented a simple rule for future inter-pretation. Holmes argued that "the question in every case is whether the words used are used in such circumstances and are of such a nature as to create a clear and present danger that they will bring about substantive evil." In other words, speech that presents a clear and present danger of causing a substantive evil is the only speech that should be prohibited. Holmes illustrated the rule with this example: yelling "Fire" in a crowded theater. This presents a clear and present danger of causing a riot, and therefore is not constitutionally-protected free speech. This is a correct interpretation. Unfortunately, the Court has strayed from this test over the years, especially in the area of obscenity where the personal attitudes of the Justices have influenced decisions in illogical ways, such as Burger's opinion in the *Miller* case.

Obscenity law has become so vague and confused that Supreme Court Justice Potter Stewart, in the 1970s, explained the Court's view of pornography this way, "I can't define pornography, but I know it when I see it." Well, that sounds like a good objective rule of law. Exasperated at the court's inability to develop any test to deal with obscenity, Justice Brennan, writing for himself and two other Justices in *Paris Adult Theater I v. Slaton* (1973), insisted that the right to publish should be protected where no one is injured by such publication. He added that through several decades the Court had not been able to establish a rule on limiting free speech (obscenity) that was concise and not a violation of the First Amendment. In light of this failure, he suggested that the Court not limit speech at all unless it actually harmed others. This was a return to the "clear and present danger" doctrine, but it was a minority position. Opponents of pornography consistently argue that it violates their rights, but they are wrong. Pornography that is viewed in a theater, in a bar, or in a home affects no one but the viewer. What the religious zealot wants is to control not only what he sees, but what everyone else sees as well. As no one's rights are violated, pornography is entitled to constitutional protection. At this point, the religious fanatic usually brings up the overused adage that the Founders would be sickened by today's pornography and would not allow it to have constitutional protection. The Founders probably would be sickened by much of today's society, but I believe they would take much more offense at these attacks on their First Amendment, which they would agree was designed to protect expression no matter how vile — and this includes pornography.

The confusion over what should or should not be constitutionally protected has continued. Without a clear line of limitation on restrictions from the Court, a hodgepodge of rulings has slowly invaded our rights to free speech and press. The Supreme Court has, to this point, created several major limitations on free speech. Five major areas of speech have been held to be not entitled to free speech protection; extensive time, place and manner restrictions on speech

270

have been allowed; and several areas of special-context speech have developed where regulation is allowed. Unfortunately, these legal limitations on free speech have been supplemented by censorship efforts from both liberals and conservatives.

The recent descent into McCarthyesque censorship began in 1985 with the creation of the Parent's Music Resource Center (PMRC). This conservative Christian group was led by Tipper Gore, the wife of former Senator and current Vice President Albert Gore, and Susan Baker, the evangelical Christian wife of former Secretary of State James Baker. It pushed for legislation mandating a government label-rating system for records containing objectionable music. Due to their husbands' names they were able to appear in front of a contrived hearing of the Senate Commerce Committee. To no one's surprise this committee included Senator Gore. The hearings considered no legislation, they were a glorified publicity stunt, at taxpayer expense. They quickly became rather lively when the recording industry, and indeed the musicians themselves, fought back against this blatant attempt at censorship. The musicians were represented by Frank Zappa, John Denver, and Dee Snider from the heavy-metal band Twisted Sister. The eccentric yet brilliantly intellectual Zappa debated hostile senators to a standstill. After some headlines and attention, the so-called "Washington Wives" were rebuffed by the recording industry, which suggested it might commit to a general warning label, but nothing more. The girls were then free to return to their soap operas and social registers where they should have stayed in the first place.

The PMRC, however, continued to agitate for labeling legislation. In order to prevent labeling by the government, the Recording Industry Association announced a uniform label system on all possibly objectionable material beginning in July, 1990. They argued that at least it would be run by the industry, instead of the government. Numerous musicians, rather than face a label on their records, toned down their message. To others, especially the heavy-metal and rap groups, a warning label became a status symbol. They also came to mean a sure hit, as kids flocked to buy the albums with labels. Kids assumed that an album with a label must really contain some good material. This just goes to show that the same government leaders who are incompetent in using their power are just as incompetent in misusing it. Nonetheless, this still added up to self-imposed censorship. It was a successful and commonly used government ploy. Make big noises and threaten serious action, which forces the recording industry into a labeling system on their own. The government then avoids any challenge on constitutional grounds, because self-censorship is not unconstitutional. Yet free speech is just as offended.

However, some state governments have passed, and are still attempting to pass, stronger warning label legislation. Missouri and Louisiana have been two of the more radical in this endeavor. Of course, there is nothing better to do in Missouri, while legislation coming out of Louisiana almost on a daily basis depicts this state as the epitome of a backwater refuge for the mentally handicapped redneck products of inter-family breeding. These states have proposed plans banning the sales of records containing lyrics about adultery, incest, illicit drug or alcohol use, violence, murder, suicide, Satanism or sex. In the alternative, they propose a strict warning label system that prohibits purchases by those under eighteen.

These warning labels are clearly attempts at censorship; however, 1990 witnessed an even more ominous threat to free speech with the story of 2-Live Crew (The Crew). The Crew were a black "rap" group led by Luther Campbell. Rap is a powerful form of expression for young blacks. It is the protest of the disenfranchised. Due to the absolute failure of the capitalist system, the realities of life and culture for many young blacks are drugs, violence and sex. As music is a form of cultural expression, these topics then become the subjects of a large part of rap music. Crew's music is typical of this genre, and as such it is crude. In 1989, Crew put out an album entitled *As Nasty As They Wanna Be*. It attracted all kinds of negative attention from the censorship forces, but sold well. The lyrics led to legal battles in state and federal court. The lyrics to the song "Dick Almighty" were typical:

Dick Almighty's of no surprise
It'll fuck all the bitches all shapes and sizes
She'll climb a mountain, even run da block
Just to kiss the head of this big black cock
He'll tear the pussy open cause it's satisfaction
The bitch won't leave, it's fatal attraction

Now, I certainly am not going to defend rap, because frankly it is a filthy, obnoxious form of noise that is totally lacking in any kind of musical value. It requires no musical ability whatsoever; one only needs a foul rhyming mouth and a bass guitar to produce this garbage. It appeals to only the most illiterate morons whose lives must be a complete waste if this is what they want for entertainment. Included in this group are those pathetic individuals who drive lowered pickup trucks loaded with 18-inch woofers so that everyone in the neighborhood can be offended by rap's low-frequency monotonous drone. The only good thing about rap is that it has so overloaded the airwaves that the inevitable fade is right around the corner. Like the three-year super craze of the 70s, disco, the fad of rap has reached its peak, and its lack of any musical talent or value will cause its inevitable decline.

With that said, it must be pointed out that no matter how offensive this trash is, it is still constitutionally protected free speech under the First Amendment. As such it should not be subjected to censorship. Expression that is protected under the First Amendment often makes people uncomfortable, but the amendment doesn't exist to promote comfort — it exists to promote freedom. Censorship begins with an outcry against offensive speech, followed by limitations which are compounded by self-censorship in the face of community criticism. Then the materials are pulled form the shelves, the result being that the expression of ideas has been stopped. The community then finds another offensive topic. Finally, there is no expression of any ideas.

Limitations on thoughts, the expression of ideas, and the consumption thereof are paradoxical to a free society. People have an inherent right to speak, think, and hear what they choose. People who don't like the content of certain forms of music don't have to listen to it. Don't watch MTV, or turn the radio dial. People can make these decisions for themselves, but no one has the right to tell others what they can listen to!

Shortly after the release of *As Nasty As They Want To Be*, a civil court in Florida ruled that the album was obscene. Broward County Florida Sheriff Nick Navarro then began a witch-hunt. He sent deputies throughout the county warning record store owners to remove the album from the shelves. The Crew sued in federal court, claiming that this amounted to prior restraint. District Judge Jose Gonzales, Jr., ruled on June 6, 1990, that the actions of the sheriff did amount to prior restraint and were therefore improper. He then added that the album was obscene and that state anti-obscenity laws could be applied to it.

Sheriff Navarro then had his deputies comb local stores to find anyone still selling *Nasty*. On June 8, an undercover deputy bought copies of the record from E.C. Records, run by Charles Freeman. Six deputies then burst in, arrested Freeman, and took him to jail in handcuffs. Released on bond, he faced one year in jail and/or a $1,000 fine. It was the most outrageous instance of a person arrested for selling music since the Ministry of Propaganda controlled cultural affairs in Nazi Germany. Freeman was convicted at trial.

On June 10, 2-Live Crew performed an adults-only show in front of 300 fans and 30 police at Hollywood's Club Futura in Broward County. After the show, the police found half the group in their limo and arrested them for performing obscene material. The impact of these events was far-reaching. The Crew were banned in at least six Florida counties. The ban on the album spread to other locations, such as San Antonio, Texas. Most record stores pulled the album from the shelves, and major record dealers throughout the South refused to stock it.

A decision in a federal district court applies only in that district. Such a court is not bound by the decision of another district court, it is only bound by the court of appeals of the circuit to which it sits, and the U.S. Supreme Court. A judge in a small federal district in Florida decided that the album was obscene, yet it ended up banned in most of the South, and some of the North as well. It was a case of government censorship in violation of the First Amendment. The Crew were faced with the choice of toning down the act or not taking their message to the entire southern region of the country. To some degree they did both. In the long run, overt censorship creates a climate of fear that causes people to limit their own expression. That is a true violation of free speech.

"Heavy metal" is another form of music that has been the consistent target of censorship from the religious fringe. Scores of scenes of album-burnings have flooded the airwaves in recent years. Amusing as these silly ceremonies are, hanging over them are the words of a German philosopher who once wrote, "Where they burn books, eventually they burn people." Unfortunately, an historic truism!

With its roots in the early 1970s with bands such as Deep Purple and Black Sabbath, heavy metal has grown into the second largest-selling segment of the music industry. Fast, hard rhythms, pounding drums, and screaming guitars and vocals are the body of this music. On a technical and musical level, heavy metal is more demanding than talentless rap, but it is also attacked because of its lyrics. I would be less than honest if I didn't admit that many heavy metal songs concentrate on similar themes to rap, including sex and drugs. Heavy metal songs have also been attacked for dealing with violence, death, Satanism and suicide. Heavy metal is the music of young whites, and preaches the rebellion that is part of adolescence. For many kids, these topics are the issues they face. It also tends to be negative and reflective of the attitude of most adolescents, who see a country with a rotten, incompetent, abusive government, an economy rigged for the rich, and the hypocrisy of organized religion. They see themselves living in a negative environment, and the music expresses this.

It is the issues of Satanism and suicide that encourage the most radical attacks from fringe elements. Many instances of church-organized record-burning parties, much like those in Nazi Germany, have taken place to rid the world of these threats. Churches have, throughout history, created and perpetuated the myth of a monstrous devil, though the actual biblical descriptions are the exact opposite of this. Its need to do so is simple. Scare the people into the churches and keep them there with threats from a supposedly loving God. This is necessary because no rational person can accept the garbage that gushes forth from religion without being threatened. The churches cannot exist without their illusions of evil. Heavy metal is just another entry on a centuries-long list of victims of religious attacks. They claim that heavy metal turns kids toward Satan. The reality is that religion cannot compete with the fact that it is more fun to be bad. Nor is heavy metal based on the hypocrisy that is the underlying principle of organized religion. Many people in today's world seem to follow the old literary bromide, "it is better to rule in hell than serve in heaven." There are now numerous groups that are openly Satanic, such as King Diamond and Venom.

> From Kind Diamond's - "The Oath"
> *I deny Jesus Christ, the deceiver*
> *And I abjure the Christian faith*
> *Holding in contempt all of its works*
> *I swear to give my mind, body, and soul*
> *unreservedly to the furtherance of our*
> *Lord Satan's designs*
>
> From the cover of Venom's *Welcome to Hell* album:
> *We're possessed by all that is evil*
> *The death of your god we demand*
> *We spit at the virgin you worship*
> *and sit at Lord Satan's left hand*

There is a clear problem, though, with any attempt to include warning labels or bans on albums containing references to Satan. San Francisco is the home of Anton LaVey's First Satanic Church. As such, Satanism is an organized religion. Any government attempt to limit lyrics concerning this would be a violation of the First Amendment right to a free exercise of religion. It would be exactly the same as requiring warning labels, or a ban, on Christian lyrics. Or the Bible. While the Bible is full of offensive sex, violence, magic, and references to Satan, no one would propose putting a warning label on it. Or would we?

The Christian argument against these lyrics is very similar to their argument against pornography. They claim that pornography must be banned because it causes people to commit sexual assault and abuse. Well, what about John George Haigh, the so-called "British vampire murderer" who sucked out his victims' blood with straws? He was influenced to do so by witnessing the ritual drinking of the blood of Christ in an Anglican church communion service. Should communion be banned because of its criminal influence? Critics are also very critical of movies and lyrics discussing violence, but would their bans and labels apply to the "Star Spangled Banner," a song full of violence?

Another criticism of heavy metal is that it encourages suicide. Ozzy Osbourne, formerly of Black Sabbath, was sued after a California teen shot and killed himself. Apparently the teen had been listening to Osbourne's song, "Suicide Solution." The parents sued Osbourne and CBS Records for having "aided, or advised, or encouraged" the son to take his life. Ironically, the song was actually telling kids that suicide is not an acceptable solution to their problems. Frankly, any kid who commits suicide because of a song has emotional problems to begin with; the music can hardly be blamed. Fortunately, the case was dismissed as groundless.

Yet the proponents of warning labels would include lyrics relating to suicide on their endless lists of "unacceptable subjects" that society must be protected from. Would we then require warning labels on literary works as well? Would this apply to classics such as Shakespeare's *Hamlet,*in which the central character proclaims that suicide may be preferable to life's miseries? Or to *Romeo and Juliet,*in which the two lovers choose suicide together rather than life apart? Or Leo Tolstoy's *Anna Karenina,*in which the heroine concludes that suicide is the only alternative? The point is, where will the line be drawn and who will draw it? This is the ultimate question behind censorship. The religious fanatics are only too willing to come forth with their answers to these questions.

Another ground for the attacks on heavy metal has been the accusation that the music contains backwards or subliminal messages. This started with the song "Stairway to Heaven" by Led Zeppelin, but took a serious twist recently involving the British heavy metal band Judas Priest. In 1985, two Nevada teens allegedly consumed alcohol and drugs all afternoon while listening to a Judas Priest album. They then made a suicide pact and shot themselves with a shotgun. One died on the spot and the other died in 1988 due to his wounds. The parents sued the band and CBS Records, claiming that subliminal messages in the songs caused the boys to kill themselves. The case went to trial and attracted national attention. Fortunately, the jury acquitted the band of the charges.

Cases of censorship and attacks on free speech are on the rise. Censorship heralded the oppression of the 1940s and 50s, a period known for its blacklisting of entertainers, and it is doing so again in the 1990s. Censorship is the traditional precursor of a conservative revival. The straying from the Constitution that has occurred in the last few years may be the beginning of a conservative period we never escape. This new conservative era may so emasculate the already seriously-weakened Constitution that the pendulum may never be allowed to swing back.

Restrictions against speech are a direct assault on the First Amendment. As far as rap and heavy metal go, most Americans probably feel that they should be limited in their expressions of vulgarity, sex and violence. They feel that the First Amendment doesn't need to "protect that sort of thing, as long as my expression isn't affected." Unfortunately, a government that begins to censor expression of one type has the authority to limit the expressions of all types. So as the people sit back and approve these limitations, they shouldn't get too smug, because as soon as their thoughts and beliefs become "unacceptable" to the majority, they will be censored too. As the nation continually turns away from organized religion, towards rationality and New-Age philosophy, its citizens should be aware that their beliefs may fall into disrepute someday, and the censorship they have so vehemently supported may be aimed at them.

Clearly, in light of the PC movement, the conservative movement to censor has been joined by the liberal movement to censor. One recent example is truly astonishing. In January, 1994, the Department of Housing & Urban Development (HUD) began an investigation into the activities of three Berkeley, California, residents. It became a persecution which lasted nine months. These three citizens lived on the main road leading into Berkeley. For 15 years they had watched as a number of homeless shelters and rehabilitation facilities were placed in their residential neighborhood. These had led to serious problems. In one case the juvenile offenders held at a half-way house nearby had formed a gang and terrorized local residents. In another case a children's park next to a female shelter was taken over by the women's boyfriends for drug dealing. Not surprisingly, local residents were less than happy when, in July, 1992, the city decided to place yet another homeless shelter for the mentally ill in their neighborhood. They reacted as angry Americans always have. The three residents organized a neighborhood committee, published a newsletter, and circulated a petition to stop the facility. Basically, they exercised their First Amendment right of free speech, and the right to assemble and petition the government for a redress of grievances, as Americans have done for over 200 years. Specifically, the residents argued that the chosen location, which was next to two liquor stores and a bar, was not an appropriate site in light of the high rate of alcoholism and drug addiction among the homeless.

HUD moved in and began an investigation for violations of the Fair Housing Act Amendment of 1988. Unbelievably HUD targeted the residents who organized to stop the facility. Eventually, HUD threatened the three with fines of $100,000 each and a year in jail apiece, unless they turned over everything they had written about the project: their files, the minutes of the meetings of the neighborhood committee, and the committee's membership list.

The Fair Housing Act was designed to safeguard the housing rights of the disabled. It is the view of HUD that these facilities for social rejects have no negative consequences for a residential neighborhood. HUD and the federal courts have defined addiction and alcoholism as federally protected disabilities. This is, of course, more of the liberal philosophy that no one is to blame for their own actions. According to HUD, organized opposition to social service facilities based on the attributes of the people involved is a violation of the Fair Housing Laws. Apparently, HUD has not read the First Amendment. Or was HUD saying that the Fair Housing rights of drug addicts and drunks outweigh the Bill of Rights? Unfortunately, that is exactly what the head of San Francisco's HUD office claimed.

This was not an isolated case. HUD is currently questioning a group that opposed a home for the homeless mentally ill in New York. The Justice Department has sued a group of neighbors in Connecticut who tried to prevent a shelter in their neighborhood. In Seattle, a community group which opposed a home for ex-convicts was investigated by HUD. Another group nearby was investigated for filing a zoning suit. Residents in Kansas have been fined for trying to block a group home in their neighborhood. All of these case have occurred in the last three years. People across the country are now afraid to exercise their rights, just as HUD intended. Is this liberty? Is it freedom when the people live in fear of the government? These practices may have been appropriate for Heinrich Himmler, but they are not proper in the United States. The only question is: when are the people going to do what the Declaration of Independence states they have the right to do?

When a government takes away the right to express oneself it has taken away freedom. The Constitution should have prevented censorship in this country, but after all, it is just a piece of paper.

CHAPTER 24
CONGRESS 1990s

If ever a government institution deserved to be overthrown it is the United States Congress. Greatly disparaged throughout the nation's history, Congress has traditionally been known to be thoroughly incompetent and corrupt, but in modern times the members have reached a new low. Some of their more infamous legislative achievements in recent years include the Savings and Loan scandal, the huge Congressional pay raise, Bouncedcheckgate, the utter failure to do anything at all about the deficit, burdensome taxes, creating lavish perks for themselves that would make a Roman emperor blush, consistently refusing all attempts at reform, and having the audacity to be offended when the American people criticized them. Recent elections have echoed a "throw the rascals out" mood from the people, but this is hardly an appropriate punishment for these deadbeats. The people are so outraged that many would now suggest that a more fitting punishment would be to take all Congressmen out back, line them up against a wall, and have them shot. (Rhetorically speaking only, of course!) Unfortunately, that would probably only lead to a three year debate among the members over whether or not they wanted blindfolds. As it currently exists, this sorry excuse for an institution is unconstitutional and an absolute disgrace to the country. For two hundred years this so-called institution has been a perpetual joke and disgrace. It is time it was stopped! And it will be stopped; if not by political action, then by armed revolution and the rhetorical wall!

Congress: A national embarrassment
(Southern Cross Publishing)

My contempt for Congress began while teaching. At one point, I was engaged in a conversation with a student who wanted to be a congressman. When I inquired as to his reasoning, he seriously replied that he wanted his share of the graft and corruption which is endemic in that occupation. That certainly puts Congress in perspective. Another event that occurred while teaching finally convinced me that Congress is out of touch with the people and that we do not have a workable representative government anymore. Unfortunately, it also proved the point to my eighth-grade students.

In the spring of 1988, I began a unit on government with my American history classes. I went way beyond what the curriculum called for in this area, but I always felt that a participatory democracy requires an informed populace. The system will not work if the citizenry does not understand the process. To those ends I designed a six-week unit that included software for a presidential-election simulation in the computer lab; a study of the Libertarian, Republican, and Democratic Parties; a county voter-election machine and voter-registration cards for a grade-wide election; a two-day simulation of the passage of a bill through Congress; and a week long re-enactment of the Constitutional Convention. The result of the course was a real interest in government on the part of the students. As a follow-up exercise, I assigned a Constitution project which required, among other things, that the students write a letter to their congressman. In this case, it was Congressman Jack Brooks (D-Tex), representing (though this is a poor choice of words) the 9th District of Texas. He had held the seat since the 1950s.

I had several objectives in mind when I assigned the letter project. First, the students were allowed to write on any topic that was in the realm of federal government control, so it was a chance to research current events, gain an understanding of issues, and practice writing. Second, and more importantly, it was a chance for the students to see how representative government works. The people write their elected officials, and by making their voices heard they influence the process. As a congressman's office is more likely to respond when they think they are dealing with voters, I took steps to make sure the letters appeared to be just the usual mail from constituents instead of a school project. The students used their home addresses and did not indicate that they were kids. After checking the letters for content, neatness, and accuracy, I mailed them from several post offices over the next few days. The students anxiously awaited their responses, and waited, and waited.

Now, every first-year political science student knows that one of the functions of a congressman is that of "troubleshooter." This most important role consists of responding to constituent concerns. But not for Jack Brooks. The first response from the congressman did not arrive for four months. During the next school year, several of my ex-students returned to the junior high to show me their letters that had just arrived after six months. They told me that they understood I wanted them to see how government works, but what they learned was how it does not work. That's a sad commentary from a group of ninth-grade students. All in all, only about 10% of the letters ever received a response.

In anger over the lack of response I fired off a nasty letter to Brooks describing these events and my opinion of his utter incompetence. A nasty reply from his office took only three days to get back to me! I reported this story to both of the major Houston papers and the campaign director of Brooks opponent in the 1990 election.

It is true, of course, that it is not the congressman, but rather his office staff that handles the letter-writing chores. Some would offer this as an excuse for these events. It must be noted that a congressional staff neglects its constituency duties only if the congressman allows this practice. Only a congressman who feels entrenched and unthreatened by challengers could take this position as Brooks does. This is the norm for a congressman who has been in office too long. Jack Brooks is a walking example of the need for term limitation!

For Brooks and many other members of Congress, the job has become a career, and the powers of incumbency guarantee re-election. In recent years these members have been enjoying a 98% re-election rate. They use their position to consolidate their power, making them almost impossible to defeat. They steadfastly refuse to initiate campaign reform laws. To run successfully now, one must have millions of dollars available. Membership in Congress is limited to the rich. The same members continue in control for decades, unaccountable to anyone. This is legislative dictatorship, and it would sicken the Founders if they could see what their exercise in democracy has become. Fortunately, this has begun to change.

Not to disparage the entire institution, however. Congress does some things well. They secretly voted themselves a pay raise, they raked off millions and sold influence while contributing to the massive S&L scandal (now estimated to be a $500 billion cost to the taxpayers), and they annually engage in the budget farce, which always seems to result in new taxes, more wasteful spending, and a larger deficit.

In the spring of 1988, the members of Congress decided they needed to raise their $89,500 a year income. It seems they were having trouble getting by on this paltry sum, and being that rare group that can raise their own pay, they did just that. A pay increase of 33% was proposed. This amounted to approximately $29,535 for each congressman. Apparently it occurred to them that this maneuver might not sit well with the American people, whose yearly per capita income averages around $18,000, so they sought to cloak the raise in deception. The final pay raise was set to take place on a particular date unless both houses voted to stop it. The vote that then followed allowed a member to vote "no" to keep the raise and "yes" to stop it. This trick enabled the members to tell the public that they voted "no" on the pay raise bill, but it passed anyway. No matter how incompetent these people are at running the country, when it comes to deceiving the American people, protecting their own jobs, wasteful spending, outright lying, and stealing from the taxpayers, money can buy no better than the members of the U.S Congress.

At this point, however, a surprising thing took place. The usually apathetic American people, alerted by the media, had a fit over the pay raise. Radio stations led the outcry by organizing protests all over the country. These tactics worked, and Congress was forced to rescind the pay raise. The members of Congress were outraged at this interference by the people, and schemed secretly to get their raise anyway. In 1989, they quietly passed another pay raise with the support of President George "Read my lips, I lied" Bush. They thumbed their noses at the people and grabbed the money even in the midst of another record budget deficit. The apathy of the people had returned, and no real protests took place. The pay raise, scaled in over two years, increased House pay to $125,100 a year per member as of January 1, 1991. The senators brought their yearly pay to $101,900 apiece with an allowance for income earned from honoraria (speaking engagements and appearances). As these pay raises applied to 435 members and several non-voting delegates in the House, and all 100 senators, the increase totaled $16,832,800 per year. Total pay for the members of Congress stood at $64,983,800 per year. But we got such quality for our money!

On July 17, 1991, another chapter was written in this pay raise saga. The Senate, in a midnight move, voted to raise their yearly income another $23,200, to $125,100 per year. Leaders of both parties agreed to bring the measure to the senate floor well after the evening network news and the departure of most reporters. And we criticize them for not thinking? Senators, bristling at the idea that this was inappropriate, claimed that it wasn't really a pay raise, it was an equalization to keep even with House salaries. In a typical argument, Senator Ted Stevens, R-Alaska, told senators considering voting against the measure that they would need to get hotel rooms for the night because their wives, who supported the bill, would be upset. Isn't that an interesting legislative priority?

The senators also claimed that in exchange for the pay raise they would give up honoraria. These speaking fees are paid to senators by special interest groups. Frankly, honoraria is thinly disguised bribery. It is in keeping with the fine traditions of the Congress that the members steal some more taxpayer dollars and try to justify it by appearing saintly and giving up their payoff money, which they shouldn't have had in the first place.

Senator Chuck Grassley, R-Iowa, an opponent of the pay raise, suggested, "Salaries should not be raised until the Congress shows it can balance the budget and run the government efficiently." This received a chorus of laughs in the Senate. As a result, the pay raise gave the 100 senators a total of $2,320,000 more per year, bringing the yearly pay of Congress to $67,303,800. And we continue to get such quality for our money!

Then the curtain rose on another act in the pay raise saga. In 1789, James Madison proposed 12 amendments to the first Congress, and ten of them were ratified by the states, becoming known as the Bill of Rights. One of the other two amendments that was never ratified dealt with congressional pay raises, and stated, "No law, varying the compensation for services of the senators or representatives, shall take effect, until an election of representatives shall have intervened." In a bizarre twist, Michigan became the 38th state to ratify it in May, 1992, thus completing the requirement of approval by 3/4 of the states. Modern-day amendments have gone to the states with seven-year limits, but this 203-year-old amendment didn't have a deadline, so it was apparently valid. Of course, Congress was not at all impressed, and declared that the amendment had expired. Incompetent boob, and House Speaker, Thomas Foley led the charge, insisting on congressional hearings into whether or not the amendment had became defunct. I think we can all guess what the results of those hearings would have been. Finally, Foley and company gave in and admitted the validity of the new 27th Amendment. As it turned out, congressional resistance gave way when the honored members figured out that the new amendment would not stop a system of automatic, yearly cost-of-living-allowance (COLA) raises that Congress passed in 1989 in order to avoid further embarrassing fights over pay raises. The COLA law had already, secretly, raised yearly congressional pay to $129,500 in 1992, with another big increase planned for January, 1993. We now pay Congress $69,671,000 per year.

This new pay raise came only days after the new deficit numbers were released, which showed the 1992 shortfall was expected to reach $362 billion, by far the largest in the nation's history. The budget projection for 1992 also included a special treat. For the first time in U.S. history, the single greatest expense in the federal budget was gross interest payments due on the federal debt. The following chart reflects some of the major components of this budget.

1992 Budget Item	Expenditure
Interest on Debt	$304 billion
Defense	$295 billion
Social Security	$288 billion
Environment	$20 billion

Paying the interest on the debt does not reduce it at all; it just keeps the government credit worthy so it can run up more debt. The $304 billion interest payment for this year equals $832 million per day. If a taxpayer had $304 billion to spend on himself, he could buy 2,080 Lambourghini sports cars (at $400,000 each) every day for a year. As it is, that money doesn't buy a damn thing. It doesn't take a rocket scientist to realize there is something dreadfully wrong here. In the 200+ years since the Constitution went into operation, the nation's accumulated debt amounted to $908.5 billion. Reagan and Bush quadrupled that number to $4.021 trillion as of October, 1991. By 1994, the debt approached $5 trillion.

Besides the extreme danger posed by such a huge debt hanging over the nation, there are other issues. What services could the government provide to the homeless, to education, to crime prevention, to health care, to the environment, and to other necessities with an extra $304 billion this year? How far could middle class taxes be lowered to obtain relief from their oppressive burden if this amount wasn't being wasted? Well, at least the members of Congress aren't doing without!

Attached to all this free spending is Congress's own operating budget, which after a 20.5% increase at the same time as the pay raise, reached $2.5 billion in 1991. That translates into $5.6 million per congressman per year. Much of this money goes to the congressional staff of 37,388 persons, which includes personal staff, cooks, beauticians, travel agents, and mail carriers. More than 19,000 of these persons work directly for the congressmen on their personal staffs, which is 10,000 more than when the reduce-the-size-of-government Republicans were elected in 1980, 1984, and 1988. And what do these people do for their taxpayer-supplied salaries? Many staff members play a direct role in the re-election campaigns of the Congressmen; they produce the massive taxpayer-funded mailings to constituents at election time; and a new part of their job is leaking confidential FBI reports so as to smear Supreme Court nominees.

Some members tried to cut corners in the congressional allotment. Representative Harris Fawell (R-Illinois) proposed stripping $375,000 which was intended to renovate the House beauty salon. After being accused of sexism by a female member for not proposing to cut the barber shop funds, and suffering a backlash by many other members, Fawell's amendment was easily killed.

The absolute fiasco that was the development of the budget during the summer of 1990 shed much light on congressional incompetence. The idea of cutting wasteful spending seems completely foreign on Capitol Hill. The only solution they see is more taxes, more borrowing, and more printing of currency. When Reagan was elected president in 1980, the United States was the world's largest creditor nation. Now it is the world's largest debtor nation. The deficit, currently approaching $5 trillion, is a noose around the country's neck that will surely strangle us. Like an individual, a nation can only go so far into debt before bankruptcy becomes the only option. When that happens to the U.S. government, it will collapse the economy of the entire world and set off a depression so deep economists will have to create a new word to describe it.

The problem is very complex and, rather than solve it, Congress simply tries to ignore it. Much of the problem is the politics of compromise. This approach is slow and cumbersome. On the philosophic level, one who compromises always gets less than one wants. Mediocrity, in other words. Another problem is that the members of Congress do not have the intellect to solve this problem. Two basic maxims of life are at work here. I have witnessed both in education and business. First, only the most incompetent, those who never rock the boat, climb to the highest levels of authority and, second, most people are not courageous enough to attempt to solve problems. In my opinion, if one isn't a part of the solution then one is a part of the problem. With these operating to the extreme in Congress, there really is no hope of ever solving the budget mess. An economic collapse then becomes inevitable.

The budget of 1990 included some interesting items. In one example, a North Dakota woman had attempted to raise funds to restore the boyhood home of band leader Lawrence Welk. The fund raising went slowly until someone suggested she investigate federal funds. She wrote to senator Quentin Burdick (D-N.D.), who turned the matter over to his press secretary, who then contacted Rocky L. Kuhn, clerk of the Agriculture Subcommittee of the Senate Appropriations Committee, which was chaired by senator Burdick. Kuhn then wrote in a $500,000 grant under the heading of "rural development" as part of the agricultural appropriations. No hearings were held, no witnesses called, no explanation of how the money was to be spent. A subcommittee clerk authorized the spending of a half-million dollars of taxpayer money, and people wonder why the deficit will be about $362 billion in 1992. If businesses practice this kind of financial planning, they go bankrupt. If individuals do it, they go to jail. If Congress does it they vote themselves a pay raise. What a country!

The Welk story continued in March, 1991. After several months of attempts, the House rescinded the $500,000 grant. This move was led by Jim Slattery (D-Kan.). North Dakota congressmen then made political threats against Kansas lawmakers for stopping the project. Senate Republican leader Bob Dole stated that "the matter may be bubbling into a little civil war." Rep. Dan Glickman (D-Kan.) summed this up well, saying, "the grant fiasco became a national embarrassment." It sure is an interesting way to run a country.

Another classic example of government spending came to light in July, 1991. It was revealed that $300,000 had been provided for a three-year environmental study titled "Methane Emissions from Ruminant Livestock." The goal of this project was to determine how much methane gas enters the atmosphere when cows burp.

Then even more examples of congressional waste of taxpayer funds were revealed: $3.1 million to convert a ferry boat into a crab restaurant in Baltimore; $107,000 to study the sex life of the Japanese quail; $150,000 to study the Hatfield-McCoy feud; $320,000 to purchase President McKinley's mother-in-law's house; $1 million to study why people don't ride bikes to work; $144,000 to see if pigeons follow human economic laws; $219,000 to teach college students to watch television; $1 million to preserve a Trenton, New Jersey sewer as a historic monument; $6,000 for a document on Worcestershire sauce; and $10,000 to study the effects of naval communications on a bull's sexual potency!

The 1990 Deficit Reduction Act, as that year's budget farce became known, purported to cut the 1991 deficit by $40 billion. It supposedly would reduce the deficit by $500 billion over the next five years and balance the budget. Didn't Reagan make that promise in 1979, and 1980, and '81, '82, '83, '84, '85, and so on? Wasn't the Gramm-Rudman Act supposed to require automatic budget cuts if a yearly deficit rose beyond target amounts so that the budget would be balanced by 1990, or '91, or '92, or so on? Didn't Bush make the same promise in 1988, and '89, and '90, and so on? At least with Bush the explanation is simple — he lied, again! The deficit reduction act was a charade, a planned hoodwinking of the American people. The Congress attempted to make the people think they had reached a lofty solution and that, with just a little more sacrifice, we would finally achieve a balanced budget. So the people grudgingly accepted a new round of tax increases in the belief that this was the cure. The only problem is that no Congress is tied to the decisions of a previous Congress, and the same bunch of irresponsible incompetent congressional deadbeats who created this problem are still in control. The next few years will see them moving away from the cuts that they established, the enactment of new spending measures, and a new budget crisis requiring tax increases.

In July, 1991, Budget Director Richard Darman reported to Congress that the government had overestimated their anticipated tax revenues for the next five years, which was the basis for the 1990 Deficit Reduction Act. The new numbers anticipated $132.9 billion less in revenues than originally forecast. Most of this difference was said to be "technical re-estimates." When pinned down, Darman explained this to mean a "mathematical goof of $132.9 billion." Oops! Budget Committee Chairman James Sasser (D-Tenn.) pointed out that the Deficit Reduction Act raised taxes by $137 billion over the five years, and that this error essentially canceled out the tax increases, so that no progress was actually made by the Act. It was all so predictable.

The new taxes themselves were not very well thought out either. They hit gasoline, air travel, luxury items, alcohol, and cigarettes, among other things. Our lying no-new-taxes-president, who swears he was coerced into accepting these increases to protect the country from the Democrats, proposed a 10-cent increase in the federal gas tax. The Democrats in Congress managed to reduce this amount to a 5.1-cent increase. A mobile country whose people depend upon transportation in a time of rapidly escalating fuel costs, and the government after much study decided that the cure is to raise fuel taxes. What stupidity! These new gas taxes were projected to raise $5 billion a year. I guess we have nothing to worry about since that covers .0012% of the deficit.

A year after enactment we saw one typical result of the short sighted congressional tax policy. The luxury tax placed on boats helped sink the American boating industry. The law established a 10% excise tax on boats costing more than $100,000. Like the colonists before them, modern Americans decided not to buy the products, and so not to pay the tax. The National Marine Manufacturers Association estimated in June, 1991, that due to severely reduced sales, caused by the tax, 10,000 American jobs had been lost and another 10,000 would be lost. Following this news the IRS informed Congress that the tax was "revenue negative"; that is, its cost of collection exceeded the projected $3 million it was expected to bring in during 1991. Finally, it was estimated that the lost payroll taxes, increased unemployment benefits, and welfare costs of the displaced boat builders would exceed collected revenues from the tax by $30 million in 1991 alone. What a brilliant plan!

American boat builders have historically set the standard for innovation, quality, and competitiveness, but not anymore. The ridiculous tax from our consistently inept Congress broke the backs of the industry, but all is not lost; after all, the Japanese will now be able to supply us with better boats. The Congress clearly deserves a raise for this!!!

More final straws came in a September, 1991, report from the General Accounting Office, a congressional agency. According to the GAO, from July 1, 1988, to June 30, 1989, congressmen bounced 4,006 personal checks. These accounts existed in a bank set up by Congress in the Capitol Building to serve congressmen. When we, the common folk, bounce checks we pay typically $20-$25 as a penalty, but the members of Congress do not pay such penalties. And they say that power doesn't corrupt! When the GAO originally discovered this problem and reported it, a new set of procedures was implemented in an effort to stop the check-bouncing. For the six-month period (July-December 1989) following the new procedures, congressmen bounced 4,325 checks, an 8% increase. This number works out to an average of nearly 10 bounced checks per congressman. What's more, the GAO reported that 134 Congressmen cashed 581 bad checks for amounts of $1,000 or more. Congressional procedures allowed the bad checks to be "floated" until the writer could redeem them, in some cases up to a month, thus protecting members from embarrassment and plunging credit ratings. When this debacle hit the fan, House Speaker Tom Foley (D-Wash.) announced that the names of the bad check writers would be kept secret from the public. Republican House leaders joined in with Foley's cover-up and agreed that the offenders should remain a secret. The real reason for this cover-up became apparent when media investigations discovered and revealed some of the offenders. The ranks of the check-bouncers included Speaker Foley, House Majority Leader Dick Gephardt (D-Mo.), and Republican Whip Newt Gingrich (R-Ga.). In an attempt at political damage control, Speaker Foley agreed to an Ethics Committee investigation into the banking abuses. Washington insiders said about half of the ethics panel, including its chairman, would have to remove themselves from the investigation, because of the hot checks they had written. We can be sure that any congressional investigation of a scandal involving House members and leaders will be a whitewashing, as the Keating 5 investigation proved. At the end of this dismal week, Foley announced the matter was closed. The following model is provided as the ultimate example.

The Eight-Step Congressional Problem Solving Technique

1) Discover a problem.
2) Bumble around directionless while it gets worse.
3) Try to fix it.
4) Make it worse through inept, poorly thought out legislation.
5) Try to cover it up.
6) Set up a whitewashing investigation only after severe criticism.
7) Forget about it.
8) Vote selves a pay raise.

It was noted that after the pay raise took affect on January 1, 1991, the number of bounced checks dropped somewhat. Well, I guess the pay raise was worthwhile after all.

In the aftermath of the stir over "Bouncedcheckgate," several other congressional mini-scandals came to light. On October 3, 1991, a House subcommittee disclosed that some 300 current and former House members had stiffed the House restaurant for more than $300,000 in unpaid bills. This restaurant is subsidized by tax money so that the prices remain low for the House members. It is absolutely incredible, in this situation, that the congressmen still don't pay their bills. Is it any wonder the country is in such a disastrous financial condition?

More indignation developed in December, 1991, when the media began to investigate the long list of congressional perks that are provided to members at taxpayer expense: 1) three private gyms with pools and tennis courts; 2) Library of Congress check-out privileges which the voters do not have; 3) free parking at Washington National Airport; 4) cheap haircuts, car washes, and child care; 5) free airfare home and to exotic locations around the globe on government business; 6) parking tickets "fixed"; 7) a pension plan that pays $50,000 a year to members with 10 years experience.

Not paying restaurant tabs, knowingly writing bad checks, and taking expensive perks are just more indicators that many members of Congress are deadbeats who consider themselves above the law. In *Animal Farm*, George Orwell wrote the ultimate essay on the corruptive influence of power. The story begins with a group of farm animals whose lives were tormented by an abusive owner. This treatment eventually brought about an animal revolution. After throwing off the bonds of human control, the animals agreed to live by a series of commandments. Painted on a barn wall, one of these commandments stated "all animals are equal." As the pigs assumed control and eventually totalitarian dictatorship, they began to separate themselves from the conditions and laws under which the other animals lived. Finally the pigs, in order to justify their corruption, took advantage of the fact the other animals were barely literate, and modified the commandment, under the cover of night, to read "all animals are equal, but some animals are more equal than others." The members of the Congress, who seem ever-determined to bring about an Orwellian future, must consider themselves the most equal of all.

In a related note, it was revealed in June, 1992, that Congress had spent millions of tax dollars building and maintaining a posh congressional bomb shelter alongside the luxurious Greenbrier Resort Hotel in the West Virginia countryside. Apparently this was only one of several such installations built by the federal government to protect Congress, the President, the Cabinet, and the Supreme Court Justices in the event of nuclear attack. I can see it now, as millions of the American people are vaporized by hydrogen bombs, remembered only by their shadows burned into walls, the leaders of our government reside safely underground in luxury ready to emerge and rebuild the nation to the same level of incompetence as before. They do such a good job I think they deserve the right to live and re-create the country. There ought to be a law that in case of nuclear attack the members of the government have to stand outside and act as a shield. After all, they are the ones who start conflicts. The revelation of this story by the media caused an immediate outcry from enraged congressmen, some of whom had tried to prevent the story from being printed.

It seemed to be a very bad two years for Congress, but actually it was business as usual. The only difference was that the media kept the people's attention focused on the congressional circus more than usual. During all this time polls showed a dramatic decrease in the already-abysmal approval ratings for the Congress. Even President George "Read my lips, I lied" Bush had suffered a 50-point drop in the polls due to his criminally negligent mismanagement of the economy. With an election year right around the corner; it was clear that something had to be done to turn around this trend. For those of us familiar with American politics it was clear that it would soon be tax-cutting time. Sure enough, in the spring of 1992, Congress and the President began to talk tax cuts. One would think the people would see through this transparent charade, but alas they never do. Various proposals abounded and the debate, as planned, shifted the attention of the nation. The people love tax cuts and the government knows this. This device is consistently used in an attempt to make the people believe the government is doing a good job because they are cutting our taxes, and it seemed to be working once again. One of the ideas gaining momentum was to give a one-time $300 credit to each filer. Well, if 150 million people made use of this credit it would cost the Treasury $45 billion in 1992. That kind of responsible legislation will surely help eliminate the unbelievable 1992 budget deficit of $362 billion. Such a move to cut taxes at that point was financial suicide, but this does reveal the priorities of Congress and the President — get re-elected no matter what it does to the nation!

Another brilliant example of American government incompetence was revealed in protectionist legislation to deal with the trade imbalance with Japan. Talk on this issue became quite intense following the 50-year anniversary of the December 7, 1941, Japanese attack on Pearl Harbor. As the United States slides inexorably into decline as a world power, the nations of the Pacific Rim, especially Japan, are on the upswing. This has created numerous difficulties in trade between the U.S. and Japan. Essentially, our shores are open to most of their exports, while the reverse is not true. This has been dramatically proven with cars. The results can be readily seen in the December, 1991, announcement by General Motors to lay off 74,000 workers and close a number of plants. This was forced on GM due to a decreasing market share as a result of foreign competition and, of course, poor management practices. To combat this situation the U.S government is increasingly resorting to the same policy — protectionist measures — that have failed for 200 years. Congress and the President feel that if Japan won't allow our products in, then we won't let theirs in; this will be implemented through high tariffs placed on Japanese imports. This can only force Japan to respond with further protectionist barriers of their own. As prices rise due to the tariffs, purchases go down. Historically, this approach has worked to cut trade. If there is anything the U.S. economy can't stand at this juncture it is a trade war. Since we take the same protectionist approach to Europe, we may find the new world order is dominated by trade between Japan and Europe while the U.S. sits on the sidelines and quickly fades.

The Japanese have a very good reason for not wanting American products, especially cars — they are exorbitantly-priced garbage. The reputation of American products is known world-wide, and that's why this nation faces shrinking markets. The major portion of blame for this reputation belongs to the labor unions. They greedily consumed ever-increasing amounts of overhead until American products became priced out of the market. A typical auto worker, who is (by the way) a high-school dropout, makes approximately twice what a college-educated classroom teacher makes. At the same time, these beer swilling couch potatoes produce a product that is absolute crap. A common, yet typical, joke about American cars is the explanation of the acronym FORD — Fix Or Repair Daily. Frankly, these unions have gotten exactly what they deserve. Now they act like the Japanese are to blame for their misfortune, but even most American auto industry workers now drive Japanese imports. It's simple: Japanese cars are cheaper and they are better. That used to be true of American products; as a matter of fact that is how the U.S. built itself into a manufacturing giant, but now we are being beaten at our own game. Past Presidents and congresses have clearly been accomplices to this modern industrial collapse. Their pro-union policies, especially from Democrats, allowed the unions to strike their companies into unprofitability while at the same time encouraging lazy, slovenly work. No wonder the Japanese laugh at this country. The U.S. may have won the military war against Japan, but the Japanese have won the economic war, and in the long term that means we lose! Until U.S. industry is able to shed the yoke of union control, bring their prices down to a reasonable level, and rebuild a reputation for quality, we will have a trade problem with Japan. In the past we have been able to intimidate nations into less restrictive trade policies, but unfortunately, this time we are up against a Goliath and our slingshot is broken. (It was made in the USA.)

One step that is imperative at this point is congressional term limitation. This idea has gained a great deal of momentum recently. Several states have passed such limitations for their state legislators. The state of Washington even attempted to limit its members of the U.S. Congress. Unfortunately, this is unconstitutional; the only way to bring about term limitation for the Congress is through the Constitutional amending process. Even President George "Read my lips, I lied" Bush supported the plan, although he was not motivated by any interest in democratic government, but rather in breaking the control of the Congress held by the Democrats and replacing it with Republican control. Seems the G.O.P. wants a chance to run the graft and corruption for awhile.

A constitutional amendment should be passed to limit the members of the U.S. Congress to 6 years. This change would mean three two-year terms in the House of Representatives and two three-year terms in the Senate. Opposition to term limitation comes, not surprisingly, from Congress and their hordes of moochers who claim the Founders did not intend for there to be such limitations. It is interesting how these people consistently trample the Constitution, but when they are threatened they hide behind it.

The topic of term length was debated at the Constitutional Convention. Views ranged from lifetime terms to one year. The current two-year term in the House and six-year term in the Senate were more the result of compromise than any strong feelings, though most delegates agreed these terms should be short. The Convention also debated term limitation. The delegates were almost unanimous in the feeling that a limit on the number of terms was not necessary. Many, however, supported a term limitation on the president. This reflects their belief in the inherent goodness of the legislature. At that time legislative bodies were a relatively new phenomenon and so there was no experience with the legislative dictatorship we have witnessed in this century. Had they concluded the legislature was as easily influenced by the nature of power as the executive, they would have had a different view on term limitation for Congress. Nonetheless, the delegates decided the people should be the final arbiters of an elected official's destiny. The Founders assumed the people would revel in their freedoms and constitutional powers and would vote to remove any unresponsive official, so term limitations were not considered necessary. That is republican government at its most basic, and is certainly a laudable principle, but things have changed. Following the four terms of President Franklin Delano Roosevelt, the people experienced the potential for abuse and passed the 22nd Amendment in 1951, which limited the president to two terms. The same conditions now demand a limitation on the Congress.

The American people take their rights for granted, and many others rightly feel that the entire electoral process is pointless, as nothing ever changes. Voting is a privilege that is exercised by an increasingly shrinking disillusioned minority. It is time for a change and it is one that the Founders would have approved.

The major drawback of term limitation, and a prime complaint of those opposed to it, is the loss of experience in Congress that will result. It was a concern over this that led the Founders to stagger the election of senators to one-third every two years. This was designed to avoid the possibility of all members of the House and Senate being removed at the same time. Unfortunately, the choice becomes one between an inexperienced Congress or a corrupt abusive Congress. Given these two options, the better choice is self-evident! However, until the 1994 elections, Congressman Jack Brooks not surprisingly, prevented any term limitation legislation from getting out of the House Judiciary Committee, which he controlled. Another case of democratic government at work!

On the other hand, maybe we won't need term limitation. As the election season approached in 1992, 62 members of Congress decided to quit. They quit for a variety of reasons: many of them, alienated and frustrated, left due to the utter inability of the institution to affect the nation's problems; some of them are left because they knew they would be defeated in fall elections; and 21 of them called it quits in order to benefit from a loophole that allows them to convert millions of dollars of reserve campaign funds into personal wealth as long as they retire by 1992. Of course, once they quit they get to live off one of the best pension plans anywhere.

And then in November 1994, an amazing event took place. Apparently, the American people finally woke up. In elections at the local, state, and federal levels the public voted overwhelmingly for Republicans thus sweeping hordes of Democrats from office. The list of defeated incumbents included such career politicians as Speaker of the House Tom Foley, Congressmen Jack Brooks and Dan Rostenkowski, and Governors Mario Cuomo and Ann Richards. This reflected a very serious anti-government, anti-incumbent, anti-tax, and anti-Democrat sentiment. It was nothing less than a complete rejection of the old socialist principles of the Democratic Party. But more importantly it was a warning to both parties to get things in order. The most surprising outcome of the election was a Republican majority in both houses of Congress for the first time since the 1950s. There were great celebrations and predictions that nirvana was at hand.

For some months Ross Perot had been campaigning for such a Republican majority. It was his view that since the Democrats had failed so miserably to solve any of the nation's problems, it was time to give the Republicans a try. Republicans, having been unified by the slick Contract With America hype during the campaign predictably began to go to pieces immediately following election day. Essentially, they resorted to the same stupidity as that generally reflected by the Democrats. Like Clinton, who in his first week in office pushed the extremely divisive issue of allowing homos into the military, the Republicans promised an immediate vote on a school prayer amendment thus alienating just about everyone. What an absurdity, but it was all so predictable. As a side note, anyone who thinks returning prayer to the schools will fix a damn thing is an idiot. Period! So, instead of leading the nation in a resolution of serious and potentially fatal economic problems we get the same old simplistic whining and preaching about moral issues. Not that the Republican program was appropriate or even original. Nothing more than a rehash of previously popular Reaganomics, the Republicans sought to cut taxes, raise military spending and promised a balanced budget would be the result. Well, that is exactly what Reagan promised, but the result was a budget deficit which quadrupled in only 12 years. And it will be again. And the mess continues. Was this the major revolution the voters thought they had wrought or was it final proof of the inadequacy of democratic government, a system based upon allowing the leaders to hide behind a continually shifting majority which avoids responsibility and therefore blame and therefore resolution?

Considering the criminal negligence of Congress raises a philosophical concern about the law. The people are raised in the propaganda institutions (the schools) to revere the law. But is there any reason to respect the law? Laws are made by men in Congress and the state legislatures. They are just men. The fact that they have bribed or swindled their way to power gives them no inherent right to pass divine judgment for the rest of us. These men are incompetent and corrupt, not omnipotent. And are the judges who enforce these decrees entitled to any more respect? The fact is that none of these men deserve respect or even attention. Their decrees are the useless words of the unjust. And the law, as statements of the unjust, deserves no respect.

The Congress as currently functioning is not what the Founders had in mind when they planned a democratic body representing the needs of the people. In the Declaration of Independence, Thomas Jefferson stated, "A Prince, whose character is thus marked by every act which may define a Tyrant, is unfit to be the ruler of a free people." Every act of Congress now defines a tyranny, and they are unfit to be the rulers of this nation. It is now time to heed another Jeffersonian principle. It is the Right, indeed the Duty of the people, to alter or abolish a government that becomes abusive, and institute a new government. Following the original intent of the Constitution would have prevented this sad state of affairs from developing, but after all, it is just a piece of paper.

CHAPTER 25
THE COMMERCE CLAUSE 1990s

The government sues a small business into bankruptcy attempting to force it to spend tens of thousands of dollars on renovations to accommodate one crippled customer; the government forces an airline to put different seats in all its planes as a result of a suit by a grossly fat person; the government tells private restaurants and hotels who they must serve; the government orders a car-rental company to install hand controls so that cripples can drive the cars; the government mandates all companies to give 12 weeks off to their employees; the government forces a college not to drop their women's gymnastics team; the government requires racial and gender quotas in hiring. Unfortunately, these scenes are not taken from George Orwell's *1984*, but rather are headlines today. Such unbelievably intrusive federal government power represents a recent phenomenon of greatly expanded government power under a little-known phrase in the Constitution, the Commerce Clause.

Congress has no power, under the Constitution, to enact any legislation unless it can point to a specific source in the Constitution. The listed powers of Congress can generally be found in Article I, Section 8. Under the Founders' concept of Federalism the powers of government were split between the states and the new federal government. The states agreed to give up a few limited powers to the federal government in order to assure an orderly national authority sufficient to hold the nation together. The concept of federalism developed out of a fear of strong central governments. It was hoped that this split in power would avoid future abuses. It was clearly understood that all government power not specifically given to the new federal government in the Constitution would be retained by the states and the people. This limitation was adopted officially in the 10th Amendment to the Bill of Rights in 1791. The list of powers given to Congress includes the powers to lay and collect taxes, coin monies, establish post offices, declare war, and others. It also includes the power "to regulate Commerce with foreign Nations, and among the several States, and with Indian Tribes." This became known as the Commerce Clause.

Determining the original intent of the Founders concerning the Commerce Clause is a simple matter. There were serious and clear problems between the 13 States during the disastrous Articles of Confederation period. One of the major failings of the Confederation government was its inability to regulate trade between the states or between the United States and foreign nations. As we have seen, the American leaders who drafted the Articles of Confederation in 1781 were almost pathologically afraid of strong government. To this end they had prohibited the national Confederation government from regulating trade. The abuses committed by the British under the guise of regulating trade were still fresh in their minds. From the Navigation Acts to the Tea Act, the British had abused the rights of the American colonists for more than 100 years. It was thought that the control of trade was a matter best left to the exercise of sovereign power by each state. This decision really reflects the extent of the paranoia American leaders felt about government at that time; prohibiting this power to the central government assured the continuation of conflict between the states and an eventual breakdown of the "perpetual union." And that is exactly what happened.

During the American Revolution the 13 States had more or less cooperated with each other against the greater evil of Great Britain, but make no mistake, there was extreme animosity between some of the states. At the most critical point in the war, as American nationalist leaders attempted to institute a centralizing government to run the war effort, the states fought over western land claims for land they had not yet won from Britain. This delayed the implementation of the Confederation for four years. The states simply acted like, and believed they were, 13 separate nations temporarily tied together. When the war ended, so did the need for cooperation, in the view of many states. In 1783, after seven years of war, what was left of the American economy began to collapse. As conditions worsened, the states began to discriminate against each other in trading matters, which guaranteed a complete economic collapse. The states resorted to a number of discriminatory techniques: they implemented use taxes on the products of other states which crossed their roads; they restricted the use of waterways; they continued to fight over boundaries; those with ports bilked those without them; they implemented protective tariffs against other states to such levels that the British trade paid less; and they refused to accept the printed paper money of other states. Eventually, armed conflict flared between several states. Virginia and Pennsylvania fought over the Pittsburgh region, while Pennsylvania and Connecticut fought over the Wyoming Valley in northeastern Pennsylvania.

The international trade scene was a mess as well. When the Confederation Congress attempted to gain some control over international trade to respond to European trade restrictions on American goods, the states refused to allow it. Instead, the states openly competed with each other for trade treaties, thus forcing potential trading partners to negotiate with 13 separate entities. With the states printing stacks of worthless paper money, a lack of exchange rates, and the inability of the Confederation Congress to coin money, the government fell into a $40 million debt. This earned the distrust and disrespect of European governments. As a result, Europeans became reluctant to engage in trade with America.

Finally, in August 1786, Shay's Rebellion in Massachusetts revealed the beckoning road to civil war if something was not done soon. At that same time, James Madison and other leaders from five states held a conference in Annapolis, Maryland, to work on resolving trade problems. While the conference failed to take any action on trade, the delegates voted to recommend that another convention be held in Philadelphia the following May. When the Virginia Assembly called for the same the Confederation Congress agreed. This would turn out to be the Constitutional Convention which gave Congress the power to regulate commerce.

At the Constitutional Convention the delegates debated the need for Congress to have the power to regulate commerce among the states. There was general agreement, as all recognized this failing in the Articles of Confederation government. Specifically, they addressed the power of the new federal government in three areas: its ability to tax imports and exports; its ability to stop states from levying taxes on the shipping of other states; and requiring a 2/3 vote for Congress to pass any navigation/commercial laws. The new government was given these powers, but the 2/3 vote requirement was dropped in place of a simple majority.

As is the case with every other provision in the Constitution, the intended meaning of the Commerce Clause comes from the experience of the Founders. Their intent can readily be seen in *The Federalist Papers,* a collection of 85 essays written in 1787-88 by James Madison, Alexander Hamilton, and John Jay, which explained to the people of New York the meaning of each provision of the Constitution as that state considered ratification of the new plan. The intent of this clause was to allow Congress to pass legislation to give the nation one united voice in the area of international trade and to prevent the states from discriminating against each other in trading matters. In *The Federalist* #22, Alexander Hamilton, in discussing the proposed commerce power, does not do more than simply mention the interstate power. On the other hand, he goes into some detail in explaining the extent of the power of Congress to regulate foreign trade.

In *The Federalist* #42, James Madison adds a detailed explanation of the foreign and interstate trade powers. He begins by concentrating on what the Founders clearly understood to be the most serious problem: foreign trade. The goal was to establish an organized basis on which to conduct foreign trade. Madison goes on to say that "without the supplemental provision for Congress to regulate commerce among the states, the great and essential power of regulating foreign commerce would have been incomplete and ineffectual." The power to regulate commerce among the states was then a secondary power designed to support the nation's foreign power. Madison added that the past conflict among the states, as they taxed the products of other states, would, if not regulated, "nourish unceasing animosities and not improbably terminate in serious interruptions of the public tranquillity." He concludes by examining the lessons of European confederations. In Germany the lack of central commerce regulation had led to precisely the evils which were occurring, and predicted to worsen, in the United States. Meanwhile, in the Netherlands and Switzerland a central authority was regulating commerce among confederation members without such problems.

The intended meaning of the Commerce Clause in the area of interstate trade is quite clear: to regulate trade "among" the states. Obviously, this means trade involving more than one state. In *Gibbons v. Ogden* (1824), the first case to deal with the extent of the Commerce Clause, Supreme Court Chief Justice John Marshall, the most influential member in the Court's history, stated that "It is not intended to say that the words 'among the states' comprehend that commerce, which is completely internal, and which does not extend to or affect other states. Such a power would be inconvenient, and is certainly unnecessary. Comprehensive as the word 'among' is, it may very properly be restricted to that commerce which concerns more states than one."

There is another element to this discussion; the ability of Congress to regulate "commerce." This meant intercourse of a business nature. As Judge Bork has pointed out, "a regulation of commerce had to be done for commercial reasons and not as a means of effecting social or moral regulation."

It was never intended, not even by those Founders who supported a very strong national government, that the Commerce Clause should allow Congress to reach into the power of the states, into the operation of business, or into the lives of individuals for the purpose of social and moral regulation. But that is what the clause has been perverted to do.

In the decades that followed ratification, there was never any real question as to the extent of congressional power to regulate commerce with foreign nations or Indian tribes. However, in the area of interstate commerce there were some questions which arose. First came the question of whether a state could regulate interstate commerce co-extensively with the federal government. In *Gibbons v. Ogden* (1824), the Supreme Court held that any state legislation that acts to regulate interstate trade is unconstitutional; the regulation of interstate commerce is a power given exclusively to Congress. This was a correct decision necessary to avoid a repetition of the problems of the Articles of Confederation. The second question concerned the extent of this congressional power. Until 1936 a "geographic analysis" was followed in this area. Under this analysis commerce conducted solely within a state was not within the reach of congressional power. In other words, Congress could regulate interstate commerce only if it crossed a state line. Even this was read narrowly to hold that the manufacturing of products which would eventually cross a state line were not within the reach of Congress to regulate. The geographic analysis was a commonly accepted doctrine which was recognized repeatedly by the Supreme Court. [See *The Daniel Ball* (1871), *United States v. E.C. Knight Company* (1895), *Champion v. Ames* (1903), *Hammer v. Dagenhart* (1918), and *Carter v. Carter Coal Company* (1936)].

By the 1930s a new attitude had developed among liberal politicians that government should be more progressive and involved in controlling economic conditions such as working hours and minimum wages. This was a response to the Great Depression. For the American nation it was the beginning of the misguided and totally inaccurate belief that government should, or can, fix social problems such as poverty. Not only is government inherently abusive, but it exhibits another unfortunate characteristic as well: incompetence. And really, this is to be expected. It is a simple truism that no competent individual will go into government service at the level of pay which is offered. Those willing to do so fall into two categories: the corrupt who look to get rich off of graft, and those unable to obtain work elsewhere. It is sheer nonsense to think that a government composed of such fools can fix anything. The result can only be scandal and ineptitude. This has been unquestionably proven correct in this country. Nonetheless, this absurdity gained ground in the 1930s led by the crippled President Franklin Delano Roosevelt. Coming to power in the midst of a severe economic downturn, and looking primarily to ensure his continuation in power, Roosevelt proposed a number of government programs to end the Depression. Such programs amounted to the same government controlled economy which exists under a socialist system. Roosevelt's agenda included social spending programs such as Social Security and jobs programs such as the WPA (Works Progress Administration). It also included legislation which intruded heavily into the operation of business and private affairs as the law began to regulate commerce conducted solely within individual states. This was the New Deal, and while the populace was willing to trade their liberties for food, the judiciary stood against this unconstitutional grab for power.

New Deal legislation was challenged at every turn. The Supreme Court struck down several key provisions including the Agricultural Adjustment Act of 1933 and the Railroad Retirement Act of 1934. It was feared that the Social Security Act and the National Labor Relations Act would also be struck down, thus destroying the New Deal. Since Congress had no clear constitutional power to pass such legislation, a new creative argument was needed: the Commerce Clause. The Supreme Court, following sixty years of precedent based on the geographic analysis, disagreed. In most cases the Court voted 5-4 against Roosevelt's New Deal legislation. Roosevelt responded with an attempt to corrupt the Supreme Court. This was the infamous Court Packing Scheme. Thinking, as all politicians do, that the American people are morons, Roosevelt proposed a plan to expand the number of justices on the Supreme Court. He suggested that for each justice over seventy years old the president could nominate an additional justice. At the time six justices were over seventy. This would have allowed Roosevelt to add six justices to the court bringing the total number to fifteen. Roosevelt then hoped to win these economics cases by a 10-5 vote. If he had simply told the truth — that his program which was supported by the American people was being held up by a retrenched judiciary — he might have won the day. But instead he claimed that this plan was designed to solve the heavy work load placed on the Justices. No one believed this lie, and the plan went down to a humiliating defeat.

Unfortunately, many of the elderly justices retired and others were intimidated, so that by 1936 the constitutional interpretation of the Commerce Clause began to change. In *Carter v. Carter Coal* (1936), the Supreme Court was faced with the issue of the constitutionality of the Coal Conservation Act of 1935. This law established a tax on coal production which occurred solely within individual states. Under the law, coal producers were to receive a reduction in the tax if they accepted a series of codes which set minimum prices, wages and hours for workers, and recognized the right of workers to collectively bargain. The Court again applied the geographic analysis and held that since coal production was an activity that occurred entirely within a state this was beyond the power of Congress to control; therefore the act was unconstitutional. The Court's opinion included language which admitted that coal production did have an indirect effect on interstate commerce and inferred that commerce conducted wholly within a state could be regulated by Congress if it had a direct effect on interstate commerce. This was unfortunate because this language became the basis for a new test which sounded the death knell for the geographic analysis and the end of the strict interpretation of the Commerce Clause.

In *National Labor Relations Board v. Jones & Laughlin Steel Corporation* (1937), the Court was faced with the constitutionality of the National Labor Relations Act. This law regulated union rights, working conditions, and minimum wages at steel plants whose operations took place solely within individual states. The Court upheld the law. In a major change of direction the Court stated that the Commerce Clause allowed Congress to regulate a commercial activity conducted within a state if Congress could perceive any effect on interstate commerce from the regulated area. In other words, if the activity Congress sought to regulate had any effect, in the opinion of Congress, on interstate commerce, then regulatory legislation was legitimate. In this case Congress perceived poor working conditions in steel plants as reducing steel production and thus affecting the interstate trade of steel. It was one of the most disastrous Supreme Court decisions ever.

In *Wickard v. Fillburn* (1942), the expansion of government power under the Commerce Clause grew exponentially and into the lives of private individuals. The Federal Agricultural Act provided for growth quotas and subsidies for farmers to artificially maintain agricultural prices. The defendant accepted these rules and then grew a small amount more than the quota for his own personal consumption. When fined by the government, he sued, challenging the constitutionality of the act. The Supreme Court upheld the act. This time the Court refined the Congressional Perception Test from the NLRB case, holding that "if Congress could perceive a situation, when multiplied by similarly situated individuals across the nation, that could affect interstate commerce, then it was a legitimate regulation." In other words the act of one small farmer in growing a tiny amount of food beyond his federal quota, if emulated by everyone, would have an effect on interstate commerce. This was to be known as the Cumulative Impact/Aggregate Effect Test. And it was still based on the congressional perception process. The reasoning here was that this man, by exceeding the quota, grew and consumed crops he would have had to buy elsewhere, and since he did not, this acted to reduce interstate commerce. The Court went on to say that in the future they would not examine data on this question; if Congress claimed it perceived a need to regulate commerce, then the Court would defer to that judgment. By this decision Congress was left with the power to regulate any activity for which it could imagine any effect at all on interstate trade. The Supreme Court had even given Congress a mandate to do so without any fear of such laws being overturned, no matter how abusive they might be. Suffice it to say that since 1942 no act of Congress has ever failed the Cumulative Impact/Aggregate Effect Test. The gross intrusions that followed were predictable, considering the nature of power.

By the early 1960s liberals in Congress began to perceive more social problems in the area of race. As a result a whole new spate of social legislation based on the Commerce Clause began to appear. The Civil Rights Act of 1964 was the penultimate example. Included in Title II of this law was the Public Accommodations Act, which was designed to end prohibitions against blacks in hotels and restaurants. The act led to two major cases in the Supreme Court.

In *Heart of Atlanta Motel v. United States* (1964), the motel refused to rent rooms to blacks. When sanctioned under the act the motel sued, challenging its constitutionality. The government argued that such race restrictions affected interstate commerce. The claim was that when blacks could not find a place to stay they would decide not to travel. Therefore they would not spend money on products in other states, thus reducing interstate commerce. As silly as this argument was, the bottom line was that Congress claimed it could perceive race restrictions as affecting interstate commerce, and based on the previous cases, the Supreme Court agreed.

In *Katzenbach v. McClung* (1964), an Alabama restaurant, which refused to serve blacks, was sanctioned under Title II. The owner sued, challenging the constitutionality of the act. The government argued that Congress could perceive an effect on interstate commerce. This time it was claimed that restaurants receive items from out of state and that if blacks are not served then less items will be bought from out of state, thus harming interstate commerce. The Supreme Court agreed.

The Commerce Clause also allowed a Fed intrusion into the day to day operation of employers through the 1964 Civil Rights Act. Under §703 (Title VII), employers are prohibited from discriminating on the basis of race, color, religion, sex, or national origin with respect to hiring and firing as well as terms, conditions, or privileges of employment. This legislation spawned legions of lawsuits as the Court delved into every decision made by employers. The effect of the litigation was to force employers into unofficial quotas so as to avoid the appearance of impropriety.

The addition of "sex" to §703 has an interesting history. For many months in 1964 Congress had been locked in a bitter battle over this civil rights legislation. One day prior to the passage of the bill, Representative Howard Smith, who was an opponent of the entire bill, proposed an amendment to add "sex" discrimination. Smith knew that the final vote would be very close and he hoped to swing a few more votes against the bill by adding sex discrimination. Much to his, and our, chagrin the bill passed with the amendment. Such is the way Congress functions.

The next step under §703 was a judicial creation called "disproportionate impact." This allowed employers to be sued for unintentional discrimination. Under this doctrine, employment policies neutral on their face that have a disproportionate impact on minorities are also prohibited. In *Griggs v. Duke Power Co.* (1971), Duke Power operated a power-generating facility. The company, due to the complexity of the work, required a high-school education as a condition of employment in certain departments. The Court held that, even though there was no intentional discrimination, this violated §703 because it disqualified blacks at a disproportionately higher rate than whites. Since blacks had received an inferior education, fewer had a high school diploma, and thus fewer were able to get these jobs. The Court's solution was to punish employers and begin Court supervision of almost every decision made by an employer.

The 1964 Civil Rights Act led to a wide assortment of new laws. Some of the more infamous include the Age Discrimination in Employment Act, the Americans With Disabilities Act, and the Family and Medical Leave Act, to name some of the more offensive.

In 1989 Congress came up with the Americans With Disabilities Act to provide even more rules for businesses to follow. It mandated companies across the country to make expensive changes in their physical facilities to accommodate handicapped people. It also allowed those with handicaps to sue businesses directly for violating the law. Those brain dead dumbasses in Congress were vague enough with their definitions that in 1994 a grossly fat guy sued an airline under this law, claiming that their small seats violated his rights as a disabled person. Obesity was, then, a disability.

The latest development on the PC front is the hoax which amounted to a lynching of Clarence Thomas: sexual harassment. In their efforts to make everyone think and act properly so as not to offend others, feminazis came up with this wondrous creation. Recently, frivolous sexual harassment lawsuits have even been brought by the parents of elementary girls who have been called childish names such as "flat" by elementary school boys. In the workplace the courts expanded the employment discrimination laws to cover hostile work environments resulting from sexual harassment. Under this doctrine an employer is liable when employees, through words or acts, cause other employees to feel they are in a hostile work environment. And with such vague terms the courts assured a whole new round of litigation as the ultra-sensitive across the country saw the potential for a quick buck.

In 1993, Congress passed the Family & Medical Leave Act. The first piece of legislation signed by that dumbass incompetent Clinton was another major step towards American socialism. This law requires employers to provide employees with up to 12 weeks of unpaid leave in a 12-month period in order to provide care for a newborn or adopted child or a seriously ill child, spouse or parent. An employer is required to keep the employee's job open and cannot reduce their benefits during the leave time. Employers, anticipating complex staffing problems as employees come and go at their leisure, fought the legislation intensely. The actual effect of the legislation, which Congress and President Bill claimed was a marvel of social consciousness, was an unexpected result of being poorly thought out. The wealthy, who can afford 12 unpaid weeks off, had already hired nannies, so to them this was a moot point, while the poor, who cannot afford 12 unpaid weeks, refused to take the time off. Basically, no one used the time off. So much for social consciousness. Unfortunately, this led to rumbling from the liberal fringe in Congress to mandate paid leave as is done in European socialist states.

In 1994, as election day neared, scumbag congressmen, fearing the wrath of voters, attempted to reform health care. The American medical system is the best in the world. It has some problems, primarily its high cost and numbers of people without medical insurance. Liberals stirred up the people with horror stories of those unfortunates who could not get medical treatment. The people salivated like Pavlov's dog at this tactic and screamed for reform. Through the summer the battle raged. Finally, Republicans managed to defeat the Clinton Plan. By that time the people had begun to see through the charade. They realized that people without insurance were the same people who dropped out of school and had lousy jobs. The bottom line is that's what they get for not getting an education. The majority of the people do not scheme every year to cheat on their taxes so that the few dollars they do send the IRS can be spent on government support for the useless. Lurking behind all of this debate was the concern about the ability of Congress to fix such a complicated problem as the medical system. The same institution which cannot even stop its members from bouncing checks is really not the group to put in charge of anything remotely difficult, let alone health care.

All of this legislation, which is clearly on the rise, has allowed Congress to stick its incompetent nose farther and farther into the private lives of individuals. Liberals are now agitating to expand anti-discrimination rules to homosexuals. How far will this go? Some city governments have prohibited discrimination against AIDs carriers, so this may be the next breakthrough in national civil-rights legislation.

In the public education arena the federal government, using the Commerce Clause, has also intruded heavily on the rights of the states and the people, beginning with the 1964 Civil Rights Act. Under Title IX of the act, the Feds established guidelines mandating equality in sports programs administered by schools receiving any federal monies. This eventually expanded, as courts held that if a student received a federal student loan and used it to pay a school, then that brought the school under Title IX. Today that has led to court control over school sports teams to ensure absolute gender equality in spending, facilities, uniforms, offered sports, and travel. It is an interesting situation as numerous girls' sports must be offered, though no one really has any interest in coming to see females compete. Ironically, all male sports are required to allow girls to participate because equal protection mandates this; however, boys may not participate on girls' teams because, as the courts have put it, they would dominate the sport and reduce girls' chances for participation. This is typical feminazi doctrine: demand total equality at the expense of males, but preserve some areas exclusively for females.

From this, the power hungry Feds moved on to develop guidelines in numerous other areas such as special education. It was the precursor to a whole spate of legislation to protect the handicapped. At the same time, the Court-created nightmare of "due process" reared its ugly head and led to the establishment of complex legal forms, procedures and meetings for educators ill-trained to teach, let alone function as lawyers. The final leap was to be expected: the Feds dictated that all schools must follow these guidelines. This then took in all public and private schools, even though they received not a dime of federal money.

This process represents an unbelievable and thoroughly illegitimate intrusion of the Feds into areas of state concern and control. Not only does this offend traditional control over education on the local level, it also violates the essence of Federalism upon which our entire system rests. The Constitution does not grant Congress the power to control education. If ever one questioned Lord Acton's famous aphorism about absolute power, this unparalleled and Constitutionally prohibited grab for power should settle the question.

Granted, the state-run public school system is a complete failure and national embarrassment, but it is a sick joke to assume that federal intrusion into this area will do anything except make it worse. In September, 1994, I attended a seminar on new federal civil-rights legislation and its requirements for the schools. The local school district was attempting to figure out this nonsense and avoid lawsuits. This meant the establishment of "due process" procedures. Such began with the Rehabilitation Act of 1973 and continue today with regulations concerning access for the handicapped under §504. Congress has based all these laws on the Commerce Clause. Basically, this absurdity takes the bureaucratic maze of special education and applies it to the entire system. The bottom line is that a teacher must, under threat of dismissal and penalty of law, diagnose every child in their class who is not achieving and make modifications so that the child does achieve. These modifications include: shortening or eliminating tests, not assigning homework, excusing work which is hard, writing the student's notes for them, allowing students to turn in work whenever they can, and not enforcing discipline on students who cannot control themselves. The seminar presenter explained that not even the government attorneys were able to define the criteria that were to be used to identify legitimate problem students. Without definitions, the school district was playing it safe by deciding to consider all students eligible for modifications. So if a child is just plain lazy and not achieving, all his teachers must undergo the torture of special forms, procedures and meetings while the student is told that he is a good person and does not have to do the work. He is then given a passing grade. Really, no one should have expected any less from this federal intrusion into education. This also presents another problem: the new American motto, "I'm not responsible," under which no one accepts responsibility for their actions and seeks to place blame elsewhere. Under these educational rules, if child is not achieving, it is expected that everyone else except the child must work harder.

This nonsense has been around since the 1970s, but a new trend has developed from the federal requirements. Mainstreaming, also known by its PC label as "inclusion," is the latest educational fad. It forces all students, brilliant, average and stupid, to be mixed together rather than grouped according to ability level in separate classes. The United States is the only country in the world that practices this silliness; it is no wonder American schools are the world's worst. Regardless, numerous school officials, all of whom have Ph.D.s, declare that studies show the success of mainstreaming. This raises two points. First, why does an educator get a doctorate in philosophy instead of education; and second, everyone who has ever studied statistics knows the first lesson taught in that subject is that anyone can manipulate statistics to say whatever one wants.

Ivory tower academics aside, mainstreaming creates two major problems. First, the teacher who is ill-trained to teach to begin with must now teach to three subgroups within each class: the brilliant, average and stupid. Each group has its own peculiarities; the brilliant are often accompanied by emotional problems and the stupid are accompanied by a whole range of abbreviations such as ED, LD, and FU. It does not take a rocket scientist to predict the result: that teachers will teach to the middle. It is simply impractical to ask a teacher to develop lessons and assignments for 3 subgroups when they are overburdened already by an assignment that includes six classes and 160 students per day. The teacher is frustrated and angry. The first problem leads to the second. Students at the bottom cannot ever compete and do not achieve, thus setting themselves at risk of dropping out. Meanwhile, the advanced students, who used to have challenging advanced classes, are bored. Their talents are wasted. Of course, laws such as §504 require modifications for the stupid students so they get a passing grade without earning it. It is the responsibility of every educator to resist this patent absurdity!

At the seminar, the presenter was pinned down on this point. He responded with a truly classic example of Ph.D. thinking. He stated that a slow student in a regular level class was like a golfer with a 32 handicap playing a person with a 10 handicap on an even basis and that was unfair, so requiring modifications simply leveled the field. My question was this: when that student has modifications made for his entire school career and he graduates and goes into the work world, isn't that like putting a player with a 32 handicap in the Masters Tournament? The presenter had no response, so I asked, "But I guess we could cure that with new federal laws requiring employers to make modifications for their employee's jobs?" The presenter was no longer smiling stupidly. Neither was I, because such regulations are inevitable.

The bottom line is that in our utopian wishful endeavor to educate everyone we are educating no one. Two hundred years from now, when the historians ponder the collapse of the American nation, they will pinpoint this period as the critical time and they will blame the failure of education as a primary cause. They will be only partially right, as the real blame lies with the federal government and its incompetent and illegitimate grab for power over every area of American life through the Commerce Clause. If the courts had kept Congress limited to its original power of only regulating commerce among the states we could have avoided all this.

As if there were not sufficient reasons in the historical record for limiting congressional power in the area of commerce, then the 10th Amendment should have been the trump card. The fact that the powers of Congress are listed in Article I shows that the Founders did not intend for Congress to have unlimited power. This is reinforced by the 10th Amendment which states, "The powers not delegated to the United States by the Constitution, nor prohibited by it to the States, are reserved to the States respectively, or to the people."

The historical development of the 10th Amendment makes its meaning clear. In 1787, under the proposed Constitution, the states were to give up a limited amount of their power to the federal government. There was great concern on the issue of the federal government being limited only to those powers listed in Article I and the states retaining the remaining powers. As the states fought over ratification of the new plan, eight states voted to approve the Constitution only after proposing amendments to be adopted after ratification. All eight of these states included in their amendments a statement that the states did indeed retain all the power not specifically given to the federal government. These were later incorporated into the 10th Amendment. The states, and indeed most Americans, were worried that the federal government would grow and expand its power at the cost of the states, and become dictatorial.

That protection has worked well until recent years. Unfortunately, if the modern steamroller of federal power was to continue, this Amendment needed to be, and indeed was, ignored. The 10th Amendment has a very short litigation history. It has only been involved in two cases recently, the second of which spelled its death.

In *National League of Cities v. Usery* (1976), the Supreme Court dealt with an attempt by Congress to add state public employees to those covered by the Federal Fair Labor Standards Act. The law set a minimum wage standard for such state employees. As usual, Congress claimed the Commerce Clause as its basis for the legislation. In reality, it was just another reach by Congress into the powers of the states. The Court struck down the Act, holding that it was a violation of state sovereignty under the 10th Amendment. In other words, the 10th Amendment was a real limit on the power of Congress. Unfortunately, the Court said that the states are immune from congressional control in areas of traditional state governmental functions. Lower federal courts perceived this to be a test and began to judge state immunity from congressional control based on whether Congress was attempting to control a traditional state governmental function. This created a great deal of confusion as lower courts tried to figure out what traditional state government functions were. It took only nine years before the issue returned to the Court.

In *Garcia v. San Antonio Metropolitan Transit Authority* (1985), the Court faced the same problem as in the National League of Cities case, as Congress again attempted to use the Fair Labor Standards Act to set a minimum wage standard for the employees of a mass transit system owned and operated by the city of San Antonio, Texas. Congress claimed that mass transit was not a traditional area of state governmental function. The district court held that it was, and that the 10th Amendment prohibited congressional control in this area. However, three federal appeals courts had come to the opposite conclusion. Because of the disparity the Supreme Court agreed to hear the case.

By a 5-4 vote the liberals on the Court held that the *National League of Cities* case was overruled. They cited several reasons for this. First, they held that the *National League of Cities'* "traditional state government function" standard was so ambiguous that it had created confusion and had to be scrapped.

Second, the Court stated that the *National League of Cities* decision was actually bad for the states and violated Federalism — an interesting statement in the face of the effect of this decision, which effectively killed the 10th Amendment and removed the last constitutional impediment preventing total domination of the states by the Feds. In a thinly-disguised and disingenuous assertion the Court said that the ambiguous *National League of Cities* test required constant federal intervention by the courts to determine whether a state function was a "traditional" one, and that this decreased the power of the states and weakened federalism. This was true to a small degree, but not a regular problem for the states. It is beyond question that the states would have preferred this limited federal intrusion rather than the total intervention which was the result of this decision. It should be remembered that the majority included Justices Marshall, Brennan, and Blackmun; a group of Justices whose entire careers were marked by rulings abusing the Constitution. This was a case of claiming the ruling helped the states at the same time it gutted the only real protection the states had left.

The Court's next assertion was even more amazing. The Court claimed that the Founders intended to protect the states from the expansion of federal power, not through the 10th Amendment, but through the political system set up in the federal government. This was indeed an ironic statement. Brennan, Marshall and company, who voted with the majority in this case, have always been vicious opponents of even looking at what the Founders intended, let alone following those intentions. Nonetheless, since there was no real intellectual or legal basis for this decision, the majority needed to try to base it on something. The Court claimed that since the states had a hand in selecting the members of the Congress and the President they were ultimately in control, and therefore they easily could easily control the federal government. This statement is as untrue as it is ridiculous. Today, the states do not play an important role in selecting the national leaders. To claim otherwise is simply a lie. It also ignores the fact that once a person is elected to national office he is a part of the federal government and acts accordingly, to the detriment of the states. All one needs to do to refute this alleged idea is to look around. In recent years, the federal government's regulatory intrusion into the power of the states has increased to involve incredible attention to details. Even the age at which states can retire their law enforcement officers and the agenda which must be followed in state utility commissions has been dictated by the Feds. With a federal invasion on this scale and this detailed, does it look like the federal system has protected the states from encroachment by the Feds?

Finally, the Court held that the 10th Amendment is only violated if the congressional regulation under the Commerce Clause is actually "destructive of state sovereignty or violates an express constitutional provision." Under this new test the Court held that the minimum wage standards of the Fair Labor Standards Act were not destructive of state sovereignty and were not prohibited by any express constitutional provision; therefore they were constitutional. It is quite clear that, just like with the Commerce Clause Congressional Perception Test, the Court has abandoned any role in reviewing the acts of Congress in this area. If dictating the wage scale of a state's own government employees is not violating the sovereignty of a state, then nothing will ever be found to be so.

The dissent by four Justices very poignantly points out that "by usurping functions traditionally performed by the states, federal overreaching under the Commerce Clause undermines the constitutionally mandated balance of power between the states and the federal government, a balance designed to protect our fundamental liberties."

The result of the *Garcia* decision is that the 10th Amendment is now completely dead. Considering how broadly the Court has interpreted congressional power under the Commerce Clause through the Cumulative Impact/Aggregate Effect Test there is no chance that it will use this "destructive to state sovereignty" test to curtail that power. The last constitutional provision restricting the power of the federal government is now gone. The people are now at the mercy of Congress.

The extent of the commerce power today is unlimited. Under the Cumulative Impact/Aggregate Effect Test, every activity which occurs in this country could be perceived by Congress as having some effect on interstate commerce. If Congress were to decide that the disorganized condition of divorce law, or state criminal laws, classroom curriculum, local cable television bills, dog licenses, or driving license requirements needed to be regulated by Congress, then all they have to do is pass new legislation based on the Commerce Clause, and those areas of traditional state power simply cease to exist in the hands of the states. With the death of the 10th Amendment there is absolutely no barrier to stop Congress as they finalize the destruction of Federalism and consolidate all power in the federal government. Federalism, the Separation of Powers Doctrine, and the Checks and Balances Doctrine were the three bedrock principles designed by the Founders to prevent the abuse of power by our government and to protect our liberties. One leg of that triad is now dead. It only remains for the government to hammer in the nails on the coffin lid.

The end result of this abandonment of another constitutional principle is a rush of legislation which allows the government to intrude into the affairs of private business and individuals on a level commensurate with government control in a socialist system. This expanded power is totally out of line with the original intent of the Commerce Clause and represents the most dangerous trend toward totalitarianism in this nation.

Regardless of the fact that some of the achievements — protecting opportunities for all — may be worthwhile, this does not get around the fact that the use of the Commerce Clause in this way is an illegitimate abuse of the Constitution. That is the ultimate difficulty with constitutional interpretation; one must take out the issue of the morality of the act and look simply to what is the outcome required by the Constitution. If such social legislation was truly necessary, the Constitution could have been amended to grant Congress the power to pass it. But perhaps the government knew that the people would never allow such an increase in government power if it were done in the light of day. Hence the deception, done without recourse, by the courts. This is all so unnecessary, but after all, the Constitution is just a piece of paper.

CHAPTER 26
AFFIRMATIVE
DISCRIMINATION 1990s

The 1960s and 70s saw the creation of affirmative action, though it could be more appropriately titled "affirmative discrimination," a misguided and unconstitutional practice of establishing racial quotas that has produced nothing but negative results. This policy was devised to correct past discrimination against blacks, but has been broadened to include women and other minorities. A better name for it is "reverse discrimination against white males." It requires government, businesses, schools, and other institutions to give preferential treatment to minorities, especially in the area of employment. The results have been three-fold. First, companies are saddled with inferior employees. Second, it promotes mediocrity on the part of the various minority groups who are guaranteed jobs and other benefits without earning them. Third, it creates racial and gender animosity. Unfortunately, it is not the only divisive racial policy pursued by the government, as minorities increasingly demand a free ride. The concern for the future, though, is not black rage, but white rage!

The Supreme Court decisions in the area of affirmative discrimination have been muddled. After years of liberal support the Court changed direction in the landmark case of *University of California v. Bakke* (1978). The medical school at the University of California maintained an affirmative discrimination program that reserved 16 of the 100 entering seats for minorities. Allan Bakke, a 37-year-old white engineer, was denied admission and brought suit against the university claiming he was better qualified than some of the 16 admitted minority students and was being discriminated against because of his race. He claimed this was a violation of the 14th Amendment's "equal protection" clause and Title VI of the Civil Rights Act of 1964. Section 601 of Title VI states that "No person in the United States shall, on the ground of race, color, or national origin, be excluded from participation in, be denied the benefits of, or be subjected to discrimination under any program or activity receiving Federal financial assistance." The University of California did receive such financial assistance and was therefore affected by this law. Ironically, these two laws were used to establish affirmative discrimination in the first place. It is ironic because they prohibit all racial discrimination in federally funded programs, including education. Nonetheless, affirmative discrimination had become the rule by 1978, until the Bakke decision. The Supreme Court, in a 5-4 decision, ruled in Bakke's favor saying that, "the 14th Amendment and Title VI required that race could not be the sole factor in determining admissions." It was an interesting reversal because past Court decisions had upheld affirmative discrimination as consistent with these laws. Until Bakke, the rationale was that since discrimination existed, these laws required preferential treatment for minorities, at the expense of whites, so as to give minorities an equal opportunity. In other words, to end discrimination the government required discrimination; to gain equality it mandated inequality.

In the *Bakke* case, the four justices in the minority (Brennan, White, Marshall, and Blackmun) voted to uphold the perverse practice of affirmative discrimination. These liberal justices had for decades called for equal treatment under the law for minorities, but in this case they ignored that theory and went to great lengths to reject the idea that the Constitution should be color-blind, that all people should be treated equally without regard to color. They argued that "the court had never taken, and should not take that position and that racial classifications could be justified upon an overriding statutory purpose." To support this position they cited *Hirabayashi v. United States* (1943) and *Korematsu v. United States* (1944). How ironic! These were the two cases that legitimized Japanese-American internment during World War II. It seems that Justice Jackson's "loaded weapon" had found a hand.

The bottom line from the supporters of affirmative discrimination is that laws are not to be color-blind. They are to be used to help minorities, and used against whites. Their justification for this asininity is that past discrimination against minorities must be corrected through special preferences. Unfortunately, the Justices don't realize that this puts them in the untenable position of sacrificing a white who did not inflict discrimination to advance the interests of a black who did not suffer discrimination. No old injustice is undone, but a new injustice is inflicted. Even if the leftist members of the Court who supported this nonsense really believed it was necessary social policy, did it not occur to them that the result would be alienation on the part of whites which would lead to worsened race relations and then to increased discrimination by whites?

It is beyond understanding how one can read Title VI, which prohibits discrimination against *all persons* including whites, and the 14th Amendment, which guarantees "equal protection" *for all*, and then rationally assert that the government can require programs to give preferential treatment to minorities by discriminating against whites. These minorities deserve the backlash that is coming!

Following *Bakke*, court decisions continued to head away from quotas in the 1980s, much to the chagrin of black leaders and many of their constituents who had become accustomed to the free ride. The idea of making up for past discrimination, though, took a ludicrous turn in the late 1980s when a Massachusetts state legislator demanded that the federal government make a cash payment to every black as compensation for crimes committed against their ancestors during the time that slavery was legal. There was even serious debate on this absurdity.

This reflects a basic problem in race relations at this time. No politician, or anyone else for that matter, is willing to speak out and to criticize blacks, because their attacks will be construed as racist. A recent Houston, Texas, incident reflects this well. An extensive investigation into financial oddities at Prairie View A&M University, a black college, revealed numerous infractions. Three former officials were blamed for a lack of accountability for some $15.1 million over a four-year-period. One of the officials countered by saying, "It's curious to me that the three people accused are all black employees at Prairie View. I think this attack against me and my colleagues is racist." Besides being poor English it was a rather feeble attempt to interject a diversion. Many people, however, jumped on this bandwagon. I guess it didn't occur to them that the administration of an all-black college would just happen to be black too. Very often this kind of defense is used by minorities to cover up their criminal behavior. Too often it works.

Another example arose in June, 1992. Democratic presidential nominee Bill Clinton appeared before Jesse Jackson's Rainbow Coalition and during his speech criticized the appearance of a black female rap singer named Sister Souljah at the same meeting. The rapper, whom few had ever heard of before, had made the comment in a May newspaper interview concerning the Los Angeles riots that "If black people kill black people every day, why not have a week and kill white people?" This attempt to justify the killing of whites by blacks was an outrageous racist remark. One would have expected a backlash against this disgusting assertion. Clinton, in criticizing her appearance said, "Wouldn't it be nice to have a week when no one killed anybody." Unbelievably Clinton was attacked by blacks led by Jesse Jackson for making a racist attack on Sister Souljah. Jackson, who was given every opportunity to refute the rapper's racist comment, refused to do so. It becomes painfully clear that the only color in Jesse Jackson's rainbow is black. I have had a lot of respect for Jackson in the past and would have voted for him as a presidential contender, but he lost all his credibility on this one.

In a related story, which occurred simultaneously, another black rap/thrash metal singer, Ice-T, became embroiled in controversy. In a song entitled "Cop Killer," Ice-T rapped about using a shotgun to "dust some cops off." A storm erupted as law-enforcement agencies across the land demanded the record company pull the album from the shelves. Three major record stores banned it and police groups tried to organize a boycott of Time Warner Inc., the producer of the album. Ice-T eventually pulled the song from the album after months of free publicity, which led to huge sales. He promised to give out free singles of the song at his concerts. While these are highly offensive lyrics, Ice-T has every right to utter them under the First Amendment. The reaction of the black community, though, was even more offensive, yet predictable. In one example, an association of black Southern California police officers attacked the boycott, stating that it was racist. So suddenly the debate shifted to white racism instead of the song's lyrics about killing cops. These three affairs, however, reflect the double standard that now exists in race relations in this country.

This racial situation is now almost completely out of hand. One would think that blacks were the majority in this country, judging by the way people knuckle under to them, but according to the 1990 census they make up only 12.1% of the population. In light of their criminal conduct in Los Angeles and the ensuing threats of a race war by some segments of the black community, they would be well advised to remember that fact.

In 1990, an uproar arose over the use, by the PGA, of a Birmingham, Alabama country club that had no black members. The black community threatened protests unless the club immediately admitted a black. As the PGA considered moving to another site, the club was cajoled into accepting racial blackmail and an honorary black was accepted. Another black without credentials, without qualifications, without effort was handed something for nothing. People have a right to associate with people of their choosing, and if there are those who wish to participate in clubs, groups, employment, or neighborhoods without blacks, or any other group, then they should be allowed to do so. Government pressure in this area can only backfire and cause racial animosity. We are seeing a recurrence of such at this time, and no amount of spoon-fed multicultural propaganda in the colleges or the media is going to change this. Whites are fed up with being treated like second-class citizens. They are mad as hell and not going to take it anymore.

Stories of racial unrest in America are now a regular occurrence in the media, extending even into the traditionally quiet heartland. Between July and November, 1991, there were at least 10 incidents of cross-burnings in Dubuque, Iowa, and when a national Ku Klux Klan leader came to town to speak he was greeted by a cheering crowd. These types of incidents are spreading rapidly because of the animosity whites feel towards blacks. This is the harvest reaped from affirmative discrimination.

Of course, the ultimate example of racial unrest occurred in May, 1992, with the Los Angeles "Rodney King" Riots. This sad chapter began with an incident of apparent police brutality by a group of white L.A. police officers beating a black motorist named Rodney King who had led them on a high-speed chase. An eyewitness with a video camera caught some of the action as the police continued to beat King even after he was down on the ground. A nationwide stir erupted, and several of the officers involved were prosecuted. Amazingly, the jury trial ended in acquittal for the officers, and when the verdict was announced it set off protests in black communities across the country. Almost immediately riots broke out in Los Angeles, which turned into a three-day nightmare. Rioting on this scale had not been seen since the 1960s. The results were frightening: thousands of businesses in South Central L.A. were burned down; innocent people were attacked on the streets and even pulled from their cars and beaten; thousands were injured and almost 50 were killed; thousands were arrested; and millions of dollars of goods were stolen by looters. Finally, the National Guard and the Army were called in to stop the bloodshed.

The most offensive incident of the riots occurred when a group of black youths stopped a truck in an intersection and pulled white driver Reginald Denny out and beat him. Even as the unconscious Denny lay bleeding and seriously hurt in the street, these blacks smashed bricks into his head, took his wallet and danced around laughing. The entire scene was filmed from a helicopter. Afterwards, blacks would justify this outrage by claiming it was no different from the beating of the black motorist. I beg to differ. The black motorist was chased by police in a legitimate attempt to stop his criminal behavior. They were led on a high-speed chase which threatened the lives of the public as well as those of the officers. The physical confrontation which resulted was justified, while the attack on Reginald Denny was the cold, calculated, inhumane act of animals against a totally innocent person.

Both of these incidents led to criminal trials. The police who beat the motorist were acquitted on state charges, and immediately the federal government jumped into the fray, bringing federal civil rights charges against the police. Two were convicted and sent to prison. In the Reginald Denny case the defendants were acquitted of all but a few minor crimes. This time the federal government said not a word about the civil rights violations committed against Reginald Denny. Is this equality?

Inconceivably, blacks attempted to justify the LA riots on two grounds: first, they charged that blacks were rightly outraged at the obvious failings of a criminal justice system which allowed white cops to get off after ruthlessly beating a black man; and second, they charged that years of neglect by the federal government had created and perpetuated terrible poverty in these inner city neighborhoods, and the people were rightly outraged. This outrage then logically turned into violence as the futility of life under these circumstances became unbearable.

It became quite apparent, however, that the overwhelming majority of rioting looters were just out to do some damage and get some free stuff. Simple criminal scum! There was no evidence of social consciousness, just common criminal behavior; indeed, many of these hoodlums didn't even care about the trial verdict. To claim that their actions were valid socio-political protests was just absurd. Still, the debate revolved around the horrible conditions that caused these poor people to revolt and how to help them, instead of discussing their criminal behavior. That lying scumbag Bush jumped into the fray seeing an opportunity to improve his re-election chances by proposing a billion dollars in aid, loans, jobs, and opportunities for these damaged areas. Everybody made a big fuss about improving conditions so that these people are not forced to riot again. More emphasis was placed on disputes about minority contractors getting their fair share of the rebuilding contracts than on the fact that lawlessness ran rampant. What a wonderful way to run a country: hoodlums burn down their neighborhood and the government rewards them for doing so. That is a tremendous message to send out to frustrated inner-city youth across America. More riots are sure to break out in the near future.

Following the riots, dangerous threats began to issue from the black community. Young blacks threatened that L.A. was only the first skirmish in the coming race war. Their position was that it is time for blacks to take what they want. Unfortunately, the continuing disintegration of race relations in this country, due in large part to the incompetence of the federal government, almost guarantees such a result. However, if blacks succeed in provoking a race war, the result won't be a victory for blacks, but the destruction of the black race in America!

Blacks also want to rewrite history and remove symbols they find offensive. After 23 years, the Fort Worth, Texas, Southwest High School Rebels were forced to change their Confederate mascot because blacks claimed it caused racial tension. What we had here was a couple of loud-mouthed individuals, you know the type: the ones who read somewhere that their ancestors were kept as slaves at one time. Now they will never let us forget, and they think they can keep milking white guilt with ever escalating demands. Somewhere in this debate has to be some consideration for what the majority wants. Or is this no longer a nation of majority rule?

Southern states have been increasingly criticized by blacks for symbols representative of the Confederacy. The uninformed, that is those who still believe the Civil War was fought over slavery, view these symbols as racist. They attack school mascots, flags, statues, and memorials. They whine and whine until they get their way, though this is usually because people are tired of their whining. In July, 1994, the NAACP organized a protest march in Myrtle Beach, South Carolina, to protest the fact that South Carolina was flying a Confederate battle flag atop its statehouse. The small march was led by the executive director of the NAACP, who, ironically, would be fired in disgrace a month later for secretly using NAACP funds to pay off a sexual-harassment judgment against him. The streets were lined by hundreds of whites supporting the flag. Scores of state, local, and federal police were needed to prevent violent clashes. So much for racial harmony. The protesters threatened a nation-wide boycott of South Carolina if the flag was not removed by Labor Day. Another meaningless threat. Poor people have no economic value to withdraw.

The Confederacy was, and is, deserving of immense pride and its symbols should not be desecrated because blacks don't like them. The Confederacy stood, like the patriots of the American Revolution, against tyranny and abusive government. Their cause was just and right. The path pursued by the regime since 1865 proves the wrong side won.

A symbol of resistance to tyranny
(Southern Cross Publishing)

Since 1986, Arizona, a state with a black population of only 3%, has been embroiled in a controversy over a holiday for Martin Luther King. In that year the governor illegally created a paid holiday for state workers, by executive order, after the legislature failed to adopt it. A new governor was promptly elected who immediately rescinded the holiday. In 1989, the legislature enacted an unpaid holiday, and in 1990 a referendum question, to make it a paid holiday, was put to the voters. Just two days before the vote the National Football League threatened to pull the 1993 Super Bowl away from Phoenix if the state voted against the holiday. The polls showed that 60,000 people decided to vote against it as a result of the NFL threat. So much for the involvement of professional football in complex socio-political issues. The proposition was defeated by a few thousand votes and the reaction was swift. The NFL pulled the Super Bowl, the NBA decided not to allow any events such as the All-Star game to be played there, five major golf tournaments were pulled, major league baseball spring training was affected, recruiting at the two state universities was jeopardized, and numerous organizations threatened to pull their conventions. No one questions the right of these associations to play where they choose, but what ever happened to democracy? Arizona already had a holiday for King, the referendum was to make it a paid holiday for state workers, and in a time of financial difficulties the people said "no."

Not everyone has been blinded to the reality of Martin Luther King — adulterer, convicted criminal, plagiarist and communist fellow-traveler. It is a national disgrace that he has been elevated to the same plane as real American heroes like George Washington.

Elections are increasingly cast in the context of racism. In November, 1991, Houston, Texas, faced elections for mayor and city council. There very nearly was no election at all due to lawsuits filed by assorted minority groups concerning the issue of at-large city council seats. It was primarily Hispanics who claimed that city-wide elections with the decision rendered by a majority of the voters was discriminary. I thought this was a democracy! Anyway, they asserted that Hispanic candidates cannot win city-wide elections. First, they fought for a referendum on the issue. They got it, and the people of the city voted overwhelmingly against the plan. It was defeated because the plan included an unnecessary expansion of the city council to 16 seats. Just what we needed, more taxpayer-funded high-paying jobs for career politicians. In another slap in the face to democracy, these Hispanics declared the defeat was the result of racism, refused to accept the outcome of the referendum, and sued in federal court to force the plan on the city. The federal court ruled it was too late to do anything about it, so the elections took place.

Several of the races were forced into run-off elections in early December. Finally, Bob Lanier (white) defeated state legislator Sylvester Turner (black) in the race for mayor. Lanier received 73% of the white vote and 3% of the black vote. Turner supporters loudly announced that Turner's defeat was due to racism and they pointed to Lanier's percentage of the white vote to prove it. To these people it is racist for 73% of whites to vote for a white candidate. Does that mean the 97% of blacks who voted for the black candidate are racists too? To this, Turner supporters say "No, this is supporting the vitality of the black community." Seems a bit inconsistent, not to mention a bit hypocritical, to me. Interestingly, racism is defined by the American Heritage Dictionary as "believing one's own ethnic stock is superior to, separate from, or above others." With all the constant cries of racism by blacks, I am reminded of the story of the boy who cried "Wolf" and of what happened to him!

A major factor in Turner's defeat which his supporters ignored was the barrage of stories in the media concerning Turner's past financial improprieties. It was reported that he had bounced checks, not paid bills, failed to pay his bar association dues, was sued by Harvard for law school tuition he owed, and may have been involved in a fraudulent insurance scam. Voters perceived a man who couldn't even balance his checkbook, let alone deal with a city budget. After the defeat, the city's black groups and churches, angered over the negative reporting against Turner, attempted to organize boycotts against certain TV stations and newspapers. Unfortunately for them, poor people don't have any economic leverage to withdraw, so this was ineffective. These groups also threatened class action lawsuits against these media sources. Maybe they should read the First Amendment? There will be an impact, though. The Houston media, in the face of these assaults, will be less willing to attack minority candidates in the future, and that is a loss to the entire political process. The people have a right to be informed about the candidates and any past difficulties that could affect their ability to govern.

All of this conflict over the mayoral race wasn't an isolated incident. In a city council race, incumbent Beverly Clark (black) lost to Gracie Saenz (Hispanic). Afterwards, Clark claimed racism was the cause of her defeat because she only received 30% of the white vote. Again, she also received over 90% of the black vote - and that wasn't racist?

First Amendment free speech is clearly becoming a victim in the attempt to placate minorities. Some universities across the land have passed rules forbidding students to express opinions that are derogatory to minorities. The punishments include expulsion. In February, 1991, Brown University, in Rhode Island, disciplined a student for shouting racial epithets. While celebrating his 21st birthday, Douglas Hann, a junior, yelled an anti-black comment involving a common obscenity. The remark was yelled into the air in a courtyard and was not aimed at any individual. A student in the dormitory then opened his window and shouted, "Keep it down!" Hann then used the word "faggot" and an obscenity combined with the word "Jew," directing his shouts at the student in the window. Hann was immediately expelled from the university. This only goes to prove that as far as college administrators go, a Ph.D. is not a sign of intelligence and certainly not an indicator that they have read the Bill of Rights. This policy is an affront to the Constitution and should be struck down in the federal courts!

In an era of ever increasing crime, the police are being dragged into the racial mess. Any time a white cop shoots a black there is a public outcry by blacks and their liberal white-politician slaves. Houston, Texas, dealt with several such occurrences during 1990. In one incident a cop pulled a car over and approached the driver. The black male had a gun on the seat next to him. He allegedly reached for it, and the cop shot him dead. A justified act! The typical black whining began. Then marches, protests, and memorials took place, though they only seemed to be made up of about 20 people in a city of four million. The cop was fired by the black police chief after intense pressure from the black community. The solution to this kind of problem is really quite simple. If blacks would stop committing the lion's share of crime, then the police wouldn't have to shoot so many of them. Just after this event a young white couple drove up to a convenience store, the man got out to make a phone call, and was surrounded by a mob of black youths. They shouted racial slurs and then shot the white man to death as he tried to escape to his car. The story was buried on page 20 and nobody cared. Is this equality?

White attitudes on this subject are a peculiar thing. We just keep letting minorities push us around, and we act as if we think prejudice is ending. It has been my experience that many whites, especially in the North, do not like blacks, and this is getting worse. They do not like the crime, the welfare, or the expectations of special treatment. While in college, a typical small-town Pennsylvania school, I witnessed a scene that exemplified white attitudes towards blacks. At a party, a black entered the premises and stayed a short while. After he left, the owner of the house used disinfectant to clean every place the black had touched. This kind of attitude and racial animosity can only escalate as a result of forced integration and preferential treatment.

I wonder if these blacks realize the level of prejudice against them in other parts of the world. While I was living in Australia, the government pursued the "White Australia Policy." They did not even allow blacks in the country, because its people believed that to do so would cause an increase in "black blight": poverty, crime and welfare.

During the 1980s, blacks decided to spread their cause of racial justice to foreign nations, so they set their sights on South Africa. Some blacks even began to wear small maps of Africa, in the colors of the African National Congress, around their necks. Interestingly, many blacks cannot find Africa on a map and cannot spell "apartheid," but they think they have the right to interfere in the internal matters of another nation. The white government of South Africa built a modern westernized culture and, just as in America, the blacks wanted control of it (without earning it, of course). In early 1994, the South African government succumbed to the pressure of world community economic sanctions, and dismantled apartheid. The world has seen this particular act before. Rhodesia went through the same sort of change. Their white minority government was forced to turn over control to the blacks, who immediately declared their intention to follow Marxist principles and promptly ran the country into the ground. Everyone was worse off! The future for South Africa is bleak. Ignorant tribal leaders have no clue how to run a civilized nation and this, added to a militaristic white neo-Nazi element, spells civil war. But at least the foreign policy wizards like that dumbass incompetent hillbilly Clinton will surely be able to handle it.

During the summer of 1991, Thurgood Marshall announced his retirement from the Supreme Court. Our lying president nominated Clarence Thomas, a conservative black Court of Appeals judge with almost no experience, to replace Marshall. The confirmation hearings that followed turned into a nasty brawl. Thomas was picked because he was black, and George "Read my lips, I lied" Bush was afraid of the political backlash that would result if he replaced the Court's only black with another white. When Bush denied this fact he was absolutely lying, again! Bush also had another plan in mind. Thomas was an anomaly: a black conservative who opposed affirmative discrimination. Bush intended to split the black community by making them fight over Thomas' positions on the issues. That is exactly what happened. Most blacks supported Thomas, but their out-of-touch leadership fought against him. Most of the debate surrounded his views on abortion and affirmative discrimination. Liberals knew that another conservative on the Court would make an unbeatable 7-2 conservative majority which would reverse many practices such as these quota programs. Fearing this, the liberals attacked viciously. The debate came down to the liberal position of giving everything to minorities or Thomas' position of requiring minorities to earn their way. The last two decades have proven the total failure of the liberal welfare/quota position; it is time for a change. Contrary to the liberals' promise to "Bork" Thomas, a reference to the disgraceful liberal campaign of lies launched against Supreme Court nominee Robert Bork in 1987, the nomination of Thomas was reported out of the Judiciary Committee and sent to the whole Senate. On October 7, 1991, the day before the final Senate vote, a Senate staffer leaked a secret FBI report concerning sexual harassment allegations against Thomas by an Oklahoma law professor who had worked for Thomas a decade before. In one of the most embarrassing scenes the nation has ever witnessed from its government, the Senate Judiciary Committee reconvened to hear these charges. The nation sat glued to the televised hearings, as if it were a popular soap opera, which is what it sounded like. The accuser told the committee of Thomas pressuring her to go out with him. She also referred to his habit of discussing the size of his reproductive organs, and his sexual abilities with women, along with pornographic movies he had seen. Thomas angrily and vehemently denied the allegations and claimed they were concocted by liberal enemies as a last-ditch effort to block his nomination to the Court. He refused to withdraw his nomination. As the drama spread overseas, Republican senators launched a broadside against the accuser's credibility, branding her as an ambitious woman who was jealous of Thomas due to her inability to rise in government; a liar who was part of a Democratic conspiracy to defeat the nomination of Thomas through blackmail; and an unstable woman caught up in a fantasy love affair with Thomas.

Finally, on October 15, 1991, the Senate voted 52-48 to confirm Thomas. After hearing the testimony, one could not help feeling that the last minute unsubstantiated allegations were a setup by Democrats. Nonetheless, the ploy failed, taking the Oklahoma professor, and probably several senators, down with it. A serious repercussion of the whole affair is that good talented people, in and out of government, will not allow themselves to be nominated for these positions if this is what they can expect to be subjected to in the highly politicized process the Senate has created.

At last, the tide began to turn against racial blackmail and preferential treatment. As a teenager, David Duke became involved in activities that he now admits were the stupid indiscretions of youth. A former Klan and Nazi Party activist who has long since moved away from these extremist groups, Duke created quite a stir in national politics since being elected to the Louisiana state legislature in 1989. A fiery young orator, whose message is not racist, Duke argued for an end to affirmative discrimination, welfare programs, increasing crime, and the expenses they spawn. He easily won election to the state legislature and in 1990 ran, as a Republican, for the U.S. Senate. In that race he took 44% of the statewide vote against a popular middle-of-the-road Democrat. The national Republican Party establishment lined up against him. Numerous major party bigwigs, including George "Read my lips, I lied" Bush and Ronald Reagan, campaigned for the incumbent Democrat. Yet Duke still came close to a victory. This reveals how disgusted whites are with business as usual. He also received a surprisingly large number of black votes. These people see their own leadership as caught up in the pursuit of their own wealth and patronage at the expense of whites. Blacks who voted for David Duke realize that the way to improve the black community is to do what he wants: stop crime, welfare, and affirmative discrimination programs and let the black community earn some self-respect.

Duke continued to bring these issues to the forefront of the national agenda when he ran for governor of Louisiana in 1991. He lost after the most vicious nationwide attack from the media, minority groups, and the Republican Party that the nation has seen since Abraham Lincoln. He again received 40% of the statewide vote and gained financial contributions from every U.S state and from several foreign nations. In December, 1991, Duke announced his candidacy for president. The campaign of 1992 was one of the most divisive ever. Duke's meteoric rise can only be attributed to white discontent. The backlash was beginning!

As the presidential primary season began the Republican Party committed yet another example of the fascism that has become their historical trademark. Republican organizations in several states, including Florida, Massachusetts, and Georgia refused to allow David Duke on the ballot as a Republican. He had met the legal qualifications required by law, but the state party organizations claimed that Duke did not represent the ideals of true Republicans. Duke, of course, contested this abuse of democracy, and the battle with Georgia led to the Supreme Court. It should be remembered that the Court was dominated at that time by conservatives appointed by Republican presidents. The Court predictably toed the party line ruling that the Georgia Republican Party did not have to place Duke on the ballot. Duke was finally forced to withdraw from the campaign. What has this country become when a political party can keep people off the ballot because of differing views? As if the Republicans are some kind of saintly group? Ironically, this was the same party that would proudly run Oliver North — convicted criminal and liar — on the Republican ticket in the Virginia governor's race in 1994.

In large part it was the recent racially divisive campaigning of the Reagan/Bush years that created David Duke in the first place. Television ads like the Willie Horton piece, used by Bush in 1988, encouraged subtle racism. These ads worked only too well to spawn an atmosphere of intolerance, which was the basis of Duke's appeal. With the disgraceful and disgusting past of the Republican Party, they are the last ones who should attempt to appear pious. The only good news in all of this is that the approval ratings of our lying president dropped to such a point that his defeat was then a real possibility in 1992. This affair alone should convince every American to vote for someone else besides the Republicans in order to send the message that people have a right to differing views without being kept off the ballot.

Following on the heels of the Duke threat came another protest candidate. Pat Buchanan jumped into the primaries to challenge Bush, claiming that the President lied about taxes and had deserted the conservative wing of the party. Buchanan actually represented many of the same views as those expressed by Duke. He was firmly opposed to affirmative discrimination and demanded immediate welfare reform. These types of views were becoming acceptable as whites expressed their rage. Buchanan fought viciously through the entire campaign season, gaining as much as 40% of the Republican vote in some states. He did not win a primary, but he severely tarnished Bush. Of course he was brought down by the usual Republican tactics of smears, lies, and distortions. By the beginning of June, the President's approval rating was down to 37%, and polls showed that the people had not been this dissatisfied since the malaise days of Jimmy Carter's presidency.

In the midst of all this political maneuvering, however, a Supreme Court decision seemed to indicate a willingness to return to support for affirmative discrimination. In this 1990 Florida case, the Federal Communications Commission's policy of requiring preferential treatment in awarding television licenses was challenged as an unlawful discrimination against whites. In a 5-4 decision, the Court upheld federal policies that favor minorities in awarding broadcast licenses. There does not seem to be any logic to this decision. If the commission tried to award licenses only to whites there would be an outcry and the act would be immediately declared illegal, but when they give away licenses to lesser qualified blacks, it is legal?

Following a few changes on the Supreme Court the issue of affirmative discrimination arose again. In *Richmond v. J. A. Croson* (1992), the Court held that an affirmative discrimination plan initiated by a state or local government will be struck down as a violation of the Equal Protection Clause of the 14th Amendment unless that government is able to prove it is currently discriminating and that the plan is designed to remedy this. This case lays the groundwork for challenges across the nation to these programs. The practical difficulty for state and local governments now is that to implement these plans they have to publicly admit they are currently discriminating. And to do so could open them up to major liability. This is not something government entities want to admit. Unfortunately, these rules do not apply to the federal government.

Blacks are not the only minority jumping on the welfare/quota bandwagon. After witnessing black successes, Hispanics are pursuing similar tactics. Following the 1990 census, came the redistricting conflict that arises every ten years as the various political authorities attempt to redraw their election district boundaries. These districts must comply with the one-man, one-vote requirement of the Supreme Court's decision in *Baker v. Carr* (1962). In that famous case, blacks forced states to stop using racial gerrymandering. Gerrymandering was a term used to describe the bizarrely shaped district created for Representative Gerry for the election of 1812. In recent years this process was used to design bizarre districts which either consolidated all blacks into one district or split them up into strong white districts. Both approaches limited the political power of blacks by lowering their ability to elect black candidates.

The Gerry-mander.

A new species of *Monster*, which appeared in *Essex South District* in January last.

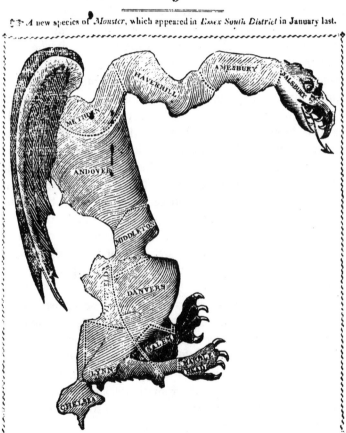

Cartoon from 1812 showing bizarre congressional district
(Reproduced from the Collection of the Library Of Congress.)

By 1993, Hispanics and blacks in Texas, North Carolina and other states began to demand that redistricting be done in such a way as to create black and Hispanic districts, thus guaranteeing that black and Hispanic representatives are elected. The idea is to create election districts at the county, state, and federal level that are dominated by these minorities so that they can be assured of electing members to these bodies. This is a total reversal of the liberal philosophy which has been the law since *Baker v. Carr*. It also has a certain logical failing to it. Since blacks and Hispanics comprise only a small segment of the total population, the result of this practice can only be a very few minority representatives elected. And what will that accomplish? Amusingly, in 1992 in a newly created Hispanic district, a white was elected over a Hispanic candidate.

The courts are going along with this charade and no one seems willing to protest. What would happen if a group of whites demanded a white district? The outcry would be loud and swift, but when the minorities suggest the same thing, people applaud. There is discrimination in this nation and much of it is caused by the actions of the courts and minorities. Whites are angry about being treated like second class citizens while the government gives minorities everything they demand.

Fortunately, the conservatives on the Supreme Court have stood against these racial set-aside districts. In *Shaw v. Reno* (1993), North Carolina had developed a congressional redistricting plan with one minority set-aside district, but this plan was rejected by the Justice Department. Under Section 5 of the 1965 Voting Rights Act, Southern states must get approval from the Justice Department for any and all changes in their voting procedures, practices, and standards. The Justice Department insisted on a second set-aside district and the state complied. At that point a group of North Carolina residents sued, challenging the plan as an unconstitutional racial gerrymander in violation of the 14th Amendment's Equal Protection Clause and *Baker v. Carr*.

The district court dismissed the case, holding that the plaintiffs had failed to state a sufficient claim upon which relief could be granted. The Supreme Court reversed. The case was then remanded for further action in the lower court. It was one of several cases handled by the Court during 1994 as residents in several states challenged these minority districts.

Thirty years ago, former Supreme Court Justice William Douglas, one of the most liberal justices ever, warned, "The principle of equality is at war with the notion that District A must be represented by a Negro, as it is with the notion that District B must be represented by a Caucasian, District C by a Jew, District D by a Catholic, and so on." But recent decisions have rapidly progressed to this point. Justice O'Connor has led the way with stinging criticisms of this inequitable approach. In *Shaw v. Reno* she stated, "We have involved the federal courts, and indeed the Nation, in the enterprise of systematically dividing the country into electoral districts along racial lines — an enterprise of segregating the races into political homelands that amounts, in truth, to nothing short of a system of political apartheid which may Balkanize us into competing racial factions." This system is a divisive force in our nation. As a practical matter, our drive to segregate political districts by race can only serve to deepen racial divisions by destroying any need for voters or candidates to build bridges between racial groups. The results of this liberal social engineering were predictable and have indeed come true. Polarization of the races is taking place at a rapid pace as blacks and Hispanics fight for their districts and whites fight against a double standard which allows special treatment for minorities to the detriment of whites.

During 1994 two California state senators began a grass-roots petition drive for a ballot question on affirmative discrimination. Known as the California Civil Rights Initiative, it would prohibit the use of race, sex, color, ethnicity or national origin as a criterion for either discriminating against, or granting preferential treatment to, any individual in the operation of the state's system of public employment, education, or contracting. If passed, the measure will invalidate any affirmative discrimination programs currently in place. Its passage will mark a great victory for equality. That such a measure is necessary at all shows just how badly skewed the notion of civil rights has become.

This double standard was clearly exposed in another context in a 1993 Texas controversy. The federal government, with its usual brilliance, decided to integrate public housing complexes in rural Texas counties. Their justification was the usual nonsense about the public policy benefits of cultural diversity in our communities. These benefits have never been explained, probably because there are none. In one such community, Vidor, Texas (an historical hotbed of Ku Klux Klan activity), the expected protests by whites materialized. This included harassment, threats and vandalism. So much for the benefits of cultural diversity. Finally, all the blacks left.

Thereafter, the Texas Commission on Human Rights began an administrative investigation of the Vidor situation. In this endeavor the Commission issued a subpoena against Michael Lowe, Grand Dragon of the Texas Knights of the Ku Klux Klan, to force him to give up the organization's membership lists so that the State could interview these people with an eye towards prosecutions against those who drove the blacks out of town. Lowe refused to turn over the records and the Commission brought an enforcement action. Still Lowe refused, was found to be in contempt of court, and sent to jail. Lowe hired Galveston attorney Anthony Griffin, who is black, to fight the case. Griffin was the state's leading attorney for the NAACP and the ACLU. While the ACLU stood behind him, the NAACP attacked him personally and viciously for taking the case. He was fired from his position with the state organization, and a movement developed to kick him out of the national organization. Griffin made his distaste for Lowe and the Klan quite clear, but he also pointed out that he was standing up for the constitutional right of association. He felt that it was a right that applied to all Americans, not just the NAACP. It was an incredibly courageous stand to take. If only this nation was made up of people like Anthony Griffin, who respect the Constitution and even make personal sacrifices to protect it, then we would not be on the verge of losing our liberties.

It was interesting, and indeed ironic, that Griffin was able to rely on a U.S. Supreme Court decision from 1958 which involved the NAACP. In *NAACP v. Alabama*, the State of Alabama had sued and won a court order forcing the NAACP to give up their membership lists to the state. The State hoped that by revealing the membership lists publicly, pressure could be brought to bear on NAACP members, thus harming their integration efforts. The NAACP refused and appealed. The U.S. Supreme Court reversed the state court and declared, for the first time, a right of association under the First Amendment. The Court found that advocacy of views is undeniably enhanced by group association, thus representing a close relationship between the freedoms of speech and assembly. Since the state action posed a substantial restraint on the NAACP's right of association, it was unconstitutional. This precedent is absolutely clear and has not been watered down by later case law. It is, then, beyond comprehension how some state bureaucrat in Texas, seeking solely to score points with minority groups, could attempt to do the exact same thing to the Ku Klux Klan. The fact that it was exactly the same thing was made perfectly clear when Lowe filed a petition for writ of habeas corpus to the Texas State Supreme Court and won. The court did not even hear oral arguments in the case, and the short opinion briefly reviews the applicable federal law and ends by lecturing Texas authorities on the simple fact, known by every first year D- law student, that federal constitutional law must be followed. There were no dissenting opinions.

The NAACP fought tooth and nail to support the state's efforts to get the Klan's membership lists. And when a black attorney stood up to defend the constitutional principle involved, he was lynched by the modern day racists of the NAACP. What an incredible hypocrisy! But what a revelation of the racial double standard presently at work in this country.

During the summer of 1994, Congress debated the infamous Crime Bill. At the time, Clinton's support among the people was abysmal, which led Congress, not having to fear the people, to revolt against his proposals. He was hardly able to get any legislation passed. In this atmosphere the Congressional Black Caucus assumed an inflated importance. Clinton and these blacks realized he desperately needed their support if he was to pass anything. Blackmailed into this corner, Clinton was forced by the Caucus to add the ridiculously inappropriately-named "Racial Justice" provision to the Crime Bill.

Under this provision, a defendant sentenced to death could challenge the sentence on the basis that the jurisdiction in which they were judged had applied it more often to one race than another. Blacks were, of course, upset at the large number of blacks on Death Row. As usual they claimed this was a result of racism. It was a new low in the movement by weak-kneed liberal politicians to appease blacks. Fortunately, so many whites in Congress were offended by this provision that it was clear that the bill had no chance of passing. The racial justice provision went down in flames. And eventually the Crime Bill barely passed.

Another brilliant example of hillbilly Clinton's racial policy is reflected in the activities of the Department of Housing & Urban Development (HUD). No part of the federal government has a more infamous reputation for decades of abuse, incompetence, scandal, misguided social engineering and waste than this bunch. In 1992, hillbilly Clinton appointed Henry Cisneros to run HUD. As a result of typical liberal quota philosophy, Cisneros was appointed because he was Hispanic. An insignificant bureaucrat, his greatest claim to fame came in 1994 when the FBI placed him under investigation for lying during his confirmation process about the amount of hush money he paid to a former mistress. Remember that to a Democrat, quotas are more important than quality.

In June, 1993, Cisneros admitted to Congress that "HUD has exacerbated the declining quality of life in America." An unusually candid response from a politician, it is true nonetheless. HUD began to pursue a socialist housing agenda following the passage of the National Housing Act in 1968. The act created the Section 235 program to provide heavily-subsidized loans for the poor to allow them to buy homes in middle-class neighborhoods. The program was an unmitigated disaster, as these people trashed the properties and the neighborhoods and then abandoned them. Tens of thousands of homes were left to rot. The program devastated the housing markets in numerous cities. Detroit and Chicago suffered the worst. *The Chicago Tribune* stated in 1975, "No natural disaster on record has caused destruction on the scale of the government's housing programs. It took only four years of this program to reduce a neat, middle-class neighborhood into a shattered, decaying slum." City officials declared HUD "the greatest enemy of community stability." It was only just the beginning.

HUD continued its campaign to help with housing by developing the mass public housing concept. Inner cities across the nation are dominated by row upon row of huge towering apartment buildings for the poor. Supposing that building these monstrosities was enough to help the poor, HUD was either incompetent or simply ignored them. Left to their own devices without adequate security, the residents of these tenements were left to suffer as the buildings deteriorated into crime-ridden sewers where violence became the way of life. Another success for HUD.

In 1993, hillbilly Clinton and his socialist yokels decided that the main problem faced by America was that poor people who do not work cannot afford middle-class housing. And the reason for this: racism. Spewing propaganda that would please Lenin and Marx, the Democrats decided that the best communities are those with income integration; that is, mixed income levels. As a result, they then defined unfair housing patterns as any community showing a lack of income integration. This, of course, gives Cisneros and HUD the power to declare every community in America an unfair housing market susceptible to federal intervention.

In order to solve this illusory problem, HUD developed another program. The target beneficiaries of this repeat of the disastrous Section 235 program, now called Section 8, are not the working poor, but only the residents of public housing or other HUD handout recipients. The plan is designed to move large numbers of inner-city slum dwellers into every suburban community in America.

Section 8 is the key to the Clinton administration's efforts to force racial and economic quotas on American suburbs. Their idea is to end the stigma of welfare by giving welfare recipients an upper-class lifestyle. The program is planned to grow to a cost of $14 billion by 1996. HUD comes into a community and sets subsidy levels. The Section 8 recipients then are asked to pay only 10% of their income for rent while the government, at taxpayer expense, picks up the rest. In May, 1994, in Plano, Texas, HUD established the subsidy levels at

$750 for a two bedroom apartment. At the time the median apartment rent in the city was $586. This then allows these welfare recipients to live in better housing than most of the working residents of the city. HUD officials opined: "Our residents will be given better choices of where to live." Why? These people are the useless, those who contribute nothing to society, and the government gives them luxury apartments? In most of these cases the welfare recipients live in housing which offers indoor swimming pools, racquet and tennis facilities, libraries (as though any of them can read), spas, and billiard rooms.

The results of this program give one a twisted sense of *déjà vu*. Instead of scattering the poor through middle-class neighborhoods, Section 8 families have been grouped together. In Chicago, several towns on the southern outskirts have been turned into a Section 8 corridor. City officials decry this change of nice neighborhoods into slums. The worst aspect of this invasion is the crime. HUD assumed that public housing residents would be less likely to rob and steal if they were surrounded by more affluent neighbors. That sentiment succinctly sums up the level of incompetence in the American government. Of course, quite the opposite has come true. Gangs of unemployed Section 8 recipients have nothing to do except commit crimes and terrorize their new neighborhoods. Crime rates in Section 8 areas are 10-20 times higher than the national average. A typical example of public-housing crime occurred on October 13, 1994. Two boys, aged 10 and 11, tried to force a 5-year-old boy to steal some candy for them. When he refused, the older boys grew angry, grabbed him, and dangled him out a 14-story window. After fighting off a rescue attempt by the little boy's brother, the two offenders dropped the young boy to his death. This sort of bestial behavior runs rampant in public housing complexes. Yet Cisneros and Clinton want to force this upon the people in the suburbs. The American people have a message for these two: not now, not ever! Whatever it takes, lawful or not, the line is drawn!

To add insult to injury, landlords are forced to admit Section 8 residents, and then must follow an entire catalogue of special rules. They must accept only a $50 down-payment, not the usual one-month's rent-in-advance, and they must follow lengthy procedures to evict a resident. It is then almost impossible to remove this blight once they move in.

As crime rates in public housing have escalated, the government response has been typical. In June, 1994, the Chicago Housing Authority began warrantless sweeps of homes for guns and drugs. When hillbilly Clinton visited the city he praised the program. It seems that he had forgotten a little thing called the Constitution. A federal judge reminded him of it a few weeks later when he struck down the program as a violation of the 4th Amendment. Clinton's response was to call for legislation requiring public-housing residents to sign a housing contract requiring them to give up their constitutional rights as a condition of getting public housing. Simply astonishing! How far will these idiots go down this road before they admit their mistake?

HUD's original intention of bringing harmony through race and income mixing has not fared well either. Whites in these invaded communities greatly resent the government's free giveaway to the useless. Many blacks and Hispanics who have worked their way up to a better life also resent these programs. The worst part of the program for these people is that it has led to a tremendous drop in property values.

For most Americans, communism — a classless, government managed society — was something this nation fought tooth and nail for 70 years. Now the government shoves it down our throats. It a sign of true American government brilliance that this system failed and has been rejected in the Soviet Union and everywhere else that it has been tried, yet we try it now. In the 1960s it was thought that some temporary government assistance would help the poor. Misguided social policy though has led to government creation of a permanent crime-ridden underclass by paying generations of people to become government dependents.

If we are to end the racial discrimination problem, to the extent that it can be ended, we must have fair laws that apply equally to all. That will reduce the problem by itself. In addition, laws prohibiting discrimination in certain "public" areas must be maintained. Prejudice will still continue, but it is not the place of government to change attitudes, nor is it within the remedial capacity of the courts; the attempt to do so can only create animosity. The people of this nation will not be able to continue co-existing together when the laws allow blacks and Hispanics to call for and benefit from clear discrimination against whites.

This nation now faces the great danger of following in the footsteps of numerous foreign nations that have gone the way of racial conflict. When the citizens of a country focus on their various ethnic heritages to such a degree, conflict with other groups becomes inevitable. The people of this nation are drifting away from their traditionally strong national identity as Americans and becoming a nation of European-Caucasian Americans, African Americans, Hispanic Americans, Native Americans, and Asian Americans. Maybe we should look to India, Iraq, the states of the former Soviet Union, and Yugoslavia to see the racial conflict of our future. Is America on the road to Balkanization? Absolutely!

No white in America today was around when slavery was legal and we owe no apology, no remuneration, no preferential treatment, and no guilt for it. Let there be no mistake, this is not a racist attack on blacks. They deserve equal opportunity and equal justice in society which should be intensely enforced through the law. People must accept that there is some amount of division between the races that cannot be reduced. It is not racist, it is simple human choice not to mix with certain types of people. Legislative attempts to do so have been and will always be counterproductive. The bottom line is that we will no longer allow preferential treatment to be given at the expense of whites, nor will we let blacks use accusations of racism to prevent us from revealing their improprieties. And the government can accept this or have it forcibly shoved down its throat by the white majority!

Affirmative action is a typical government program. It does not work, creates animosity and a whole range of negative results, and flies in the face of the very equality it was supposed to promote. It is creating a large number of minorities who expect to do nothing and yet be given jobs and other benefits they have not earned. The old axiom about there being no free lunches needs modification in modern America. There are no free lunches unless you are a black/Hispanic/Jew, handicapped, gay, woman, or person with AIDS. There is absolutely no place for affirmative discrimination in a country ruled by a Constitution that includes an equal protection clause, but after all, the Constitution is just a piece of apparently worthless paper.

CONCLUSION

My intention in writing this book was to tell the truth about America in an attempt to create serious dialogue about the present crisis. A by-product of such an endeavor undoubtedly is to offend everyone. Sometimes it takes a full-scale attack to wake people to a danger, and if we are to have any hope of reversing the totalitarian trend I have described, it must be done now. If the PCers or any racial, gender, religious, or sexual preference group are bothered by the content of this book, good. As that great American comic Andrew Dice Clay says, "Well, fuck them!" This is not a nation of liberal minority rule, and these groups are going to have to be taught that fact, one way or another.

Unfortunately these chapters describe only the tiniest fraction of the disgraceful history of this country. Volumes could be written expounding on the rape of the Constitution. This is the real history of the United States. I have made no embellishments or exaggerations. Yet it is not the American history that we are taught in school, for obvious reasons. If we were taught the truth, we could not be successfully raised as mindless patriotic taxpayers, nothing more than fodder for any war in which the government chooses to engage. But our history is there — all one needs to do is look it up to witness the reality of America. This type of behavior has gone on and on and on in the face of the Constitution. To these arguments the typical brain-dead American will respond, "Well it's the best country in the world." That may be true, but being the best of the worst doesn't really mean much. Looking back over our nation's past I feel a sense of disgust and embarrassment, but I hope that can be changed by our future acts.

DECLARATION OF INDEPENDENCE 1994

The history of the present government of the United States is a history of repeated injuries and usurpations, all directed toward the establishment of an absolute tyranny over its citizens. To prove this, let these facts be submitted to a candid world:

It has denied the right of the people to free political speech through sedition and subversion laws;

It has denied the people their right to free expression through the burning and banning of literary and musical works and through government-sponsored intimidation;

It has attempted to control our thoughts and make us good little puppets;

It has denied the people their right to a free press by censoring materials that the people wish to have available;

It has unconstitutionally promoted religion;

It has attacked and brutally beaten protesting citizens attempting to exercise their rights to petition the government for a redress of grievances;

It has denied the right of the people to keep and bear arms by prohibiting the ownership of certain guns;

It has stopped the people from going about their business through the use of roadblock checkpoints;

It has violated the sanctity and privacy of our homes with warrantless searches;

It has violated the sanctity of our persons by administering drug tests;

It has deprived us of life, liberty, and property without due process of law;

It has deprived us of the right to confront all witnesses against us in court;

It has burdened us with excessive bails so as to constitute imprisonment without a trial;

It has involved this nation in illegal and immoral wars resulting in the deaths of many for imperialism, greed, and paranoia;

It has utterly failed to protect the people from the ravages of crime;

It has placed multiple layers of abusive taxes upon us without our consent;

It has subjugated the people by means of terror in tax collections;

It has deprived us of our right to consume as we please;

It has at times enslaved the young of this nation under a draft system;

It has forced the nation into an illegal civil war;

It has forced illegal constitutional amendments upon us so as to attempt to justify its wrongs;

It has placed American citizens in concentration camps for extended periods;

It has committed genocide against the American Indians;

It has bound us under a monstrous bureaucracy so as to frustrate any attempts at change;

It has actively lied to the people;

It has denied the civil rights of white males in preference for other groups in violation of equal protection;

It has denied the legitimate right of states to secede from the union;

It has allowed greed and corruption to control every aspect of itself;

It has allowed incompetence to become the standard of government;

It has conducted witch-hunts;

It has attempted to force the races together in violation of their inherent rights to associate freely with persons of their own choice;

It has failed to provide quality education for the people;

It has failed to ensure adequate health care for the people;

It has aided and abetted in the destruction of the environment;

It has wasted billions of dollars on useless weapons while
   Americans are homeless and starving in the streets;
It has forced the people to submit to a criminally incompetent
   Congress, a lying President, and a Supreme Court whose
   justices disregard the Constitution in favor of their own
   views;
It has allowed federal judges to raise taxes in violation of the
   Constitution;
It has operated for the benefit of the rich at the expense of the
   poor;
It has enslaved the people under a capitalist economic system;
It has abandoned the principles of liberty upon which this
   nation was founded.

Only one conclusion can be reached at the end of this examination
of our past. We have disregarded our Constitution, and continue to do
so. The government, and in many cases the people as well, have
violated not only the letter, but the spirit of the document. It is a great
experiment in democracy, the greatest that the world has ever known,
but it has failed. The nature of power, corruption, incompetence,
greed, ignorance, intolerance, paranoia and apathy have destroyed it.
The Constitution is indeed a worthless piece of paper, and our liberty
may indeed be lost.

Maybe if the people wake up and realize the implications of
what's going on they will stand up and do something about the drift of
our country towards totalitarianism. Learn the issues, vote, sue, speak
out, and protest government action that is wrong; these are the
necessary steps. We cannot have a participatory democracy if the
people don't participate. The government counts on the people
remaining apathetic, and now because of it we are well on our way to
a police state where there is no freedom at all. It is probably too late to
do much about it. Frankly, considering the intellect and character of
the American people, I'm sure we won't turn it around. A recent
survey by the American Bar Association proves this to be true. In this
survey it was found that only 33% of the people even know what the
Bill of Rights is.

But at least the former Soviet Union is going in the other direction. In a few more years their people will enjoy the blessings of liberty and ours will not. The final chapter of the story of the United States before its inevitable and desired collapse will be a fitting one, as this nation puts up a wall to prevent a mass exodus of Americans escaping the abuses of our police state to the freedom of Soviet society.

A warning to the government, though. In the words of Alexander Hamilton, "Let us not establish a tyranny. That promotes rebellion." It surely will for there are those of us who will resist the direction our country is taking, and our weapon will not be just a worthless piece of paper.

Sachsenhausen Concentration Camp:
This will be the price of our lost liberties.
(Southern Cross Publishing)

BIBLIOGRAPHY

After many years of studying and teaching history, I have accumulated a fair amount of knowledge — the source of which is unknown. Much of this manifesto is based on that knowledge. In some cases, I have done extensive research. In those cases I have done my best to credit all the works I have used. The last half of the book was written during law school. All material quoted from legal cases comes from an assortment of law review articles, law school textbooks, legal seminar research, and case reporters. For much of the up-to-date political material and facts which make up most of the later chapters, I have relied upon several national newspapers and news magazines. The following bibliography includes sources I used in my research as well as a few recommended texts for those interested in analyzing these topics further.

Bacque, James. *Other Losses: The Shocking Truth Behind the Mass Deaths of Disarmed German Soldiers And Civilians Under General Eisenhower's Command*. Prima Publishing, 1991.

Barnwell, John. *Love of Order: South Carolina's First Secession Crisis*. University of North Carolina, Chapel Hill, 1982.

Barrett, Anthony A. *Caligula: The Corruption of Power*. Yale University Press, New Haven & London, 1989.

Bealer, Alex W. *Only the Names Remain: The Cherokees and the Trail of Tears.* 1st ed., Little, Brown, Boston, 1972.

Black, Henry Campbell. *Black's Law Dictionary.* 6th ed., West Publishing Co., St. Paul, Minn., 1990.

Bork, Robert H. *The Tempting of America: The Political Seduction of the Law.* The Free Press, New York, 1990.

Bosworth, Allan R. *America's Concentration Camps.* W.W. Norton & Co., Inc., New York, 1967.

Brant, Irving. *The Fourth President: A Life of James Madison.* Bobbs-Merrill, Indianapolis, 1970.

Buchheit, Lee C. *Secession: The Legitimacy of Self-Determination.* Yale University Press, New Haven, Conn, 1974.

Catton, Bruce. *The Bold Magnificent Dream: America's Founding Years 1492-1815.* 1st ed., Doubleday, Garden City, NY, 1978.

Craven, Avery O. *The Coming of the Civil War.* C. Scribner's Sons, 1942.

Daniels, Roger. *The Bonus March: An Episode of the Great Depression.* Greenwood Pub. Corp., Westport, Conn.,1971.

Davis, Daniel S. *Behind Barbed Wire: The Imprisonment of Japanese Americans During World War II.* Dutton, NY, 1982.

Epstein, Jason. *The Great Conspiracy Trial.* Random House, NY, 1970.

Foreman, Grant. *Indian Removal.* Norman Oklahoma Press, 1953.

Feuerlicht, Roberta Strauss. *Joe McCarthy & McCarthyism: The Hate That Haunts America.* McGraw Hill Books, 1972.

Handlin, Oscar. *Abraham Lincoln & the Union.* Little, Brown, Boston, 1980.

Langguth, A.J. *Patriots: The Men Who Started The American Revolution.* Simon & Schuster, New York, 1988.

Peters, William. *A More Perfect Union: The Making of the United States Constitution.* Crown Publishers, Inc., New York, 1987.

Rossiter, Clinton C. *The First American Revolution: The American Colonies on the Eve of Independence.* Harcourt Brace, NY, 1956.

Rotunda, Ronald D. *Modern Constitutional Law.* 3rd ed., West Publishing Co., St. Paul, Minn., 1989.

Shirer, William L. *The Rise & Fall of the Third Reich.* Mandarin Paperbacks, London, 1960.

Waters, W.W. *B.E.F: The Whole Story of the Bonus Army.* Arno Press & The New York Times, New York, 1969.

Williams, John S. *Thomas Jefferson: His Permanent Influence on American Institutions.* AMS Press, Inc., NY, 1967.

The Federalist by Alexander Hamilton, James Madison, John Jay: A Collection of Essays, Belknap Press of Harvard University Press, Cambridge, Mass, 1961.

The Third Reich Series: The Apparatus of Death. Time Life Books, Alexandria, VA, 1991.

YOU WILL ALSO WANT TO READ: